Human Rights in Canadian Education

Editors
Douglas Ray
University of Western Ontario

Vincent D'Oyley
University of British Columbia

KENDALL/HUNT PUBLISHING COMPANY
Dubuque, Iowa

Many authors have been cited throughout the text for their ideas concerning human rights. The sources cited below are credited for quotations in one or more passages. Permissions have been secured as necessary:

Stacy Churchill, "So Why Aren't the French Ever Satisfied? Educational Rights for Franco-Ontarians", from *Interchange—A Journal on Educational Theory,* 914:59–66, published by the Ontario Institute for Studies and Education, Toronto.

Robert M. Stamp, *About Schools: What Every Canadian Parent Should Know,* Don Mills, Ontario: New Press, 1975.

Douglas Myers, "The Teaching 'Profession'? A Demystification", *This Magazine,* 11/3:14–16, published in Toronto.

"School", Lyrics and Music by Richard Davies and Roger Hodgson, © 1974 by Rondor Music (London) Ltd. and Delicate Music Ltd. Controlled in the United States and Canada by ALMO Music Corp.

Richard Ares, *Les positions,—ethniques, linguistiques et religieuses—des Canadiens francais a la suite du recensement de 1971,* Montreal: Editions Bellarmin, 1975.

The Report of the Royal Commission on Bilingualism and Biculturalism. Ottawa: Queen's Printer, 1967.

The Charte de la langue francaise, Quebec: Gouvernement du Quebec, 1977.

Federation des francophones hors. Quebec, *Deux poids, deux mesures,* Ottawa, FFHQ, 1978.

Thomas Berger, *Northern Frontier, Northern Homeland,* Toronto: James Lorimer, 1977.

Peter Jones, "Theology and Etunicity" in Keith McLeod (editor) *Multiculturalism, Bilingualism and Canadian Institutions.* Toronto: University of Toronto, Faculty of Education, Guidance Center, 1979, 53–60.

Gary Onstad, "Working with Racism", *Working Teacher,* 1/13 13–13 published by the Working Teacher Educational Society, Vancouver.

This preliminary edition has been printed directly from the authors' manuscript copy.

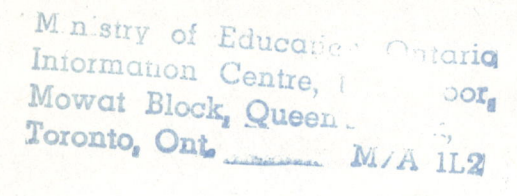

Copyright © 1983 by Kendall/Hunt Publishing Company

Library of Congress Catalog Card Number: 83-80817

ISBN 0-8403-2983-0

All rights reserved. No part of this publication may be reproduced, stored in a retrieval system, or transmitted, in any form or by any means, electronic, mechanical, photocopying, recording, or otherwise, without the prior written permission of the copyright owner.

Printed in the United States of America

This collection is dedicated to two
Canadians who made human rights
widely known and respected:

John Humphrey, O.C.

J. Roby Kidd, C.M.

ACKNOWLEDGMENTS

<u>Human Rights in Canadian Education</u> includes selected, refereed, revised and edited original papers from a symposium of invited Canadian experts in education and social sciences and community work, which was conducted in Vancouver Theological College in 1979. Certain chapters were added to address topics that were identified by the participants attending that symposium. Several excellent submissions to the symposium were not included in this volume because their topics were too particular or the papers had been published elsewhere.

The deliberations were financed by a grant from the Secretary of State, preparation of the manuscript was undertaken by The University of Western Ontario and the Centre for the Study of Curriculum and Instruction at the University of British Columbia with a grant from the Social Science and Humanities Research Council of Canada. The United Nations Association and particularly its Executive Director, Greg Wirick, encouraged and facilitated on many occasions and agreed to assist with sales and distribution.

Assistance in preparation of the manuscript was most welcome. Particular mention: Rene Fallsberg and the late John Main from the Publication Office of the Ontario Institute for Studies in Education; John Humphrey and Philippe Leblanc for insightful suggestions and Jeanette Tran for checking and rechecking. But a special tribute has been earned by Henny Vlasman for patience and encouragement.

Susan Gmiterek and Derek Allison were photographed by Les Ste. Marie (all from the University of Western Ontario) for the cover.

TABLE OF CONTENTS

FOREWORD	Walter Tarnopolsky	
INTRODUCTION	Douglas Ray and Vincent D'Oyley	1

RIGHTS AND OBLIGATIONS IN EDUCATION

Parents' Rights and Obligations	Janet V. Collins	6
The Rights of Teachers	Anthony Burton	25
Students' Rights	James Brown	38
Lifelong Education: An Emerging Human Right	J. Roby Kidd and Douglas Ray	53

THE PROVISION OF EDUCATIONAL RIGHTS

Strategies for Human Rights Education	John Kehoe	68
Special Education	Grant McMurray	110
Self and Other – The Right to a Human Education	MarySue McCarthy	129

GROUP RIGHTS AFFECTING EDUCATION

Racism in Education: Old and New	Michel Laferriere	153
Minority Official Language Education: Where Can It Be Secure?	Jacques Lamontagne	176
Contested or Non-Assured Educational Rights	Vincent D'Oyley	198
Human Rights in Canadian Education	Douglas Ray	213

BIBLIOGRAPHY	228
NOTES ON CONTRIBUTORS	250

FOREWORD

The Charter of Rights and Freedoms was entrenched in the Canadian Constitution on April 17th, 1982. It proclaims the fundamental freedoms of conscience and religion, of thought, belief, opinion and expression, of assembly and of association; it provides for democratic rights of participation in government; it lists a large number of legal rights which have to be provided in the administration of justice; and it provides that every individual is equal before and under the law and has the right to the equal protection and benefit of the law without discrimination based on race, national or ethnic origin, colour, religion, sex, age or mental or physical disability. The rights of women and men are specifically affirmed as equal. The Charter names French and English as official languages with equal status at the federal level and in New Brunswick, and requires the provision of official language minority education facilities in all provinces. Aboriginal peoples have their existing aboriginal and treaty rights recognized.

Having an entrenched Charter of Rights is one important tool in assuring basic rights and liberties. The Charter offers a context and a challenge. The challenge is to provide the people of this country with a knowledge of their rights so that they can exercise and protect them. Education is the first step by which these and other human rights may be safeguarded. Access to education of an appropriate kind is itself one of the most widely sought after and enjoyed rights in Canada, even though it cannot claim to be extended equally and without discrimination. Since the rights and obligations of students, teachers and parents underlie the provision of educational opportunities, this book provides an important focus on them.

Human Rights "education" has been or is being developed and promoted by many levels of the educational establishment. It is also an important element in the work of various social movements in this country. However, it is very piecemeal; the tremendous efforts of individuals and groups are often very localized and others do not benefit from the research, creative thinking and experimentation that is going on. The authors represented in this volume address many issues and themes which are central to human rights and education and should be applauded for their efforts. Making this kind of specific material available to the public is essential.

Since the Human Rights Research and Education Centre at the University of Ottawa has been established to stimulate research and education about human rights and to make important links between information and users, whether the users be educators, students, professionals, workers, judges, police or others, it is an honour and a pleasure to be given the opportunity to welcome and lend support to this book.

The economic difficulties of the eighties must make us all watchful of the erosion of our rights in this country and elsewhere. A collection such as this one will assist us in this responsibility.

Human Rights Centre
University of Ottawa
Walter Tarnopolsky

INTRODUCTION

Douglas Ray and Vincent D'Oyley

This book is intended for Canadian citizens who are interested in human rights and whose work may affect the rights of others. Such persons are very numerous: parents, those involved in community and social projects, school teachers, specialists in moral and social issues, journalists. The discussions are non-technical to the extent possible and are intended to promote discussion and analysis of local circumstances.

As the book was being written, human rights emerged as a central issue in Canadian politics. Within this debate there are at least three well-defined and ably championed positions.

At one extreme, human rights are claimed to exist everywhere: they are neither created nor necessarily safeguarded by being placed in constitutions. According to this view, rights exist in people's minds, and people know when their rights are being violated. The remedy which follows is to persuade an appropriate government to pass the legislation or to establish another procedure to protect the right. This position has a long tradition in Canada, reflected both in legislation and in common or case law. Where no violation has been charged, none is assumed to exist.

A second view is to acknowledge the need for constitutional protection of rights and to make general statements that would be clarified over time by the courts. This position has the advantages of flexibility and durability. It has been noted that detailed and specific constitutions (for example with lists of examples or exceptions) are always incomplete and difficult to apply to cases that were not mentioned. This second view of human rights relies upon interaction between legislators and courts.

A third view is that rights ought to be specified in considerable detail, with protections being extended to enumerated groups. This position advances the power of the courts substantially and, by the same token, apparently diminishes the power of legislators. It has the disadvantage that the details of clauses may soon be obsolete. Both women and native Canadians recognized that they should seek specific protection in the Constitution rather than trust in future legislation or judicial interpretations of general clauses.

The 1981 Canada Act moved the primary responsibility for protection of human rights from parliament to the courts with important roles to many other offices and boards. It is too early to write with confidence about the effects upon educational rights, the rights of women, of linguistic, religious or ethnic groups, or the rights of the poor persons in disadvantaged provinces. We can select among an array of Canadians who really argue about how best to achieve that which is generally wanted. This list is very extensive and includes politicians, judges, writers and others from all parts of the nation.

Nor should international influences, particularly the influence of Britain, France, the United States and the United Nations be ignored. In particular, the Universal Declaration of Human Rights and the International Covenant on Economic, Social, and Cultural Rights have great significance for all forms of education. The rights of women, children, and the disabled are special groups that have internationally proclaimed standards of protection. Canada has taken these obligations seriously, with both federal and provincial governments involved in ratification procedures and in exploring how best to accomplish the needed changes in practice.

A great deal has been written concerning the educational interests and problems of several Canadian groups. Although these analyses are not repeated here, the protection of educational rights is in principle embedded in several clauses of the 1981 Canada Act. Poverty must never be an excuse for depriving any child in Canada of a good education. Migration from one province to another must remain unfettered by educational barriers. Sex, marital status, ethnicity, religion, political affiliation, and associates of a person must never determine his/her educational opportunities. Language - particularly official language - and need for special facilities or procedures will remain educationally significant, but the ways by which these matters will be addressed will continue to vary among provinces.

These observations underline three aspects of educational rights that are recognized internationally. (1) Certain rights in Canada are safeguarded by tradition, legislation, and affirmation: schooling will be free and compulsory to ensure that no person deprives a child of his/her birthright. Violent treatment of pupils is forbidden. (2) Standard setting anticipates or directs evolving practice to ensure consistent policy development in several fields: there should be equal opportunity for women, and persons with special needs should receive education in the least restrictive environment possible. (3) Where a group or individual has been victimized by the past, affirmative action may include educational advantages.

The first section of Human Rights in Canadian Education deals with groups of people most directly, but differently, involved. Parents have traditionally been charged with providing for their children's education, selecting among available schools, fostering special interests, freeing them for effective study, sponsoring their higher education. Collins examines the implications of these expectations. What do parents need to learn of the opportunities available if they are to help and guide their children? Some parents are evidently more influential than others in securing the best for their family.

Burton portrays the teachers' dilemma with its unrelenting expectations and circumscribed authority as a study of natural versus invented rights. He shows teachers to belong to a profession that is easily buffeted by society and thereby diverted and disarmed from their real task.

Brown considers pupils' rights -- including their fundamental rights as human beings in disputes that may arise. Educational access, diversity, quality education, uninterrupted by disputes in which the students have no voice, are discussed in the light of international documents, current situations and emerging possibilities.

Kidd and Ray examine how life-long education might develop in Canada. A series of arguments for more attention to this field is followed by suggestions for achieving better results.

How certain educational rights are provided best is discussed next so that readers who agree with the objectives will receive some reliable direction. Kehoe reviews several approaches usually advocated within the social studies, then summarizes the research that bears upon them. Few of the usually recommended methods work well in all situations.

McCarthy explores ways to sensitize teachers to human rights. Her account draws upon psychology from a value perspective and applies it to the affective impact of literature, the media and personal experience.

McMurray reviews education for those with special needs, from the recommendations of current literature and in a survey of practices across

Canada. His work concludes with a challenge for all educators to be more sensitive to the needs of the learner, a message that reflects the ideas of all the contributors.

Remedying the disadvantages of the past is best addressed in Canada in the fields of language and race. Laferrière deals with the Quebec situation, Bill 101 and the need to be masters in their own house. Lamontagne shows the disadvantages faced by the French in Ontario to be far worse than those of the English in Quebec. D'Oyley discusses the educational concerns and prospects of those who are not protected by special status, despite general clauses prohibiting discrimination. His analysis of Indians who have not signed treaties and of Canadians with African or Asian roots will promote some reappraisals.

The concluding chapter establishes the philosophical and political context within which legislation and regulations may seek to promote human rights. It is recognized to be a process without clearly established objectives and means of securing them, reflecting in part the diversity of the Canadian population, in part the impact of rising expectations.

RIGHTS AND OBLIGATIONS IN EDUCATION

PARENTS' RIGHTS AND OBLIGATIONS
Janet V. Collins

Introduction

It is generally accepted that parents have prior rights to the control and rearing of their offspring, subject only to the limitations that parents' rights neither supercede nor infringe unduly upon the rights of the child. It was not always so. Once children were regarded as chattels, so parents could inflict upon them any mental or physical cruelty. They could be whipped, starved, given away, sold or sent to work under the harshest conditions (Radbill, 1974).

Canadians have recently recognized several forms of child abuse as a current social ill, leading to new legislation and changes in professional practice directed toward the protection of children. The background to current attitudes about childhood and treatment of children in English-Canada has been described by Sutherland (1976). But children are no longer regarded as miniature workers of the family and society; they are now assumed to be immature individuals being prepared for the adult life ahead. This change in emphasis is required of parents if they are to fulfil current social expectations concerned with child nurture.

Parents must provide more than before if they are to satisfy both the physical, mental and spiritual needs of their offspring as well as the demands of society that the "product" will be acceptable. Parents usually accept schools as the principal agency for preparing the next generation; this is reflected in compulsory schooling for people aged six to sixteen (Bargen, 1961, p. 62). Parents are obliged by law to send their children to school during this period; with compulsory schooling children acquire a moral right of access to schools and parents a moral obligation to learn of and to influence the education of their children.

A balance has developed between the views of parents and society which ensures some compromise among emphasis upon social responsibilities, preparation to meet change, familiarity with traditions and sensitivity to current mores. In effect the parents help to define the objectives and procedures for education.

The degree to which parental involvement is attempted or welcomed is highly variable. School boards are in some jurisdictions elected, in others appointed by local government (Halifax), by provincial government (northern Manitoba) or by a Territorial government. Direct voice may be difficult. Although parents may try to buy or rent property with an eye to their children's schooling, they may find that fluctuating enrolments or "social justice" requires their children to be bused several miles from the neighbourhood, thus making parental involvement in school activities less convenient and therefore less likely.

Within the schools, teachers and principals may reject the notion of parental involvement in school matters. For example, Stamp (1975) quotes several examples of teachers who prefer that parents have little if anything to do with schools:

> We had a Home and School Association. But the teachers felt that we did not need the organization as we were able to accomplish the same goals with the splendid cooperation of the staff.
>
> I have no particular plans to involve parents in actual curriculum planning, defining objectives or school organization since the staff consists of highly professional people well qualified to handle things in these areas.

If we examine the contributions parents are usually allowed to make in the planning, execution and evaluation of the work of society's schools, we are led to conclude that parents are merely custodians of the students during those times when teachers enjoy statutory respite, or even unreliable interlopers who would wreck a functioning, albeit imperfect, system. Stamp (1975) reported that

> Parent organizations are suspect as far as teachers are concerned. They have enough people telling them what to do. They have borne the brunt of enough criticism and aren't eager to open up other sources by encouraging well-meaning but mis-informed people to add new dimensions to already unrealistic expectations.

This extreme view may be a reaction to what are at times strident and vehement attempts by parents to influence or perhaps dictate a particular course in the schools. But excessive manipulation of the schools by a few need not lead to the effective exclusion of all parents, creating a state monopoly of child rearing. Compromise is possible.

The Mandate to the Schools

Canadian schools have been expected to reflect the character of traditionally acknowledged culture(s) and to further assimilation into the cultural mainstream (Gaskell, 1977, p. 263; Sutherland, 1976, p. 204). Immigration has resulted in an increasingly multiethnic population, and cultural pluralism is perceived by many as a desirable goal. Recent governmental changes such as the formal recognition of minority cultures (since 1972 there has been a Ministry of State for Multiculturalism) have led to differing expectations of schooling, both at the local level and nationwide. If schools are to meet these expectations then it is desirable that all partners in the compact know the basic assumptions and their implications. In particular, it is necessary to reconcile three quite different interpretations of the school's role: (1) as a mirror of society with all its possible imperfections (e.g., poverty, cruelty, sexism, racism, disregard for human rights), (2) to develop children's talents to the fullest extent, and (3) to promote some idealized myth as a common goal.

Teachers, textbooks, and other resources reflect this imperfect consensus. After reviewing materials, Pratt (1975, p. 121) reported that Canada was considered to be "...a white, Christian, homogenous, middle-class country where liberal democracy and free enterprise have combined to produce the ideal society". He recognized that this was inaccurate both for the past and the present. Whether Canada continues to attempt consensus with new ideals depends upon whether the emerging sociological and demographic realities are acknowledged. Although the conviction that equality of opportunity is a human right in this society is widespread, it is not universal. Officially, programs to extend equal treatment to all groups are symbolic of this larger goal.

Within the schools where children spend a major portion of their formative years, parents anticipate that their children will experience equality of opportunity. They do not expect that children will end their school years "less equal" than before. Although it has been suggested (Jencks, et al., 1972) that schools are ineffective as agents for social change, and are unlikely to have much effect on the status of adults in society, this claim is consistent neither with the experience of educators and the general public nor with public opinion polls (Livingstone and Hart, 1980). Contemporary Canadian society apparently accepts Sutherland's view (1976, p. 237) that "the teacher is a necessary and, potentially, an influential factor in determining the direction and strength of social movements".

To the extent that schools reflect the status quo in society, it is inevitable that there should be dissatisfaction with their performance, particularly among those who consider existing social conditions to be seriously deficient. One aspect of schooling which is potentially damaging in this regard is misused psychological testing. Although there is controversy on this point (Samuda, 1975), most psychological tests given in schools measure what has been learned, rather than native intelligence. Such tests are not often required in order to educate most children to their maximum potential, but are used to separate groups of students for different kinds of teaching. Current practice within the public schools subjects children from very early in their school life to a battery of tests that increasingly narrow their choices. These tests (and the grade level successes) are used to predict what future a child will be advised/allowed to have. The result is that a useful tool for identifying specific learning problems has sometimes been transformed into a device for placing insurmountable obstacles in the path of education.

This process maintains within the school the kind of stratification that exists outside it. When I.Q. tests are used as the basis for streaming children into classes which forever cut off their access to the kind of education that spells "success" by society's standards, parents can be forgiven for thinking that their rights, and their children's, are being infringed by the schools and by professionals within them.

Years ago, parents in Toronto and Montreal argued that the less than satisfactory performance of their children in schools arose not from any innate inability of the children, but rather from a failure of the schools and school authorities to arrange that they be taught appropriately (Park School Community Council Brief, 1971; Brief to the Protestant School Board of Greater Montreal, 1972).

Parents' concern that testing is often detrimental to their children (and indirectly themselves) often arises through poor communications. Hoff et al. (1978) concluded that parents do not always give informed consent to decisions concerning their children's placement in schools, even when they have been involved in the process. The authors ascribed this to a lack of real understanding of the discussions and procedures. Wandler (1978) urged that school psychologists should make genuine efforts to interpret test results with parents so that decisions are fully understood and supported by them, underscoring his belief that "decision making based on tests alone is a misuse of tests". Parents need to know that I.Q. tests do not provide results that can never change. Although there is continuing debate on this point, even those experts who attach overwhelming importance to the evidence that IQ is partly genetically determined admit that present evidence does not rule out the possibility that IQ scores can be raised. Herrnstein (1982) argues that IQ scores are the most effective predictors of future performance, but concedes that methods of teaching and measurement may affect the outcome of tests. When students are labelled in schools, their performance may fulfil the test predictions more because of teacher behaviour than innate ability (Samuda and Tinglin, 1978). On the other hand, young children with lower than average IQ who are taught in an appropriate manner have shown that their scores could be raised to more "normal" values (Englemann, 1970). Moreover, not only teachers but also parents of "deprived" children can participate successfully in the process (Ehrlich and Feldman, 1977). There may be similar parental roles in the education of handicapped persons (see McMurray's chapter).

Tests can be used variously: to predict what students can learn, to help identify effective procedures for teaching, to find what they do not yet know, etc. If all our faith is in predicting success, there is little hope for children whose parents are unable to contribute a great deal to the process of developing their talents fully. However, if we grant a significant reconstruction role to the schools, then parents (especially of the disadvantaged) can expect a lot more.

Sawhill (1979) considers that in America the public schools have been expected to do too much, that the schools have been too near the forefront of social change. However the opportunity to transform society and individual prospects is available only to the school if we examine affordable time and resources. This prospect cannot be forsworn nor diminished because ambitious goals are not always achieved. For some parents, the opportunities presented for their family make bearable their own deprivation and the hardships still oppressing their children. We can and must expect our schools not only to teach students the common goals of our society but also to foster the development of the individual to exploit unique talents.

Parental Expectations

Present concepts of the nature of childhood and the rights of children have rejected the notion of the child as property, though we do not yet regard children as full-fledged members of society. Children still "belong" to their parents. Parents have special rights arising from the responsibilities of custody and guardianship implicit in the parent-child relationship. As guardians, parents protect when children cannot safeguard their own legal and other rights. Children have a right to suitable education; parents have the high responsibility to ensure this. When parents enrol their children in schools, they thereby act on behalf of their children's right to an education, as is their duty. Compulsory attendance imposes obvious responsibilities upon the school which both parents and children have the right to expect that schools will fulfil. Those expectations include competency, consultation and custody.

<u>Competency</u>. Parents assume that their children's education will prepare them to lead independent, satisfying lives. They expect that at the very least they will be literate, and able to handle simple arithmetic and simple logical reasoning. Most parents demand a lot more. They have been led to these expectations not only by the recognition of the relatively advanced state of literature, science and technology of our culture, but selfishly by their increased tax burden so that more highly trained, "competent" teachers are hired. It is reasonable to expect that the competence of teachers, so dearly bought, should be reflected in the accomplishments of their pupils. Canadians may note that some parents in the United States have been so dissatisfied with the results of their children's schooling that they launched civil lawsuits against school authorities (Saretsky, 1973). In Canada both university professors and

parents have claimed that literacy and other skills have declined (Ward and Miller, 1976).

Teachers have argued that the historical comparison is unfair because of the changes in public attitudes to education and the increased numbers of students continuing to high school graduation or beyond. They argued that what is now seen as a decline in overall competence is really the result of a greater number of less competent people being maintained to the stage of leaving school. There are still highly accomplished students graduating every year - those who under rigorously selective secondary schools would have been the only ones enrolled.

Changes in public health and school practice have increased public awareness of specific kinds of learning difficulties, and of the school's competence to deal with them (see McMurray's chapter). Together with more students remaining longer in school, levels of literacy will thereby be maintained and perhaps raised. School authorities and parents must agree on the division of responsibility and participation in order to heighten the level of accomplishments of all students to acceptable standards. A first step would be to decide the best level and nature of communication and consultation with parents on various aspects of school function.

Because parents have the right to choose how their children will be educated, it follows that they influence what is taught. Parents who agree with general principles may still argue over details of emphasis or proportion. An example is the rift between those who advocate "no frills" and "back to basics" and those who consider that art, music and drama belong in the standard core curriculum.

This is not a debate to be confined to teachers and other professionals. Although innovations from research are notoriously slow to affect practice, this is partly because concerned parents and other members of the general public have not been consistently involved in the debate. This is unfortunate, for an enlightened public can help civic authorities to decide which policies and expenditures are justified.

Take the case of Arts education. There are convincing arguments that school children need "an aesthetic mode of experience" because of the relationships among images, language, thought and feeling (Broudy, 1979).

Although school is the only agency that can be relied upon to perform this function adequately, if average taxpayers and their elected representatives do not understand the issues involved, they may not demand or allow suitable aesthetic experiences to be included in the curriculum. When parents participate in this debate, they may need technical help from teachers and other professionals in education.

In an elegant essay on "The Moral Implications of the Decline of Literacy", Monk (1979) has argued that to be literate in the classical sense was to be fully adult and responsible; but that literacy in a contemporary context implies facility with many forms of communication, and those who are deficient are unable to be fully responsible participants. They are denied the basic right to be, through education, adult members of the community. Seen from this perspective, whatever facilitates and ensures understanding and communication cannot be justly regarded as a "frill". In this argument, mathematics, science, modern languages and familiarity with computers are becoming the equivalent of literacy in a simpler society. If parents are to discharge their responsibilities to their children, and to society, they have the right to know this.

Harder to resolve are the objections of parents from minority groups who find that their children are educated in matters totally alien to their culture and values, perhaps without their acquiescence. These problems are very obvious for Indians and Inuit. Such parents often feel that since they have control over neither ends nor means, they must act as responsible parents by withdrawing their children from the offending institutions.

<u>Consultation</u>. By their acceptance of tax supported schooling parents relinquish most education to the professionals. Many are content with this situation but some argue that parents and teachers should collaborate in the education process. Moreover they note that educational philosophies, theories and practice vary over time and from place to place. There are many examples of differences in classroom practice and school design: "traditional" vs "open" schools; authoritarian moral authorities or "resource person" teachings; reading taught by ignoring or emphasizing the phonetic approach; curriculum swings between a vocational and a liberal arts emphasis; students evaluated by standardized tests or non-graded continuous progress.

These changes and variations present numerous problems for those parents whose children are unable to function as well in one regime as another.

> My daughter attended a fairly conventional school where she was happy and doing well. Unfortunately we moved to a new school district where she now has to attend an open-plan ungraded school which she hates. She is so desparately

> unhappy it makes my heart bleed. She finds the seeming
> chaos overwhelming. Being naturally a quiet, neat,
> methodical child, she is unable to assimilate anything
> in the noise and confusion and constant distractions.
> She has made no progress in the six months she has been
> there. Her teachers, of course, are aware of the
> difficulty. In their blind, unthinking way, they are
> sympathetic, assuring me they will make every effort and
> take all the necessary steps to help her adapt. But mark
> well that -- the solution is for the child to adapt to
> the system, not that the system is obviously the wrong
> one for the child.... How is this different from the old
> traditional method, which progressive educationists
> condemn so righteously as narrow, harsh and cruel?
> (Stamp, 1975, p. 110).

Ray (1974) has discussed the importance of consensus on the objectives of education, and concludes that a successful program can be devised in terms of broad social goals by the public, pupils, and teachers. He argues that this approach is essential to ensure that students attain competency in appropriate areas. Arcus (1979) describes such an example from Calgary concerning Family Life Education.

One undesirable consequence of the lack of consultation and cooperation between home and school is the alienation that often develops between parent and child. This may be most serious when children observe that the right hand at home knows not what the left hand at school does, and where children surpass their parents in their ability with school work. While no one would expect uniform competency among parents, they deserve the chance to be fully involved in their children's education. In the kind of dialogue that this entails, the benefits are not all on the home side, for in helping parents fulfil their role, school people also enhance their own rewards.

An examination of the many suggested ways to improve home-school relations reveals the need not only for changes in attitude, but also additional personnel. Since many parents desire more personal involvement, it is apparent that personnel must be at hand. The problem of attitude is more refractory, for the assumption that professional teachers must stick together and support each other against "them", would alienate the parents.

Parents must rely on the judgment of professionals regarding their children's future even when their own interests and judgment suggest otherwise (Gordon, 1978). However frustrating it may be for teachers and counsellors that parents often disregard their advice, often parents perceive teachers to brush aside views or objectives which do not accord with their own. Results of psychological tests are presented without adequate explanation, so that even the most knowledgable parent may be intimidated. Parents are disturbed when pathways to their children's future are selected on the basis of tests which are used more to predict failure than to plan for success (Hutchison *et al*., 1979). This is particularly stressful for disadvantaged parents who are already convinced by the world at large that their views are not worth hearing.

One principal cause of misunderstanding and dissatisfaction is that some school authorities are secretive about records of individual students. While streaming and choice of subjects taught are decided on results of school administered tests, parents are kept from knowing precisely what information is being used. Comparable information about citizens and consumers has been made accessible so that inaccuracies can be challenged. It is not clear why parents should have any less access to confidential files on their children, especially when they are hampered from conscientiously exercising their best judgment on particular issues. This matter is examined persuasively in <u>Privacy in Jeopardy</u> (Humphreys, 1980).

There has been considerable public debate concerning the moral and ethical values which parents wish to share with their children. Usually the objections arise when specific topics such as human sexuality and birth control are included in the curriculum, and when 'obscene' texts are used in English literature classes. Although parents have a right to transmit their peculiar values to their offspring, the vociferous insistence that the school reflect only such values must be seen as an infringement on the rights of others. The public thus becomes the judge of what is obscene - not a few parents. While there is no justification for inflicting the values of a majority upon a minority who strongly reject them, the converse is also true. In many cases the different perspectives are accepted and some alternatives are available so that students are not forced to study what offends their parents. The financial implications may be more important than the educational or political consequences, but human rights may often demand that penalty.

<u>Custody</u>. All School Acts require that children be in the custody of school personnel during school hours (Bargen, 1961, p. 114). Parents expect that the safety and orderly climate of the school will equal or surpass that of the home. Parents also assume that the school will ensure an environment that is conducive to learning, and they expect to be informed and consulted when this does not prevail. If they do not, parents cannot expect that conflicts which may arise will be resolved in their children's favour.

Neither can they expect that persistent disruption of classes by their children will be tolerated. Parents have a right to expect cooperative custody, as well as a responsibility to facilitate it. But it is difficult to define and agree upon the limits to the school's custodial role. Although it is agreed that the role extends beyond mere physical safety, there may be conflict in areas like suitable clothing which parents have not relinquished. For example, dress codes have often been developed without direct parental involvement and may ignore their values. While it may seem reasonable from the point of view of instilling a type of discipline, self respect and a sense of appropriate conduct, a particular

dress code rigidly enforced may in fact infringe upon parents' rights to clothe their offspring to the best of their ability, or in keeping with their own taste and value system. In a melting pot society rigid dress codes may be perceived as necessary to ensure that all members of society fit the mold; in a multicultural society this is neither necessary nor desirable.

The Plight of the Poor. The children of the poor tend to leave school early (Adams et al., 1971). Those who graduate from high school have usually been motivated by the promise of good job opportunities, until recently a sure job. For many the sad truth is that jobs are scarce for them, even with a high school diploma. In Canada, several groups, especially the more visible minorities, are underrepresented in post-secondary education institutions and within the professions. Undesirable as this may be for the full development of a truly multicultural society, it is hardly surprising, giving the tendency for many minority youth to truncate their schooling. In addition, children in single parent families, or where illness or accident have taken their toll, or where few economic opportunities exist, are very likely to leave school early.

The problem for parents in such situations is complex. Their children may be placed in non-academic programs, especially in high school. This is usually claimed to meet the students' needs, and to have their parents' knowledge or approval; poor parents cannot ensure that their children will be able to secure the optimum education. They are less likely to know the available options, less successful at having educational decisions reversed, less able to afford alternative programs or schooling. Cycles of repeated disadvantage become translated into economic and psychological deficits which are loaded onto the children. Education is only one part of their disadvantaged status but it is an important part of their inter-generational opportunity. However, poor parents have rarely been advised and consulted for their children's programs; they may not know that their children usually start school significantly behind in measurable skills behind the children of middle class parents. Without special efforts to build on their skills, they fall rapidly behind their classmates in such things as reading ability and consequently in almost all other subjects. It is not unusual for students to progress through the entire system with reading abilities consistently and significantly below the level required to cope with the assigned work, and some graduate from high school barely literate (Jencks, 1972). Personal communication with Canadian teachers indicates similar events in Canada.

Bargen (1961, p. 114) cites a legal opinion that the authority of the school over pupils is not limited to school hours and premises. This claim is based on the view that the well-being of the school (and, by implication, of society) must be protected. It could be used to promote opportunities for the disadvantaged, an opportunity that would be most effective if parents were involved appropriately. Such programs are especially necessary where the schools are not fully meeting their mandate, where parents are unable to help their children understand and prepare for their future, but where social interests and human rights demand some joint efforts. These conditions exist in every part of Canada and led to the Black Education Fund (Education Nova Scotia IX, 2.7, 1978), community programs on Indian reservations (Snow, 1977), heritage language programs of major cities and a host of multicultural programs and facilities. In the long run these cooperative ventures hold substantial promise of recognizing parents' rights in defining and achieving what has been proposed as a just society.

REFERENCES

Adam, Ian, et al. *The Real Report on Poverty*. Edmonton: Hurtig, 1971.

Arcus, M.E. "Inservice Education in Family Life Education" in *Canadian Education*, 1979, 4 (3): 43-52.

Bargen, P.F. *The Legal Status of the Canadian Public School Pupil*. Toronto: Macmillan Co. of Canada, 1961, pp. 62, 114-115.

Broudy, H.S. "Arts Education: Necessary or Just Nice?" in *Phi Delta Kappan* 60 (5), 1979: 347-350.

Education in Transition: A Capsule Review, 1960-1975. Toronto: Canadian Education Association, 1975.

Ehrlich, P.R. and S.S. Feldman *The Race Bomb: Skin Color, Prejudice and Intelligence*. Quadrangle/New York Times Book Co., 1977, pp. 83-91.

Englemann, S. "The Effectiveness of Direct Instruction on I.Q. Performance and Achievement in Reading and Arithmetic" in *The Disadvantaged Child*, 1970, Vol. 3, pp. 339-361.

Gaskell, J. "Stereotyping and Discrimination in the Curriculum" in (editors) H.A. Stevenson and J.D. Wilson, *Precepts, Policy and Process: Perspectives on Contemporary Canadian Education*, 1977. London, Ontario: Alexander Blake Associates, pp. 263-284.

Gordon, W.R. "Parents and the Schools: Responsibilities Before Rights" in *Manitoba Teacher*, 1978, 56 (5): 3.

Herrnstein, R.J. "IQ Testing and the Media", *The Atlantic Monthly*, August 1982, pp. 68-74.

Hoff, M.K., K.S. Fenton, R.K. Yoshida and M.J. Kaufman "Notice and Consent: The School's Responsibility to Inform Parents" in *Journal of School Psychology*, 1978, 16 (3): 265-273.

Humphreys, Edward H. *Privacy in Jeopardy: Student Records in Canada*. Toronto: Ontario Institute for Studies in Education, 1980.

Hutchison, H.P., D.H. Prosser and P. Wedge "The Prediction of Educational Failure" in *Educational Studies*, 1979, 5 (1): 73-82.

Livingstone, D.W. and D.J. Hart *Public Attitudes Toward Education in Ontario*. Toronto: Ontario Institute for Studies in Education, 1980.

Monk, P. "The Moral Implications of the Decline of Literacy" in
    Halifax Chronicle Herald, 1979, May 21, p. 7.

Pratt, D. "The Social Role of Textbooks in Canada" in E. Zureik and
    R.M. Pike (editors) Socialization and Values in Canadian
    Society, 1975, Vol. 1, Toronto.

Radbill, S.X. "A History of Child Abuse and Infanticide" in R.E. Helfer
    and C.H. Kempe The Battered Child, 1974, Chicago: Chicago
    University Press, 2nd. ed. pp. 3-21.

Ray, D. "Competency Based Education: Creating the Environment for
    Learning Efficiency" in Journal of Abstracts in International
    Education, 1974, 4, 2: 3-37.

Samuda, Ronald J. Psychological Testing of American Minorities.
    New York: Harper and Row, 1975.

Samuda, R.J. and W.H. Tinglin "Can Testing Serve Minority Needs?" in
    School Guidance Worker, 1978, 33 (4): 39-44.

Sretsky, G. "The Strangely Significant Case of Peter Doe" in Phi Delta
    Kappan, 54 (9), 1973, 589-592.

Sawhill, J.D. "The Collapse of the Public Schools" in Saturday Review,
    August, 1979, pp. 17-18.

Snow, Chief John These Mountains Are Our Sacred Places. Toronto:
    Samuel Stevens, 1977.

Stamp, R.M. About Schools: What Every Canadian Parent Should Know.
    Don Mills, Ontario: New Press, 1975, pp. 30-32, 110.

Sutherland, N. Children in English-Canadian Society: Framing the
    Twentieth Century Consensus. Toronto: University of
    Toronto Press, 1976.

Wandler, J. "Interpreting Test Results With Parents of Problem Children"
    in School Guidance Worker, 1978, 33 (4): 35-38.

Ward, E. and R. Miller "Are Canadians Getting Their $12 Billion Worth?"
    Macleans Magazine, September 6, 1976, pp. 59-62.

THE RIGHTS OF TEACHERS

Anthony Burton

What rights do teachers have, and in which areas do these obtain? What is different about the rights teachers have with regard to parents and employers, and in their working contact with students? What moral and legal bases exist for the rights that teachers are accorded, or claim for themselves? And what is the relationship between rights and power, in the different levels of the teacher's existence?

Much has been said about the rights of teachers which lie beyond the narrow context of the classroom, i.e., to establish working rights through union process, and to share in areas such as curriculum development and policy formation. These discussions rarely reflect the dynamics that occur when teachers' rights are placed in conflict with other rights and with the realities of power: nor do they reflect the need for teachers to struggle for their own rights while seeking to buttress their limited and fragile power so important to control and educate students.

Natural and Invented Rights

It is essential to recall the distinction between 'invented' and 'natural' rights because the problems raised by the theme of teacher rights are very different as we look at the teacher in the schooling bureaucracy and the teacher in the classroom. These problems are reflected in two sub-themes: the importance of locating any talk of rights in cultural and political realities; and the options that may exist for action to bring about useful change.

Rights were once thought of as natural, absolute and inalienable: natural because they were given, by God or Nature; absolute because they were part of the 'human condition', the way it was spozed to be; and inalienable in the sense that they could not be taken away. Such a view of rights reflected the social facts of an earlier time. It also seemed to benefit the interests of the elite who proposed them: self-government seemed right for Jefferson, Cavour and Bismarck, and the right to own property and profit from speculation and capital seemed right to Morgan, Rhodes, Strathcona or Holt; who of course gave due attention to the ten commandments and the penal code.

Such views of human rights may be entering a new ascendancy. But it should be noted that successful claimants of natural rights are those who have some power, oil perhaps, to back their claims.

Invented rights have been emphasized during this century. We are much more likely today to accept that rights are fragile, impermanent, man-made and often in conflict with each other. They may also be in conflict with natural rights and the realities of power, but this is not new. The State, now as then, certainly has the power to take away life, liberty, property and definitely happiness. It still may lack the means or the will to protect the rights of various minorities from their neighbours or to intervene in the marketplace to protect against misused power (rights).

These competing concepts can be applied directly to the rights of teachers (Goble, 1982). Rights may be claimed by two kinds of groups: those who have some measure of power; and those who lack it, so must form together in order to get power in some measure. The problem with teachers is that they belong to both groups at the same time and their rights are fragile, impermanent, and inevitably in conflict with power and rights of others. This constant flux means that once rights have been won and stated, they quickly become static and ossified. The meaning of such statements as the duties and rights of teachers sounds silly unless you somehow embed them in the cultural flow to which they are supposed to relate.

Teachers as Employees

Teachers might seek collectively not only to protect their standard of living, job security and working conditions, but to participate in decision-making and policy about what should happen in schools, as they did with some success in Calgary in 1980 (Kratzman, 1980). Unlike doctors and lawyers (who exceed teachers in power and status) and blue collar workers (who have less), teachers have trouble both with the protection of their working conditions and with participation in decision-making. To grasp why teachers have such trouble securing their rights, we must take a closer look at where teachers stand in Canada and in other societies, particularly in professional autonomy, income and community deference. Their own view may not be that of the community (Ray, 1977).

In most countries there is a modest mystique about teachers. They are supposed to experience a sense of vocation and to enjoy a special cultural status. Doctors care for our bodies, priests care for our souls, and teachers care for our children, who are extensions of ourselves and a promise for the future.

Once this mystique is brushed away, we see that teachers are hardly professionals at all (Miranda, 1981). Within memory some Canadian teachers received their credentials only seven months after incomplete secondary education. All doctors studied for at least six additional years. Teachers cannot control entry to their own ranks nor impose their own fees as doctors and lawyers do. They must fight to participate in defining what they will teach, how and why. They are very like the lower orders of civil servants.

Teachers are not fully professionals, but neither are they blue collar workers. They are not really free to use the bargaining weapons of that group (Hennessy, 1980). Teachers, like policemen and firemen and nurses, must be very careful about withdrawing their labour. If assembly line workers strike, people still have cars. Even the strikes of mailmen or garbage workers can be tolerated as an irritation. But when teachers strike, parents and others must take up the slack. The profound irritation of parents who are inconvenienced with the need to care for their own children because the schools are closed says a great deal about Canadian society, when earning an income may supercede parents' contact with their children and the value of a school as a child tending place becomes evident. Dubious though the status of teachers may be, most parents hold most teachers to be of superior social class. This means that the teacher is not seen by the workers as one of them, so teachers' efforts to improve their own situation through the same means that workers use are liable to evoke the nastiest forms of blue collar resentment. The solidarity between one union and another is overshadowed by the distinctions that are perceived between mental and manual labourers. Doctors and lawyers obviously have the power which teachers do not, to hold that resentment to their economic advantage.

We may pause to consider how teachers came to this pass. During the nineteenth century, surgeons, lawyers and architects were among those able to claim for themselves many of the professional rights and advantages that had previously belonged to clergymen and physicians:

> The characteristics of these occupations were strikingly different from the established liberal professions. Often they were initially associated with working class (lowly trade and commercial) occupations - the surgeons with barbers, the apothecaries with green grocers, and so on. Their claims to higher income and status were not based on their general familiarity with classical languages but on their increasingly specialized and extensive knowledge and skill. In their endeavours to achieve the social status of gentlemen they both built on their solid craft foundations (e.g., apprenticeship-internship), and aped the peculiar habits and customs of the established liberal professions (e.g., fee-for-service payment).
> (Myers, 1977, 16).

Teachers never managed to acquire such status. This has led to a contradiction: while teachers possess much power over the young, they are in important ways dependent and domesticated beyond the confines of the classroom. Even the power of collective bargaining is truncated by cutbacks, attrition, and the near bankruptcy of various administrations. The rights of teachers to join in administrative and policy decision-making about their daily work are also greatly reduced in fact.

> As a young teacher in the Toronto area in the early Sixties, I became concerned about a particularly striking characteristic of teaching and teachers. Despite the fact that the Board, which employed me, enjoyed an international reputation for openness, innovation and progressive educational development, I soon became aware that its teachers, in an important sense, worked within a restricted and narrow context. A wide range of educational issues involving school and board policy were regarded as out-of-bounds for teacher consideration and comment, even though those policies affected what the teachers did. (Myers, 1977, 14).

Although the UNESCO Recommendation Concerning the Status of Teachers attempts to redress such areas of powerlessness (Thomas, 1968), it has no power to compel, but serves as a skeletal base for the consciousness shifts and collective struggles that teachers should urgently decide to undertake.

> What is important for teachers to note, however, is that no occupational group - professional or union - acquired whatever degree of power or influence it possesses, by waiting for society to 'award' it. The task for teachers, then, is to decide in the light of their present circumstances, what collective means they wish to utilize in order to achieve their occupational objectives.... (Myers, 1977, 16).

Teachers as Teachers

The rights and powers that affect teachers' relations with parents, board officials and government are but one side of the penny. When we look at the interface where teachers and students meet, the roles are reversed. It is the students for whom rights are claimed, while the teachers are seen as the power figures.

Only a few of the UNESCO Recommendations (class size, evaluation, safety and guidance) refer to rights involving teachers and students (Thomas, 1968, 74). This is significant, but most such relationships are not defined in terms of rights. In effect, classrooms are usually left to the teacher. Unless the teacher is patently unable to keep control, few principals will enter the room for more than cursory visits. Few others are (or want to be) admitted. Superintendents are too busy doing all the things from which teachers are excluded. Professors of education are reluctant to disturb teachers in their natural habitat.

Two decades of radical critique of the schools (i.e., Goodman, 1962; Friedenburg, 1964; Illich, 1970; and Gintis, 1975) have established that schools educate to some extent, they socialize the young into the attitudes and behaviours of the larger society, and they restrain an enormous number of young people who might well have better things to do but are not thought to be 'safe out'.

Teachers must juggle the twin acts of controlling and educating. Most documents concerning teachers' rights and responsibilities assume the controlling function but do not properly deal with the teaching.

The New Sociology of Education in Britain has peered closely into the interface of education and control. Willis (1976) shows how distinctions between manual and mental labour are articulated in the school. Hammersley (1976) examines how teachers force students to submit to the process of being taught. This school of sociologists observe with great care and over long periods of time, so that their empirical studies have great credibility. Simpler observations have been made in North America by Kozol (1967), Herndon (1971), Dennison (1969), Holt (1969) and several others; similar assertions about how teachers educate-and-control seem to occur in great profusion.

Hammersley notes that teachers have limited power to coerce. Although they can use such devices as strapping, lines, detentions, suspension, sending people to the office, and so on, their currency is limited, and can easily be devalued. Students who appreciate that their teacher has run out of repressive devices are dangerous and literally not to be contained. Therefore, if they are to survive, teachers seek for more artful ways to beef up their control; they claim rights which they only arguably possess (Hammersley, 1976, 105-115). They present themselves as authorities. They claim that status and the obligations that go with it are givens, a normal and natural state of affairs which the student cannot question without putting himself beyond the pale. Secondly, teachers establish this status by 'superior' behaviour. They ask questions no one can answer but themselves. They engage students in confrontations which the teacher must win. If students question the ground rules, they are defined as 'cheeky', thereby shifting the theme from teaching to control.

Third, teachers practise what Hammersley calls "Strategic Easing". They relax their controls by offering deals to the students which will make repression more bearable. Such offers come with strings which may not be the subject of bargaining. Forced in this way to accept the teacher's rules, students at the very moment of protest legitimize the rights the teacher has spuriously claimed.

Most teachers do this. Wise, experienced, loving teachers probably do it as little as possible, and insensitive, hating and callow teachers may do it most of the time. We know that teachers MUST in some degree do this, because all teachers face a structural problem implicit in the nature of schooling. Learning must take place, if necessary by coercion. The young are compelled by law and by cultural forces like their parents and peers to attend school. Schools offer credentials which are related to economic and working success, and even to the definition of reality. The last thing you can safely assume about schools is that the young attend them out of interest. They put up with them, which is different.

One may retreat from constructive discussion by saying that schools are awful dehumanizing jails, and that the problem is not how to improve them or put up with them but how to get rid of them (Reimer, 1971).

But the schools are with us for the present. Although they are in many ways lousy, they are no worse than the rest of life on the planet. The present point is that teachers seem to claim rights for themselves in order to exercise a little more power than they are given. Although this makes their daily lives a little easier, it also distances them from students, who may see through such con-games and feel an intensely adolescent revulsion at such hypocrisy. The import of Hammersley's data is that teachers tend to deny to their students the dialogic and invented view of rights they seek to impose on administrators and others. Since the problem is structural, it has no solution. However, there may be ways in which the problem could be eased slightly.

Ameliorations

Strickland, Phillips and Phillips (1976) have produced a 'practical legal handbook for the teaching profession', in which they set out all the teaching behaviours that can lead to charges of malpractice. While this book makes many points that teachers should find useful, it seems grossly to exaggerate the risk of malpractice. It deals in feelings of anger, paranoia and self-pity. In the argument proposed, it presents a manual of techniques for domestication.

A much cooler and more sensible approach is available (Ladd, 1975). It accepts that teachers must control and must educate but Ladd distinguishes among kinds of control.

> One meaning is complete power over something as in 'A driver should always have control over his car'. A second meaning is partial control for certain purposes as in, 'Mrs. X allows students a lot of freedom, but she has the necessary control. Some principals and teachers, recognizing the need for control in the second sense, believe they must achieve control in the first sense...'.

The thrust of Ladd's argument is that at the teacher-student interface, many rights compete: those of parents, taxpayers, officials, and of course the entire school community itself. The task of teachers and school administrators, he claims, is to uphold all of these rights 'as best they can', and when some of these rights conflict, to strike a proper balance between them.

Ladd repeats the teachers' claim of 'natural law' as the basis for what they do, and proposes that their rights are absolute, inalienable and given. They are thus functioning as people who have power; they tend to claim rights in order to justify what they want to do anyway.

It may be that teachers have little choice, since these actions are imposed on them by the workings of 'structural' forces. Ladd, however, raises the interesting possibility that teachers may be able to move from a view of rights as natural to a view of rights as invented. Such teachers may indeed see rights as fragile, impermanent, and in necessary contradiction. This could enable them to offer to students a consistent position in which competing rights must be upheld as well as possible, and kept in proper balance. Such a position, once it has been affirmed and presented persuasively to students, could lead to interesting new approaches to the problem of management-yet-education.

People like Gintis and Illich, who claim that the schools are illegitimate in their essence and the cause of the problem rather than targets for reforming would no doubt scoff at Ladd. For those of us who are more than half-persuaded by any of the radical analyses, Ladd offers a brief whiff of sal volatile. The law, with its implied dialectic of rights, seems a better basis for the classroom powers of the teacher than Hammersley's analysis of their present practice. One does not have to be a Polyanna to see that somewhere, somehow, it might be useful to attract attention to this point.

REFERENCES

Dennison, George The Lives of Children. New York: Random House, 1969.

Friedenburg, Edgar Z. The Vanishing Adolescent. Beacon Hill, Mass.: Beacon Hill Press, 1964.

Gintis, Herbert & Samuel Bowles Schooling in Capitalistic America: Educational Reform and the Contradictions of Economic Life. New York: Basic Books, 1976.

Goble, Norman "New Angles on the Issue of Teachers' Working Conditions", Phi Delta Kappan, 63:6 (Feb. 1982), 413-414.

Goodman, Paul Compulsory Mis-Education and the Community of Scholars. New York: Vantage, 1962.

Hammersley, Martyn "The Mobilization of Pupil Attention" in M. Hammersley and P. Woods (eds.) The Process of Schooling: A Sociological Reader. London: Routledge & Kegan Paul, 1976.

Hennessy, Peter H. "A Canadian Reaction to the Debate on Teacher Bargaining", Phi Delta Kappan (May 1980), 641-643.

Herndon, James How To Survive in Your Native Land. New York: Simon and Shuster, 1971.

Holt, John The Underachieving School. New York: Pitman, 1969.

Illich, Ivan Deschooling Society. New York: Harper, 1970.

Kozol, Jonathan Death at An Early Age. Boston: Houghton Mifflin, 1967.

Kratzman, Arthur et al. A System in Conflict. A Report to the Minister of Labour by the Fact-Finding Commission. Edmonton: Government of Alberta, 1980.

Ladd, Edward T. (with John C. Walden) Students Rights and Discipline. Arlington, Va.: National Association of Elementary School Principals, 1975.

Miranda, Evelina Oeteza y "Faculty of Education and the Development of a Body of Knowledge of Teaching", Journal of Educational Thought, 15:3 (Dec. 1981), 171-186.

Myers, Doug "The Teaching 'Profession'? A Demystification", This Magazine, 11:3 (May/June 1977), 14-16.

Postman, Neil *Teaching as a Subversive Activity*. New York: Delacorte Press, 1969.

Ray, Douglas "The Preconditions of Professional Autonomy: A Comparison of Recent Educational Experience in Canada and Britain" in Jill Moore & Peter Raggatt (eds.) *Diversity and Unity Within the School*: Proceedings of the Twelfth Annual Conference of the Comparative Education Society of Europe (British Section). London: University of London, Institute of Education, 1977, 43-57.

Reimer, Everett *School is Dead*. New York: Doubleday, 1971.

Strickland, Rennard, Janet Phillips & W.R. Phillips *Avoiding Teacher Malpractice: A Practical Legal Handbook for the Teaching Professional*. New York: Hawthorn Books, 1976.

Thomas, Jean *Teachers for the Schools of Tomorrow*. Paris: UNESCO, 1968.

Willis, Paul "The Class Significance of School Counter Culture" in M. Hammersley & P. Woods, *op. cit*.

STUDENTS' RIGHTS

James Brown

TEACHER SUPERVISES SPANKING OF GRADE TWO
STUDENT BY EACH OF HIS CLASSMATES

OUTCRY BY UNIVERSITY PROFESSORS OVER
STUDENTS' LACK OF BASIC SKILLS IN
WRITTEN AND ORAL COMMUNICATION

TEACHERS STILL ON STRIKE - STUDENTS MAY
LOSE YEAR

PARENTS CLAIM TEACHERS PREJUDICED AGAINST
THEIR CHILD BECAUSE OF GRADE ONE TEACHER'S
COMMENTS ON HER RECORDS

Headlines like these challenge educators and lay persons alike to ponder the rights to which students are entitled with regard to their education, and the degree to which student rights are being violated.

Rights for Students as Human Beings

Discussion of student rights must be premised on the recognition that students are first of all human beings and, as such, are entitled to certain rights. "Human rights accrue to all people simply because they are human. We cannot deny one's humanness because of his or her temporary status as a student" (Zimmerman, 1974).

Although educational violations of group rights have been widely discussed (e.g. Eichler, 1980; D'Oyley, 1978; Laferrière, t.b.p. 1983), it is popularly assumed that most Canadian students are secure in the rights proclaimed for them. For example the Universal Declaration of Human Rights notes several standards that have significance to students, notably -

- all human beings are born free and equal in dignity and rights (Article 1)

- freedom from discrimination (Article 2)

- right to an education (Article 26)

- protection against degrading treatment or punishment (Article 5)

- recognition as a person before the law (Article 6)

- a fair and public hearing by an independent and impartial tribunal in the determining of rights and obligations and of any criminal charge (Article 10)

- protection from arbitrary interference with privacy and from attacks upon honour and reputation (Article 12).

Although being a student does not necessarily mean being a child, it involves a dependency status in most cases. Pupils in elementary or secondary schools are usually under their parents' legal care; students in senior secondary grades, tertiary education, and full-time continuing education are usually wholly or partly dependent on some kind of sponsorship. It is thus useful to examine how this dependency diminishes any rights that the student might otherwise enjoy, and the extent to which they actually gain rights by virtue of their student status. For example the Declaration of the Rights of the Child proclaims that children are entitled to special protection so that they may "develop physically, mentally, morally, spiritually and socially in a healthy and normal manner and in conditions of freedom and dignity". Do both school curricula and professional relationships fulfil these expectations?

Fundamental Human Rights

Although there would be general public agreement that most teachers most of the time are patient, caring individuals, it is very likely that any group of students will be able to relate, from their own experiences, examples where they feel that their or their classmates' rights were violated - where teachers, counsellors, administrators did not behave as they should. These might include examples of physical and psychological abuse - teachers push, throw chalk, employ sarcasm, or ridicule students.

Even before the Constitutional Act, 1982, there was a growing recognition that corporal punishment "has the potential for creating more problems than it solves, and that physical punishment violates all the human rights known to civilized man. The present level of expertise and sophistication in our society suggests that [educators] can find better ways to deal with children in school" (van Hoose, 1975). The Constitution could be interpreted as rejecting the use of corporal punishment: "Everyone has the right not to be subjected to any cruel and unusual treatment or punishment" (Article 12). "Better ways" should be premised on the dignity and worth of the student, and should preclude not only physical abuse but also psychological abuse detrimental to the student's self confidence and self concept.

Due Process. Persons accused of a crime against society have the right to expect due process of the law including, for example:

- presumption of innocence
- the right to defend oneself
- the right to witnesses
- the introduction of an impartial authority
- explanation of consequences
- the opportunity to appeal

It would not be too harsh to say that in Canada, as in the United States, students are regularly denied due process; and the presumption of innocence is almost unheard of when young people are accused of violating school rules. Instead, "when students are accused by teachers, they already stand convicted" (Marker & Mehlinger, 1974). These same critics observed that the student rebellion of the seventies in the United States came from perceptive high school students who were "attempting to reduce the inconsistencies they perceive[d] between what they [were] taught ... and the realities of the school environment within which they live[d]. They found that the rights they learned about in the classroom were unavailable to them at school. Many students in today's Canadian schools appear to be exposed to the same inconsistencies.

The Right to Privacy. In many jurisdictions, record-keeping practices are currently being revised to ensure that information detrimental to the student and entered without students' or parents' knowledge or consent is not included in the record which follows the student through the school system. This process of revision coincides with increased parental access to and input into these files, and is an acknowledgement of student right to privacy and dignity of treatment. Paradoxically, with current reforms in record keeping, privacy will be increasingly complicated by the electronic revolution now under way (Humphreys, 1980).

Students must be assured that information volunteered, especially in the high school counselling setting, is not released, even to parents, without the student's knowledge and consent, and is not discussed without permission with non-involved persons. There can be few actions more damaging to student/teacher trust and respect than the invasion of privacy occasioned by the revelation of information which the student believed was confidential.

The Right to Education

Both the Universal Declaration of Human Rights and the Declaration of the Rights of the Child affirm that everyone has the right to receive an education, that this education is to be free at least in the elementary stages, that technical and professional education are to be generally available, and that higher education is to be accessible to all on the basis of merit (Article 26; Principle 7). In addition, education must:

- be directed to the full development of the human personality and to the strengthening of respect for human rights and fundamental freedoms (Article 26)

- recognize the students' general culture, develop their abilities, their individual judgement, and their sense of moral and social responsibility, and enable them to become useful members of society (Principle 7)

- promote understanding, tolerance, and friendship among all nations and racial or religious groups (Article 26)

- have as its guiding principle the best interests of the student (Principle 7)

- be subject to the prior right of parents to choose the kind of education that shall be given to their children (Article 26).

Access to Education. A number of factors have been related to educational disadvantage: poverty, the jurisdiction for the student's place of residence, sex, the language of instruction, and the possibility that special facilities or procedures are required. Access presumably means the right to various kinds of education on a continuing or recurring basis, and also that such education is equal in quality and equally likely to safeguard the student's rights. For example, English and French schooling are rarely equal in resources. Girls and boys may not have access to the same educational experiences. Technical and vocational education may depend upon cooperation with various employers to offer certain kinds of practical experiences. When life-long learning is proposed (see following chapter), the right curriculum and teaching conditions, appropriate hours and perhaps relief from other responsibilities, all become aspects of access.

A further ramification of continued access to education is that students should not be exploited by teachers or school boards as tools to force the solution of contract differences by strike and/or lockout. If, as an Ontario study showed, "all educators of the public system, in their moments of professional reflection and candour, see themselves pursuing roughly the same goals" (Hennessy, 1981), then the adversary system of resolving contract negotiations should give way to procedures which do not infringe on students' right to an uninterrupted education.

Quality Education. Despite the current emphasis on curbing government spending and equalizing opportunity, there are strong arguments that we "owe to our children the best we have to give" (Declaration of the Rights of the Child). It should be more possible now than before to have courses and programs well designed to bring about the full development of each child's potential...to provide "all that is necessary to the building of a questioning mind and a dynamic moral conscience" (Piaget, 1973). It is necessary, therefore, that schools accept the obligation "of not destroying or spoiling those possibilities that [students] may have that would benefit society first of all, or of allowing the loss of important abilities or the smothering of others" (Piaget, 1973).

If students are to receive such an education, teachers must be highly competent in judging student capabilities and levels of development - psychological, physical, social, and emotional, and must have a sufficient range of methodologies at their command to facilitate learning for any student for whom they are responsible. For "it is when curriculum content, the teaching/learning strategies, and the learner's capabilities form an integrated planning process, that education will best assist the learner and satisfy society's expectations" (Brown, 1978). The right to such a quality education implies on the part of educators "the utilization of the psychological and sociological knowledge of laws of mental development, and methods and techniques [to] achieve the best formative results..." (Piaget, 1973).

Curricular Content. O'Leary (1980) proposed a hierarchy of curricular discipline:

1. Mathematics
2. Physical Sciences
3. Classical and Modern Languages
4. History and the Social Sciences
5. Literature and the Arts
6. Morality, politics and religion.

In his view the higher on the list a curricular area is, the more likely those in the wider community are to defer to the expertise of educators. O'Leary says that the "margin of difference [between expert and non-expert] begins to grow less and less so that by the time we reach something like morality we have to say that either there are no moral experts or that everyone, in his or her own fashion, is an expert".

It may be observed that programs like moral and values education are likely to prove controversial to parents, to interested community members and to typical school boards. Parents have the prior right to decide what type of education is to be given to their children, and typically want the "best" for them, but may not be aware of all the alternatives. For Piaget (1973), in a democracy it is vital that educators ensure that parents are, "if not educated, at least informed and even instructed about the better education that their children should receive".

Assuming the expertise of educators in regard to content is not to imply that educators should have sole input into the curriculum. Neither does the expertise of educators imply that students have no right to expect any choice in their education. Rather as they become older, students should have an increasing choice of courses, levels, and schools from suitable alternatives provided by those with the expertise to view the whole educational process (Ray, 1979, 1981). Similarly, students at all levels should have choices about the content and process through which to meet the goals and objectives pre-determined by those responsible for their education. It is assumed that choices must be made from within a framework which will ensure that the basics are adequately mastered. Furthermore, students should have the right to expect that any diploma or certificate issued upon completion of a course or program will be recognized as valid and worthwhile by potential employers and advanced educational institutions.

The Learning Environment. The full and harmonious development of students' personalities requires love and understanding (Declaration of the Rights of the Child, Principle 6), in the school setting as well as at home. "The learning process is a highly affective experience, occurring most profitably when there is mutual trust and confidence between teacher and student" (Marker & Mehlinger, 1974). Accordingly, students have the right to expect teachers who care about students and treat them as equal in dignity and worth.

The responsibility of Faculties of Education is clear with respect to these expectations. It cannot be assumed that persons aspiring to the teaching profession are sensitive to human rights or that without instruction they will be able to respond with sensitivity to individual differences of the innumerable types which are found in all Canadian schools. [Please refer to McCarthy's chapter (editor)]. Some of these differences result from the diverse cultural backgrounds of students. According to a Report by the Ontario Human Rights Commission, teachers need to be "familiarized with the backgrounds, traditions and language of their students" and educators must ensure that teaching content and materials "reflect the very rich and diverse multicultural character of our society". Without this attention, students "can as easily learn prejudice at schools as they can learn to respect one another's differences and to value diversity". Furthermore, students have the right to teachers whose training promotes "fuller knowledge and understanding of human rights [including] opportunities for student teachers to learn to recognize and cope with prejudice and discrimination, both their own and others" (Life Together, 1977).

Rights, Rules, and Responsibilities

What is it to have certain rights? "To announce a right is to announce certain rules of behaviour" (Pring, 1979). In the case of education, announcing a particular right implies a series of complementary obligations, to be assumed by students, teachers, parents and perhaps others. For example, how can students claim an educational right if they do not attend regularly, do not prepare properly, or are too tired to enter into discussion? It implies also that someone - parents, teachers, taxpayers, the Board or Ministry - has undertaken to provide the conditions for learning. How can students be educated if teachers are disorganized and unprepared, if the Board does not offer competitive salaries to attract teachers with the particular skills it needs, or if a vocal segment of the general public confuses its legitimate input on curriculum with a power of veto over course content or materials?

To say persons have the right to an education is also to imply that, in exercising this right, they must not interfere with others' right to an education. This and "[e]very human right has within it a tacit but powerful insistence on responsibility - a responsibility to see to it that human rights are accorded to everyone else" (Zimmerman, 1974). Applied to the educational setting, the purpose "is really to create individuals capable of intellectual and moral autonomy and of respecting this autonomy in others" (Piaget, 1973).

Such consideration of the right of others to an education implies rules; however, rules should be "solely for the purpose of securing due recognition and respect for the rights and freedoms of others and of meeting the just requirements of morality, public order and the general welfare" (Universal Declaration on Human Rights, Article 29). These parameters provide educators with a framework within which to judge the necessity and fairness of the rules which they expect to be observed.

It goes without saying that school rules must be known to all students before their adherence can be expected. It may not be so evident that students also have a right to know the consequences of rule violations and the procedures which will be followed in such instances. Nothing in this discussion precludes students from participating in forming, evaluating, or employing the rules.

If it is a teacher who has violated a rule, the recognition of students as persons with fundamental human rights, implies that there should also be an established procedure by which the student(s) may seek a remedy. Because of the position of authority which the teacher holds relative to students, this process should involve an impartial third party. A counsellor may be one such person to whom students at the high school level might turn, although because of the counsellor's position as an employee of the system, able to listen but not likely to act, this may prove unsatisfactory. In addition, counsellors are not usually found at the elementary school level.

Loken (1979) suggested that the rights of students might best be safeguarded by an accessible ombudsman, who would provide an impartial hearing for the student, parents, and teacher involved, and who would also be in a position of acting on the student's behalf if such action was justified.

In the area of student rights there "needs to be some written document, such as a code, to ensure equal application" (Zimmerman, 1974). Such a code could be enacted at the school level, the divisional board level, or at the provincial level (Quebec is now doing this). Any code should be "grounded in basic human rights to which one is entitled because of his humanity, not because he has attained any particular age, grade, or status" (Robinson, 1974). Given the difficulties encountered by the federal government in entrenching a Charter of Rights in the constitution, obstacles in establishing a code of student rights would be formidable in most jurisdictions. This is not to dismiss attempts as not worth the effort involved or as bound to fail.

It is suggested that student rights codes should provide specific expectations in regard to certain areas. These specifics should not be decided by the administration and imposed on students. To be effective, such a code must reflect the peculiarities of a given school or school district, and must represent input from students, parents, educators, and selected community representatives. But it must not impede access of students to knowledge and skills needed beyond that locale.

Summary

Discussion of student rights, or the formalization of these rights into student rights code(s) should be premised on the recognition of students as human beings first, and only secondarily in their educational role. Students' rights as discussed in this chapter are categorized in Table 1.

Students' rights can be "neither more nor less than the right of [individuals] to develop normally, in accord with the potential [they possess], and the obligation that society has to transform this potential into useful and effective fulfilment" (Piaget, 1973). It is clearly the responsibility of "school administrators to provide strong, visible leadership in the area of human rights" (Zimmerman, 1974), and of teachers to serve as models worthy of imitation in their accordance of students' rights.

TABLE 1

STUDENTS' RIGHTS

ACCESS TO QUALITY EDUCATION.

    No discrimination on basis of wealth, sex, or language.
    Least possible discrimination on the basis of special needs.
    Teachers well qualified and employing sound pedagogy.
    Curriculum expertly developed and adapted to particular community and students.
    Choice from available, equally valid, alternative programs.

RESPECTFUL TREATMENT.

    Dignity and respect accorded to all students
    No physical or psychological abuse or threats.
    Teachers and administrators capable of inspiring respect and trust.

DUE PROCESS.

    Apply in appropriate ways to both pupils and teachers.
    Fair procedures - publicly proclaimed
                   - impartial hearing
                     - access to advice, council or ombudsman
                     - appeal procedure.
    Formal procedures increased for serious violations.

MUTUAL OBLIGATIONS.

    Conduct of students must not impede rights of others.

FAIR RECORDS.

    Valid, useful entries.
    No unauthorized data releases.
    Records accessible to student.

REFERENCES

Brown, J. "The middle school learner: Instructional planning for a transitional stage", The History and Social Science Teacher, 13:3 (Spring 1978), 157-162.

Constitution Act, 1982.

D'Oyley, Vincent Black Presence in Multi-Ethnic Canada. Vancouver: Center for the Study of Curriculum and Instruction, University of British Columbia and Toronto: Ontario Institute for Studies in Education, c. 1978.

Eichler, Margrit The Double Standard. A Feminist Critique of Feminist Social Science. London: Croom and Helm, 1980.

Hennessy, P. "A Canadian reaction to the debate on teacher bargaining" in D. Ray (ed.) School and Society. Lexington: Ginn, 1981, 299.

Humphreys, Edward H. Privacy in Jeopardy: Student Records in Canada. Toronto: Ontario Institute for Studies in Education, 1980.

Laferrière, Michel "Languages, Ideologies and Multicultural Education" in Ronald J. Samuda, John W. Berry & Michel Laferriere (eds.) Multicultural Education in Canada. Toronto: Allyn & Bacon, to be published in 1983.

Life Together: A Report on Human Rights in Ontario. Toronto: Ontario Human Rights Commission, 1977.

Loken, J. "Students' Rights" discussion paper at 1979 Seminar of Human Rights. Vancouver: University of British Columbia, n.p.

Marker, G.W. & Mehlinger, H.D. "Schools, politics, rebellions, and other youthful interests", Phi Delta Kappan, Dec. 1974, 244-247.

O'Leary, P.T. "Authority and rights in education" in Ayim, M. et al. (eds.) Philosophy of Education: An Introduction. London: The University of Western Ontario, 1979, 164-8.

Piaget, J. To Understand is to Invent: The Future of Education. New York: Penguin Books, 1973.

Pring, R. "In defense of authority -- or how to keep their knowledge under control" in Ayim, M. et al. (eds.) Philosophy of Education: An Introduction. London: The University of Western Ontario, 1979, 169-180.

Ray, D. "Personalized Education", Teacher Education, Oct. 1979, 82-88.

Ray, D. "Students' and teachers' rights and obligations" in D. Ray (ed.) School and Society. Lexington: Ginn, 1981, 273-286.

Robinson, D.W. "Is this the right approach to student rights?", Phi Delta Kappan, Dec. 1974, 234-236.

United Nations Universal Declaration on Human Rights and United Nations Declaration of the Rights of the Child, various publications. New York: United Nations.

van Hoose, W.H. "Children's rights and the school counselor" Elementary School Guidance and Counseling, 9:4 (May 1975), 279-286.

Zimmerman, W.G. "Human rights and administrative responsibility", Phi Delta Kappan, Dec. 1974, 243, 247.

LIFELONG EDUCATION: AN EMERGING HUMAN RIGHT

J. Roby Kidd and Douglas Ray

Representatives from most nations met in Tokyo in 1972 to discuss adult education. They agreed to support democratization of education in three ways: horizontally covering every country on the globe, vertically sustained throughout all the years of living, and responsibly so that each learner increasingly gains control over his/her education. Education was seen as a right, with many references to the Universal Declaration of Human Rights. Paradoxically, it was also recognized that many systems of education have further advantaged the comparatively well educated but neglected the needs of those less well educated; thereby deepening the social, economic, and political rifts of society.

It is time for asserting new human rights. Despite constitutional confusion and perplexity, despite our vaunted educational science, it is clear that human rights have only recently been considered seriously in discussing education beyond the stage of free and compulsory schooling. This is true not only for Canada, although certain revolutions addressed the problem - France, the Soviet Union, China and Cuba. Yet in 1976 Unesco members unanimously endorsed the objective of lifelong education, implying that no country was satisfied with progress to date.

Typically adult or continuing education has been justified primarily according to its investment value. More seriously, present estimates of the quality of knowledge and skill levels of large parts of the Canadian adult population are pessimistic: for current society, perhaps one fourth of Canadian adults are functionally illiterate which means that they can read most words but not understand or act upon their meaning. Gradually the number of years of schooling is being replaced by definitions of competence. As a result of weak backgrounds in literacy or numeracy, certain other human rights (like the right to work) cannot be realized by all Canadians without new, extensive, and continuing educational programs. Changes in education and society would entail updating purposes, levels of mastery, systems for delivery, definition of audience, and financial arrangements. Certain aspects of such changes are dealt with in several other chapters of this book; here the focus is upon claims to educational rights appropriate to adult status.

Entitlement to education has typically been justified on grounds which are now outmoded. Programs have either been universal for youth - essentially their one chance to prepare for all of life's opportunities and problems; vocational courses which were justified because they are thought to be fair investments; or avocational, inspirational and/or ideological - in which cases the gains were counted in political, social or ideological rather than economic terms. Entitlement would imply that a particular person has full and equal access to an educational resource. For adults, that may require new and different regulations or programs which have been adjusted to their financial, timetable, or educational limitations. The widespread existence of regulations allowing adults to register in programs of high school or higher education, there to pursue the usual routines for youth, is not a serious attempt to meet the needs of adults. Nor does the existence of many programs that have been organized or utilized by the more sophisticated, articulate and usually prosperous members of society signify that all needs are being identified, let alone met. The disparities in adult education have unintentionally increased the gap between the advantaged and disadvantaged.

Let us return to the claim that large numbers of Canadian adults are functionally illiterate. Although it has been noted that many school leavers and even some college or university graduates are not educated well enough to cope with the demands of society, the proportion of adults similarly ill-equipped grows roughly in proportion to the interval since they left school. Continuing education and training programs which fail to provide these basic skills of learning, reading, numeracy and perhaps language will continue to bypass many of these adults. Much of the reforming zeal and money now directed primarily to programs for youth would be better spent in dealing with the shortcomings of the past. The number of persons involved, the number of productive years that could be saved, the probability of success for such programs, would all justify a substantial redirection of efforts. The cost/benefit ratio might be better.

If adequate facilities for continuing education were in place, they would also serve certain school-age persons. For example, bored fifteen-year-olds with adult ambitions and bodies could begin to interact with the real world by various combinations of work and education. Even if they left school before learning enough of the basics, they would leave aware that programs were available to suit their needs as these emerged in the future. If they return to systematic education, it would be desirable to match their programs with both their work experience and their learning potential.

It is absurd to think that schools could possibly prepare for life. People forget. The world changes. Taken together, these processes suggest that (despite learning on the job) most occupations and avocations would benefit from periodic refurbishing or renewal of knowledge and skills. In modern society, the most sophisticated areas of progress limit the claims to qualification of their employees. For example, in military high technologies, atomic physics and advanced surgery, five years produce extra-ordinary changes. Several occupations provide for the recall and periodic reconditioning of practitioners before their skills and knowledge become marginal or defective: doctors, teachers, engineers, architects, police, pilots, auto mechanics, and sometimes politicians. In such cases, recertification is periodic and subject to knowledge and skills which are continually updated and made more demanding. But whether compulsory or not, the need to learn regularly and systematically affects all professionals and managers. Education for these more sophisticated occupations is a lifelong process, whether or not classrooms are necessary to its success. It is curious that equivalent demands have not been devised for the liberal and human occupations, although advances in these fields have been similarly rapid. The assumption that all persons with liberal educations will remain abreast of the field through private efforts seems to be unwarranted.

How far should entitlement to education be extended? A case can be made for providing it throughout life, at the option of the individual. Restrictions would be minimal, consisting essentially of priorities among various programs in areas where demand would be very limited. Financial arrangements (paid study leave or educredit, for example) would be consistent in principle with current practices for the most complex occupations - in fact, society already requires and subsidizes some programs. Economic justification is most obvious where educational benefits might lead to mid-level jobs being performed with less resentment or more effectiveness than is true for workers in competitive societies. Lifelong education would be justified economically, socially and perhaps politically, for those who are structurally unemployed or underemployed. But in the context of a modern, evolving, prosperous and democratic society, full entitlement can also be proposed emphatically *as a human right*, both in itself and as a means by which all citizens may realize more fully their other human rights: particularly the right to work (Universal Declaration of Human Rights, article 23), to a decent income (articles 23, 25), to participate in the political process (article 21), and to cultural opportunity (article 27).

It should be noted that few Canadians have yet advocated that entitlement be extended so far or to so many. Some who have benefited from education have opposed such universal entitlement, but human rights should work on behalf of all. At present it would be difficult to achieve complete coverage, but the changing distribution of the population age structure would imply that it will not only become more possible but more necessary in the future. Although the population group of "school" age is likely to continue to diminish relatively and perhaps absolutely, the retired, unemployed and underemployed will place increasingly heavy burdens upon the work force. New means, such as education at a distance, (TV, radio, correspondence, etc.), may be employed to increase Canadian productive capacity by boosting the work force or the productivity of its members.

CHANGING NOTIONS OF EDUCATION

Basic education and lifelong education are both evolving and adjusting continuously to the new social realities. Basic education was once restricted to a body of facts and skills that enable the learner to become a reliable cog in the machinery of society. Even secondary education was specialized leadership training. Basic socialization emphasized punctuality, docility and conformity appropriate to the many occupations requiring passive roles.

Increasingly, theorists for liberal democracies have advocated an extension of basics toward a more humane, more diffuse, more complex set of goals, including thinking, creating, socializing, and more participation in political processes. Some mastery of academic subjects might thereby be threatened, but no serious person has urged the neglect of basic skills and knowledge. Nevertheless those who support basic education *only* seem to see the workers' future life as being essentially like that parodied by Chaplin in <u>Hard Times</u>. It becomes clear that preparation for a first job is desirable, possibly essential, but unfortunately not sufficient, particularly if one considers education to be a lifelong process instead of a phase completed before adult responsibilities. In this long range context we see both the milieu in which the 3Rs acquire meaning, and the reason why they are, by themselves, insufficient. Priorities change over a human lifespan and as a society evolves. The need for effective adult learning skills increases; it does not diminish.

Thinking in this context means emphasizing relationships and problem solving; the kind of learning that comes when the facts are not separated and compartmentalized too much in quest of mastery. Systematic methods of thinking and a predisposition to make them a normal prelude to doing are desirable outcomes of education. They are justified as never before, if citizens are to participate meaningfully in the society of the future. Consider some exhortations that are not enforceable in our society: energy conservation, cultural harmony, civic participation. Such objectives for both adults and children are not realized easily if education is concerned only with specifics of knowledge and skills that reduce the individual to automation in society. Consequently, education must extend its objectives to fuller participation or risk the development of a society composed of docile doers.

Creating in the present context means developing skills, knowledge, ideas and feelings in special ways. As part of basic education, creating could take many forms: Through cooperation with others, the outcome could be team sports, theatre, musical programs. Individuals may create in the workshop, kitchen, studio, library. Their creations need not be masterpieces, but they should promote satisfaction. The best of them may be high art, which Emerson had in mind: "Raphael paints wisdom, Handel sings it; Phaedeas carves it; Shakespeare writes it; Wren builds it, Columbus sails it; Luther preaches it; Washington arms it; Watt mechanizes it." But creativity is not an elitist activity. Education provides the basics for recreation and self-renewal, and some windfall benefits will be truly original.

Socializing, in the context of human rights and lifelong education, would focus upon knowledge and activities that might promote better relationships among all members of society. It might promote activities outlined in the multiculturalism programs for Canada, aimed not at the perpetuation of a particular set of cultural practices imported from abroad but at their articulation and development within Canada as a contribution to society here (Tarnopolsky, 1978). It would emphasize activities involving different age groups within a community. Media would be important but, wherever it could be achieved, actual participation would be the most desirable means of demonstrating and accomplishing the aims of the program (McLeod, 1981).

Liberalizing and Humanizing. Discussion of lifelong learning has often concentrated on changes in vocation and technology, as if people need only up-to-date job knowledge and skills. Even when productivity is measured solely in economic terms, the productivity of any worker or professional is the result of many factors. Low productivity may be related to stress, boredom, marital problems, lack of meaning in life (often resulting in excessive use of alcohol and drugs), or to a preoccupation with an avocation like a part-time career or leisure activity. Continuing education of a humane or liberal character may be as vital as upgrading vocational performance; it should be widely available.

Politicizing and *Conscientizing*. There is a growing body of literature discussing the limitations of our current society which can sometimes be institutionally corrected by the people themselves (Snow, 1977). Imposition from above may be less effective. This theme has been significantly developed recently; particularly by the internationally recognized Nyerere, Freire, and Ariyaratne. Domestic voices include Donald Cameron, M. M. Coady and Georges-Henri Levesque. Freire contrasts actively questioning pedagogy for freedom with passive fact-absorption designed to mold adherents. Viewed this way, education becomes development -- the means to transcend the animal existence and become fully human. One goal for such lifelong education is to promote knowledge of and respect for human rights. This needs not focus upon knowledge of the laws but on the basis for citizens' actions in a free and diversified society.

PROVIDING LIFELONG EDUCATION

Effective lifelong education calls more for facilitation than for mandating the education provided. One important observation came when Worth (1972, 152-156) identified and advocated three modes of learning: institutional, associational and individual. Although society has been preoccupied with institutional schools, colleges, universities, courses and examinations, this may be changing. If more resources were available for those interested in learning together in the home and the community, they might accomplish much more through peer interaction. But the resources for private, autonomous, and sometimes informal study are often restricted.

Community Schools may be one part of the system for providing education to a wider sector within society. In them, almost any individuals or groups have access to the educational facilities and resources of the community at times; costs, and other conditions convenient to them. Particularly during a time of declining school-age population, schools represent convenient and underutilized resources. By concentrating on increased use of them, the cost of providing alternative centres can be saved, or at least part of the money can be used more effectively to enhance the program quality. Post-secondary institutions such as community colleges have the prospect to combine the immediate accessibility that attracts people with the satisfaction that comes from higher achievement. However, Canada has too many sparsely populated regions for community colleges to serve all needs.

Distant education through television, radio, newspapers, correspondence, and itinerant lecturers or tutors is beginning to make its impact upon adults. The Université du Québec, Athabasca University, Access Alberta, Knowledge Network of the West and similar institutions indicate some of the possibilities for provision of relatively high-level education to isolated communities. Several provinces have long maintained correspondence courses for isolates, shut-ins and thousands who are not so handicapped, but apparently not enough of these services reached those who are now adults: there are many who remained functionally illiterate. Private and philanthropic organizations like Frontier College have attracted world attention, but their efforts cannot meet the need. Community and technical colleges have devised and demonstrated practical outreach programs but often cannot expand them because of their cost. Given the seriousness of the problem in Canada, governments are necessarily involved with funding and perhaps initiating adequate programs.

Experimental beginnings like Newstart or C.Y.O. showed some promise, perhaps best demonstrated by the determination of the communities involved to maintain elements of the programs when the initial government sponsorship was cut back. Similar promise may be seen in a new community service program called Katimavik, which facilitates work/study for young Canadians.

Since basic literacy may be a priority for education for adults in Canada, what are the preconditions for reducing substantially functional illiteracy? It is evident that there must be a perceived social commitment to the success of the program, shown by adequate funding, planning, trained teachers, evaluation, and perhaps securing appropriate social benefits for those participating in the program. Society may have to adjust practices either to make adult education more possible, for example, by arranging for time off when necessary, by providing financial support and new job opportunities. Present opportunities are still inadequate.

It must be recognized that one obstacle for providing lifelong education is the divided responsibility characteristic of Canadian government: there are tensions, sometimes conflicts, between such departments as education, labour, health and welfare, trade and commerce, and regional

development. There is also the federal, provincial, municipal division.
As a result, resources and constitutional responsibility may not be aligned
with the interests of the population involved.

It is essential that learners and teachers agree upon the aims,
scope and limitations of programs if lifelong education is to be justified
as a human right. Without such agreement, planning is difficult; yet
education must be articulated with all the other programs of society. The
desired educational system would be lifelong in all its principles and would
combine formal with non-formal learning. More emphasis would be placed on
the articulation of educational programs with each other and with the needs
of various societies.

Time is one important factor. Longe-range plans must be developed
and personnel recruited and trained. Monitoring such diffuse programs will
prove difficult in the short run, perhaps even more difficult than the
evaluating of innovations in elementary education. Expectations should be
realistic, for hyper-inflated ambitions for a program usually lead to
disappointment in the long run.

CONFRONTING CYNICISM

Canada has experienced more than a decade of sustained frontal
attacks upon the objectives, methods, costs and outcomes of the formal
educational system. Much of this criticism may have been generalized from
debate in other nations, but many charges were re-examined carefully in the
Canadian context. Schools have always been criticized, but perhaps never
before has the whole provision for education been so attacked. Everett
Reimer proclaimed that <u>School is Dead</u>, Ivan Illich called for <u>Deschooling
Society</u>, Ronald Dore denounced <u>The Diploma Disease</u>. Hilda Neatby had

earlier condemned much of education for offering So Little For The Mind. The titles were sufficiently evocative and the writings both pungent and plausible enough to justify the brief existence of a book club devoted to works of the genre. Widespread coverage continues to be given to such arguments, but on the whole their contribution was restricted to well-founded criticism of the present educational system, without giving equal attention to proposals for alternative measures. Criticism of education rivaled nostalgia as a means of earning royalties. Many of the most noted authors introduced arguments that were essentially anarchistic, nihilistic, or romantic. For society to construct educational reform on nothing but such critics' suggestions would be to court disaster.

Such an event appears to be unlikely. Particular programs may well be phased out when their purposes can be better met in another way or when the purposes are no longer significant. Experiments in new ways of meeting emerging purposes are often expensive, but without such initiatives and the monitoring of their results, no real changes can occur. Canada displayed exceptional interest in the suggestions of Unesco's commission on "Education Today and Tomorrow." Learning To Be (Faure, 1972) was something of a Canadian best seller. Among the vital suggestions for Canada were these relating to lifelong education:-

> The aim of education in relation to employment and economic progress should be not so much to prepare young people and adults for a specific, life-time vocation, as to 'optimize' mobility among the professions and afford a permanent stimulus to the desire to learn and to train oneself [Faure, xxxi-xxxii].

> If all that has to be learned must be continually
> re-invented and renewed, then teaching becomes
> education and, more and more, learning. If learning
> involves all of one's life, in the sense of both
> time-span and diversity, and all of society, including
> its social and economic as well as its educational
> resources, then we must go even further than the
> necessary overhaul of 'educational systems' until we
> reach the stage of a learning society. For these
> are the true proportions of the challenge education
> will be facing in the future [Faure, xxxiii-xxxiv].

More recently, the OECD review of educational policies in Canada underlined the need for continuing efforts to equalize educational opportunity (OECD, 1976, 38-53). Since various grants make possible primary and secondary educational facilities in almost every part of the nation, it makes sense to extend the use of these facilities to those who are now functionally illiterate, who may find their objectives blocked by relatively modest educational hurdles, who need the emotional or social support that might come through continuing education. Since such opportunities already exist for some, it becomes a question of pursuing the principle of equality.

THE IMMEDIATE PROSPECTS

A current investigation by Douglas Ray, Michael Bayles, Ann Harley and others on values, aging, and lifelong education addresses the impact of age and sex on four classifications of lifelong education: functional literacy, technical and vocational education, political participation and awareness, and personal fulfilment. It is evident that several provinces are still developing their policies concerning lifelong education. Statistics probably underestimate the numbers involved because some programs are not reported. Voluntary agencies still provide a significant part of educational programs and their continuity is sometimes jeopardized. These ambiguities about the available services and their effectiveness still need to be resolved (Ray, 1981).

Until policies are more fully articulated, it seems doubtful that the kind of system advocated here can become reality. The articulation of programs will depend upon significant cooperation and various concessions among levels of government, between provinces, between departments (e.g., health, agriculture, consumer affairs, and education are likely to be involved in studies of nutrition), and between private and public interests.

Until such articulation takes place, the development of new audiences, delivery systems, teaching materials or methods, and better means of assisting or motivating potential students will remain piecemeal. A great deal of waste and inappropriate programming remains the challenge to the realization of what seems to be a human right -- the lifelong securing of adequate, appropriate educational opportunities.

NOTES FOR "Lifelong Education: An Emerging Human Right"

Dore, Ronald, *The Diploma Disease*. London: George Allen & Unwin Ltd., 1976.

Faure, Edgar et al., *Learning To Be: The World of Education Today and Tomorrow*. Paris: Unesco, 1972.

Freire, Paulo, "The Adult Literacy Process as Cultural Action for Freedom", *Harvard Educational Review*, Vol. 40, No. 2 (May 1970), 205-225.

Illich, Ivan, *Deschooling Society*. New York: Harper and Row, 1970.

McLeod, Keith A., "Multicultural Education: A Decade of Development" in Daniel Dorotich (editor) *Education and Canadian Multiculturalism: Some Problems and Some Solutions*. Saskatoon: Canadian Society for the Study of Education, 1981, 12-26.

Neatby, Hilda, *So Little For The Mind*. Toronto: Clarke, Irwin & Co., 1953.

Nyerere, Julius, *Freedom and Socialism*. London: Oxford University Press, 1968.

Organization for Economic Cooperation and Development (OECD), *Review of National Policies for Education: Canada*. Paris: OECD, 1976.

Ray, Douglas, "Assessing Continuing Educational Needs for a Progressively Aging Canadian Population Profile: An Emphasis on Values". Toronto: International Society for Educational Planning, October 1981 (unpublished manuscript).

Reimer, Everett, *School is Dead*. New York: Doubleday, 1971.

Snow, Chief John, *These Mountains Are Our Sacred Places*. Toronto: Samuel Stevens, 1977.

Tarnopolsky, Walter, "Multiculturalism - The Basic Issues" in Manoly R. Lupul (editor) *Ukrainian Canadians, Multiculturalism and Separatism: An Assessment*. Edmonton: University of Alberta Press, 1978, 141-152.

Worth, Walter H., et al., *Learning To Be*. Edmonton: Queen's Printer, 1972.

THE PROVISION OF EDUCATIONAL RIGHTS

STRATEGIES FOR HUMAN RIGHTS EDUCATION

John Kehoe

There is increasing concern among teachers about the role of the school in human rights education. The concern has been generated because of evidence of prejudicial attitudes and overt discrimination (Rosenstock & Adair, 1976; Henry, 1978; Ubale, 1977; Pitman, 1977). Knowledge of human rights documents does not necessarily lead to respect, concern, commitment, or willingness to act in support of human rights. Teachers therefore need to know what can be done in the context of the school to increase commitment to human rights and reduce prejudice.

Typical courses of study do not explicitly attempt to achieve attitudes of concern or empathy for those who experience the violation of their rights. Nor are there indications of objectives concerned with presenting or changing prejudicial attitudes; or providing students with a critical and functional knowledge of national and international human rights. Objectives are more likely to be concerned with enhancing group understanding and encouraging the acceptance of cultural diversity. The curricular approach is to present information about a national subculture or international culture. The unwarranted assumption is made that providing information leads to understanding and positive attitudes. Seldom is any consideration given to pre-assessing attitudes to determine which cultural groups the students have prejudices against and then designing programs to change those prejudices. Where evaluation is required (Elementary Social Studies Guide) there is no evidence that teachers are systematically evaluating their programs for effect. Similarly there is no evidence that curricular decisions are influenced by the developmental or personality characteristics of students. Levels of cognitive and moral development and levels of dogmatism and self-esteem are likely to be influential in determining the success of strategies designed to increase commitment to human rights. A recent analysis (Thiessen, 1977) of the related area of international understanding, found that the conceptual attainment necessary for international understanding is beyond the capability of most elementary school pupils. There is a clear need for evaluation of existing and new programs and for a consideration of the restraints of selected independent variables.

There are at least four broad strategies for achieving a greater commitment to human rights and acceptance of cultural diversity. First, strategies for teaching human rights directly in a manner appropriate to student characteristics. Second, strategies for changing specific prejudicial attitudes. Third, strategies to promote multiculturalism. Fourth, strategies to enhance developmental and personality characteristics deemed essential as preconditions to achieving commitment to human rights and providing a disposition to reject prejudice. Before turning to an examination of the various approaches it is necessary to demonstrate that while it is important to encourage the acceptance of cultural diversity, it also needs to be made clear that the acceptance of human rights could very well mean denouncing present cultural practices.

Accepting Human Rights but Denouncing Cultural Practices

In the main, students should be encouraged to accept the diversity of others. They would like their diversity to be tolerated and should therefore be prepared to extend that consideration to others. At the same time we should not accept nor promote tolerance of every practice. The Universal Declaration of Human Rights and Canadian human rights laws are necessarily and rightly in direct conflict with some cultural practices. In Canada it has been a pervasive cultural practice to deny women equal pay for doing work of equal value. This cultural practice is increasingly illegal in Canada (see Eichler), but it still is defended on traditional or economic necessity arguments by influential people. In other countries slavery remains. For example, in 1972, the London-based Anti-Slavery Society reported that tens of thousands still live in slavery in thirty-eight countries. In the sixties a public auction of children was witnessed in a Latin American city and an Englishman went into the Sahara around Timbukto and bought a slave for one hundred dollars. Slavery contravenes Article 4 of the Universal Declaration of Human Rights. Apart from the slave owners, very few persons would <u>tolerate</u> either advocating or practising slavery.

Many groups have customs which we should not tolerate either because they are inconsistent with what is known to be true or they are inconsistent with being fair. In his book, <u>Bilingual Today, French Tomorrow</u>, John Andrew pejoratively refers to Quebec as a "breeding pen", implying that the birth rate of the Province is substantially higher than the rest of Canada. When the book was being written and for some years before, the birth rate in Quebec was lower than the birth rate in Ontario. John Andrew belongs to a particular Canadian subculture that believes falsehoods which affect their behaviour toward French Canadians. It is clearly within the mandate of schools to challenge beliefs which are inconsistent with the facts. It is also within the mandate of the school to challenge practices which are unfair. Article 16-2 of the Universal Declaration of Human Rights states:

Marriage shall be entered into only with the free and full consent of the intending spouses. Forced marriages are a denial of the right of choice and yet such marriages occasionally occur in Canada and frequently in various parts of the world.

Teachers have a great deal of difficulty deciding which practices should be encouraged in the promotion of multiculturalism and which should be discouraged (Kehoe, 1977). The acceptance by some teachers of all cultural practices may be a function of their level of moral development. Subjects moving from what Kohlberg described as stage 4 of moral maturity to stage 5 experience disequilibrium, i.e., their judgments are inconsistent and there is a partial rejection of moral judgments. They begin to call into question a definition of morality as a code of fixed rules and at the same time they are concerned with validating moral values. (Kohlberg's strategy is discussed more fully on pages 35 and 36 of this chapter.

Most teachers would reject a practice in Canada or in other parts of the world if it involved the taking of human life. However, the length of time a practice has been in existence and the justification for the practice seem to influence such decisions. For example, the Cuiva Indians of Colombia are being exterminated by Colombian cattle herders. Most teachers would consider the killing to be wrong because it is recent and the justification is economic. They would be much less willing to declare a practice wrong if it has been in existence for a long time and has a religious justification. For example, on an island in the South Pacific, a son kills his father while he is still healthy and strong. A similar pattern of responses results when there is denial of equality of opportunity. Most teachers consider Apartheid in South Africa to be wrong but are less willing to make a similar judgment about the caste system in India. In their historical novel, _Freedom at Midnight_, Collins and Lapierre state that in some parts of India, Untouchables were allowed to leave their shacks only at night. They were known as Invisibles. The caste system (Like Apartheid) is racially based historically. However, it has a religious justification and has been in existence for a longer time. The principle seems to be the longer people have been oppressed within a culture the more acceptable the oppression. Many teachers will more readily declare the caste system to be wrong if the victims are attempting to resist or escape. A survey of low caste households concluded, "Stigmatized ethnic identity is experienced as oppression. It is a human day by day experience of degradation and exploitation, not simply an abstract concept. People resent that identity and that experience regardless of the rationalization offered for it. People continually attempt to resist, escape, alleviate or change that identity and that experience, even in the most unlikely circumstances ... including the remote villages and urban slums of India" (Berreman, 1971). Many teachers would be very hesitant to promote through education ideas which might lead people to conclude they are oppressed. This is an indefensible position for educators to take because implicit in a definition of Education is that people have a right to know. There is a tendency for teachers to strike poses of exaggerated objectivity when it comes to the discussion of attitudes and values. Part of the problem results from our too quick acceptance of the claim that everybody is entitled to their opinion even if it is unfair or untrue. Once the incorrectness or unfairness of an opinion is brought to the attention of its holder, why would they want to continue holding it?

Teaching Human Rights Directly

There is a clear and pressing need for the evaluation of existing published materials on national human rights; and for the development and evaluation of material designed to teach international human rights laws. In a recent search, over one thousand published items were found concerning civil liberties and human rights; but only one reported a research study. In that study, students developed more positive attitudes toward civil liberties when teacher credibility was high (Goldenson, 1978).

A seldom considered but important consideration before developing curriculum materials would be to conduct a needs assessment to determine existing levels of knowledge and attitudes toward civil liberties and human rights law. Serow and Strube (1978) found that students offer only conditional support for the exercise of individual freedoms. Little support exists for civil liberties when the exercise of these liberties is seen as threatening the interests of the peer group. Students rejected the practice of school personnel "pulling rank" or acting summarily. They agreed that there should be a hearing before a school could suspend a student and that they should be able to criticize the management of the school. Students also objected to efforts at protecting them from purportedly undesirable influences of a political or moral nature. In general the study showed students were concerned about the personal welfare of their peers and at the same time are distrustful of their schoolmates' capacity to utilize freedom of expression. Kehoe and Echols (1980) concluded that student knowledge of civil liberties and human rights law was inadequate. On slightly less than half the issues presented, students did not reach the acceptable standard of achievement. Knowledge of the law should not be influenced by the circumstances presented, although the findings indicated that such was the case. Rather than consideration of the law as a universal principle, the students responded in a particular way, being influenced by situational factors. This would suggest that a "morality of loyalty" rather than a "morality of principle" is in operation, particularly when item by item inspection reveals more incorrect responses accrue to those groups that represent considerable "out group" characteristics. A second general observation that can be made following the analysis is that students' attitudes toward civil liberties and human rights law were negative and inconsistent. With one or two exceptions there were significant inconsistencies across cases.

The overall implications in terms of situational morality are certainly disconcerting if one considers that the students are likely to enter their adult life without changing their perspective on the law. Negative and inconsistent attitudes suggest the development of cases starting from the most acceptable and proceeding to the least acceptable. The need for psychological consistency would assist in changing student attitudes toward the least acceptable cases. In addition, the results of the study suggested a need for the development of materials which show the consequences of denial of various freedoms and human rights.

The results of the latter survey suggested a need for the development of curriculum materials concerned with the issues of the right of employees to have only relevant criteria used in employment decisions. Target Canada produced a sound-slide show "The Interview" which shows a variety of people being refused employment for non-relevant reasons. The sound-slide show is accompanied by a teacher's guide which provides guidelines on how to conduct a discussion of the cases presented in the sound-slide show. The discussion approach described has students participate in principle testing discussions which increases the likelihood of making fair decisions consistent with human rights principles (Metcalf, 1971). The approach has been used successfully to change attitudes toward selected minorities but has not been tested for its effect on knowledge of and attitudes toward national or provincial human rights principles.

The strategy of principle testing discussions has shown its effectiveness in teaching greater knowledge of and commitment to international human rights principles. In one study (Kehoe and Hope, 1979) students participated in discussions of cases which are contraventions of selected Universal Moral Rules, e.g., Don't Cause Death. The instructor presented several cultural or societal customs, most consisting of at least one component which violated a universal moral rule. The customs included the Indian caste system, which denies economic mobility; killing breech-birth babies, a practice once common in a tribe in Kenya; murdering children to appease God, recently perpetrated by the Universal Assembly of the Saints in South America; the Hutterite practice of denying their children music and dancing; and apartheid in South Africa. Students were told to ignore what the law prescribed or allowed but to consider each issue in terms of fairness and justice. In effect, the instructor attempted to solicit support for the universal moral position.

The salient features of the class discussion included the four tests of principle acceptability. The following examples illustrate the procedure. The instructor stated a moral rule, "Don't Cause Death", and elicited support for this rule. Once this value principle was explicitly formulated, the instructor applied it to a new case--the act of murdering children to appease God. It was expected that students would reject this practice, but their reaction was mixed. Some of them adopted the universalist position and accepted the proposition that some practices should be disallowed in all societies at all times. Other students supported the relativist position; "It may seem unfair but it's their religion", "Abide by the culture you enter, we should respect their way of life as long as they don't interfere with us", "I think it is wrong but they think it is right, therefore it is right for them". The instructor then assembled facts about this new case so that students could subsume the value principle implicit in the case, i.e., the children should not be murdered, into the more general value principle that the subjects had already accepted, i.e., "Don't Cause Death". Again, subject reaction was mixed. When the instructor asked the students to exchange roles with the children and to consider whether or not they still maintained a relativist position, it was apparent that some did move to a universalist position. However, some students responded to the role exchange test by saying, "If I was part of that culture I would think the practice would be right therefore I would accept it". The last test presented the possibility of religious sects throughout the world adopting the tenets of the Assembly of the Saints and asked students to consider whether or not they would accept the consequences of a more universal infanticide. Again, student reaction was mixed. The four tests of principle acceptability were also used with the other customs noted above. The approach was successful in persuading students to agree that cultural practices which contravene universal moral rules are wrong wherever they occur.

A second study (Kehoe, 1980) compared two approaches to teaching the Universal Declaration of Human Rights. In the first approach subjects participated in teacher led discussion of cases which contravened the selected Articles. For example, students would be told of children being sold as slaves in a South American country in the 1960s. The teacher then asks, "Should the practice be allowed to continue?" or "Is the practice right?" During the discussion the teacher asks questions generated from four tests of principles. An effort was made by the teacher to provide a climate which would encourage subjects to change their mind if they could not make cases for inconsistencies. It was hoped that by using this approach students would make rational and consistent value judgments.

In the second approach, subjects participated in the "Investigation Approach". Learning Stations were created for each of the selected articles of the Universal Decalaration of Human Rights. Each Article was written on the top of a large piece of poster paper. A large envelope attached to the paper contained newspaper and magazine articles which illustrated a contravention of that particular Article. Students were asked to work at as many stations as they could during the two treatment days. While at a station they were asked to spend a few minutes as a small group (3-4 people) discussing their interpretation of the meaning of the article of the Declaration. They were then to work independently on one of the documents from the station envelope. They were asked to gather enough information to be able to write a brief statement describing how the document illustrated a contravention of the article. When this was completed they moved to the next station. A third group viewed filmstrips on the structure of the United Nations. The group was doing something unique but no mention was made of the Universal Declaration of Human Rights.

Regardless of approach there was no difference in willingness to say a contravention of the Universal Declaration of Human Rights was wrong. Both approaches were clearly as effective in persuading students to disagree with the proposition that if a cultural group considers a contravention to be right then it is right for them. The "Investigation Approach" was more effective at teaching students knowledge of international law on the issues. This is not surprising given that the investigation group was taught the Articles of the Universal Declaration of Human Rights directly and then investigated contraventions. The "Discussion Approach" was more effective in achieving a greater acceptance of customs which are not contraventions of the Universal Declaration of Human Rights. However, it would appear that the "Investigations Approach" is generally more effective in achieving the desired outcomes.

Efforts at locating _effective_ student materials for teaching Human Rights directly have met with little success. There are few sources of information about existing attitudes of students toward national and international human rights. There are even fewer sources of information describing empirically evaluated successful materials.

Reducing Prejudice and Enhancing Multiculturalism

The development of strategies for reducing prejudice is directly related to enhancing human rights. The practice of discrimination based on prejudicial attitudes consistently results in the denial of human rights. Anything that can be done to reduce the prejudice of students will increase the prospect that human rights will not be denied. Similarly anything that can be done to encourage the acceptance of cultural diversity both nationally and internationally increases the likelihood that members of a culture will not be denied their human rights.

Tolerance of cultural diversity is an attitudinal component of citizenship education. The perceived power of the school in many areas of citizenship education has been over estimated. Various reviews of studies have shown that political socialization has, in many important respects, been completed by the time students reach high school (Kehoe, 1973) and furthermore, school courses as they are now taught demonstrate no effect (Hess and Eaton, 1962; Hess and Torney, 1967).

However, Goldenson (1978) has reviewed several studies which show that high school social studies curricula have had rather substantial impact on the formation and change of students' attitudes. He points out that one group of researchers is concerned with the effects of what _does_ happen in schools and the second group of researchers is concerned with the effects of what _can_ happen in schools.

What Can Be Done?

Two studies have been selected because what is frequently done in schools is ineffective most of the time and what needs to be done requires careful planning and careful consideration of the nature of the population.

There have been a number of deliberate and systematic attempts to teach the democratic value of accepting cultural diversity and to teach the appropriate attitudes related to such a value. In 1939 Dr. John Granrud, Superintendent of Schools for Springfield, Massachusetts, named a committee to study the whole program of intergroup and citizenship education because for some time he had been concerned about what he perceived to be growing racial, religious, economic and political intolerance. The Springfield Plan saw tolerance being achieved through the long, slow process of teaching generations of children to accept and translate into daily living the principles of the democratic ideal. The following strategies and activities are representative of what was done in order to achieve the objectives: standing committees had a balance of different religious and ethnic groups; teachers of different races, religions, and nationalities were hired; opportunities were provided for children to work together with mutual respect; students were placed on committees dealing with every phase of school life to provide worthwhile experiences in group planning and living; a parent-teacher-student association was established and a variety of school clubs were organized.

Running through all the activities in the Springfield Plan was the conscious procedure of associating in common enterprise children of different backgrounds. In this way it was anticipated they would come to know and to understand each other. As an enterprise in one school the children wrote a book, The School Speaks. The foreign lands and languages represented in the school and in the finished book included: China, Czechoslovakia, France, Germany, Holland, Italy, Palestine, Sweden and Syria. Similar books titled Folk Music and Pioneer Spirits were written in other schools. This was all done as part of a unit, The Contribution of Nationalities to Springfield. In addition, visits were made to churches and synagogues of the various religions represented in the school. Lessons were taught on the races of mankind, the procedure of reading the daily newspaper, and the techniques of influencing public opinion. The nature of prejudice was discussed. There were many more activities of a similar nature. The program was a concerted attempt to achieve the objective of persuading students and adults of the importance of a variety of religious and ethnic groups living together in mutual respect and tolerance.

A post-test comparison between graduates of the Springfield Plan and graduates of other but similar school systems was carried out (Spoerl, 1951). Graduates of the Springfield Plan were found to be less prejudiced than controls toward outgroups with whom they had no contact, but more prejudiced toward minority groups living in Springfield.

The second more complicated study (Cohen and Roper, 1972) is not typical of school activity but it is possible. First a little background. We know that in small group settings where people know their place there is no conflict because each person plays the stereotyped role of self, and expects the same from others. Placing minority and majority groups onto an officially equal footing in the same building does not ensure that "equal status" relations will develop.

In the first part of the study minority group members were taught how to build a radio crystal set and then worked with a majority group member to assemble another radio crystal set. It was anticipated that the competence of the minority group member would be demonstrated. The group then played a decision making game (called "Kill the Bull") where significant dominance by the majority group member was shown to continue. The researchers concluded that they had not produced a competence difference between the groups that was recognized by the subjects. In the next part of the study, the part that was effective, minority group members were made competent and were prepared to <u>teach</u> majority group members the radio building skills. In addition, both majority and minority group members together were shown a video-tape of the minority group member building the radio. The minority group members then taught the majority group members to assemble the radio. Finally, the minority group members were told that the self confidence they had shown as teachers would make them good team members when they played, "Kill the Bull". These activities resulted in evidence that the competence of the minority group members was recognized by the majority group members. In this particular study there was no evidence of a hostile response by majority subjects to minority teachers. There appears to be a need to treat both minority and majority expectations if we are interested in attaining equal status.

There are a number of other tested strategies that teachers might employ in order to achieve the objective of greater acceptance of human diversity in Canada. They need to be cautioned that the strategies work only for some teachers, in some schools and with some students.

Schools as they are presently permitted to function are not powerful agents of socialization. It may be that parents and students do not consider influencing attitudes and values to be part of the schools' mandate and therefore resist efforts to change. There is a general consensus of pessimism among researchers and few would now claim that changes of attitude in the area of race can readily be achieved by educational strategies. Although there are some promising approaches, researchers emphasize the importance of assessment for effectiveness each time a particular strategy is attempted.

The strategies described may not be acceptable to all teachers. They range from variations of information presentation and rational approaches, to approaches which could be defined as indoctrination or manipulation. For example, attitude change theory notes a "primacy effect" which says that the information a person receives first influences their attitudes _more_ than information received second. If a teacher was teaching a unit on discrimination in the world the starting point could be either examining discrimination in Canada or in other parts of the world. If they start with Canada, students may become defensive. If they start with cases from South Africa there may be more commitment to the principle that - discrimination is wrong - and they may be more willing to accept discrimination in Canada as wrong. Some teachers seem to believe that if you unconsciously start with the external cases it is all right, but if you are aware of the "primacy effect" principle and use it, then it is a manipulation. It could be better described as a teaching strategy for achieving more effective learning.

Usual Strategies for Promoting Human Rights

Frequently acceptable strategies include providing information about an ethnic group, and making provision for personal contact with an ethnic group. Each of these strategies can be effective if certain principles are used in planning. Less universally accepted strategies include behaviour modification, non-directive techniques, principle testing discussions, role-playing, simulations, rational analysis and the discussion of dilemmas designed to enhance levels of moral development. The importance of selecting appropriate materials for all strategies needs to be emphasized at the outset. Criteria for selecting and analyzing material are discussed extensively elsewhere(McDiarmid & Pratt, 1971).

Information

Getting more information about an ethnic group can result in a lessening of prejudice but not to any great extent. It is likely to be effective with non-dogmatic individuals who have been taught to dislike another group. Such people are easier to re-educate than the individual whose prejudices serve emotional or economic needs. However, the more strongly people feel about ethnic minorities, the less likely they are to be changed by formal communication or propaganda about them. Furthermore, the more strongly negative student attitudes are toward a minority, the less willing are they to have the history and culture of the minority included in the curriculum. Grade eleven Japanese, Chinese and East Indian minority students and their majority counterparts were surveyed (Kehoe and Sakata, 1978) to determine their willingness to have the history and culture of each minority in Canada as part of the curriculum. A high proportion of each minority group wanted <u>their</u> history and culture in Canada as part of the curriculum. Majority culture students wanted the history and culture of the Chinese and Japanese included but did not want the history and culture of East Indians included. These results are consistent with their attitudes toward the three cultures.

In general, school courses on the nature of prejudice have not been effective in reducing prejudice and in some instances have had negative effects. Black (1973) compared an anti-prejudice series of lessons with lessons on general semantics. The anti-prejudice lessons included the following:

   I. What is prejudice?
  II. Prejudice in the world today.
 III. How we get our prejudices?
  IV. What prejudice does to us.
   V. What can we do about it?

The general semantics lessons included such topics as: Word is not the thing - Map is not the territory, Symbol and Sign reaction, Non-allness, How we select details, Multi-causation, Learning what is inside and outside our skins, Many uses of words, The Abstraction ladder, Stereotyping and indexing, Dating, Two-valued orientation, Words are like maps, Is of Identity, and the Art of questioning. Students who participated in the general semantics lessons showed significant improvement in social distance, ethnocentrism and authoritarianism. Students who participated in the anti-prejudice lessons showed significant negative change on the three measures. Another study showed that attempts to improve the attitudes of students by the use of information, rational arguments or outright persuasion were likely to prove counterproductive. The study was conducted with day-release apprentices who were older and already highly prejudiced (<u>Teachers' Manual</u>, 1978).

Three strategies for changing racial attitudes were compared in a classic study. A set of value-balanced race relations material was read and the students discussed the material with the teacher adopting the role of a neutral chairperson. The second strategy aimed "to educate for the elimination of racial tension and ill-feeling within our society - which is and will be multi-racial - by undermining prejudice, developing respect for varied traditions and by encouraging mutual understanding, reasonableness and justice". The teacher was to be critical of prejudiced attitudes. The third strategy used drama. The teachers encouraged situational improvised drama with pupils taking a variety of roles in dramatized race relations situations. The first two strategies resulted in significant favourable change in attitude. The drama strategy changed attitudes in the desired direction but it did not reach significance. It should be noted that the neutral chairman strategy was similar to that used with apprentices. However, in the latter study the subjects were younger, better educated, and had lower initial prejudice (Kagan, 1953).

The Association for Values Education and Research has also demonstrated success in using a rational approach (Goldberg, 1954).

The AVER Prejudice unit has three general goals:

1. To understand what prejudice is.
2. To understand why prejudice is irrational.
3. To understand under what conditions it is likely to be immoral as well as irrational.

The objectives of the unit included:

1. The student will be able to define "prejudice" and "stereotype".
2. The student will be able to differentiate between fact and value statements.
3. The student will be able to identify the value object and value term in a value statement.

4. The student will be able to identify the point of view contained in a value judgement.
5. The student will be able to complete incomplete practical syllogisms, and will be able to write his own syllogisms.
6. The student will be able to use principle testing in order to determine the validity of a value claim.
7. The student will be able to formulate a Reason Assembly Chart using the above skills so as to arrive at a defensible solution to a given issue.

AVER assessed effect on attitudes by using a General Tolerance Scale developed as a measure of empathy toward various ethnic groups and a Specific Tolerance Scale which was a Likert type measure of subjects' attitude regarding examples of overt discrimination directed against a specific ethnic group. There was considerable community hostility toward the ethnic group at the time of the study. The evaluation study showed significant positive changes on the Specific Tolerance measure but no significant changes on the General Tolerance measure.

Case Approach

Case approaches which allow vicarious identification with victims are typically more effective than general courses. Kehoe and Head (1978) compared the effects of indirect and direct methods in groups. The direct method had subjects participate in direct discussion of personal experiences with, and attitudes toward, the minority group. The latter was effective, but may have been effective because a majority of the group members were voicing sympathetic concern toward ethnic groups. The results could well be different if a majority of the discussants were unsympathetic.

The vicarious experience approach may be most effective. Employing movies, drama, and fiction which invite students to identify with the ethnic group can be effective. Kehoe and Hood found that an abstract film on prejudice had no effect on the attitudes of the audience, whereas films involving realistic enactment of a social situation produced a significant reduction in prejudice. Another study compared three methods with Grade eight students. One group had direct experience with minority group members. A second group had academic instruction on the problems of prejudice. The third group had a "vicarious experience" approach in which subjects read, acted and listened to the experiences of minority members. The last approach was the most effective. Vicarious approaches are essentially an appeal to sympathy. Caution needs to be exercised when this approach is used. The showing of cruelty against a weak victim may cause subjects to identify with the assailant rather than the victim. They suffer from repressed hostility toward minority groups and in showing the effects of persecution we permit vicarious gratification. We usually tend to feel sympathy only toward those we like. Appeals to sympathy, therefore, must attempt not only to show the suffering of the minority but also to make them more lovable.

A study (Kehoe, 1975) with grade five and six students in a British Columbia lower mainland school district was successful in changing attitudes of students. Subjects viewed films, held discussion and participated in activities over eleven lessons. The success of the program may in part be attributed to the selection of films which emphasized positive similarities and happy events; and to the presence of a concerned and sympathetic teacher.

Another information approach is to provide the subject with information which is likely to induce self-insight without generating psychological defensiveness. Self-insight may be induced by demonstrating inconsistencies between values which are important guiding principles and specific attitudes. One study changed both attitudes and behaviour of students by demonstrating inconsistencies between general values like being broadminded and specific attitudes toward various ethnic groups. Broadminded was ranked fifth as a desirable way of behaving; Freedom and Equality were ranked first and fifth as desirable end-states of existence. Some of these same students held negative attitudes toward specific ethnic groups. Demonstrating the connection between value and the attitude and the inconsistency between them can bring about a change in attitude. Another strategy which may be effective in inducing self-insight is to show students the results of a survey of students' knowledge of and attitudes toward civil liberties and human rights issues. The survey had students respond to cases on one of three forms. Each form contained a mix of cases which students were likely to find more or less acceptable. High school students:

1. were willing to grant freedom of assembly to Consumers and Native Indians but not to the F.L.Q. or teachers.
2. were willing to have Anglicans build churches but not Hindus or Jehovah Witnesses.
3. were not willing to give the same rights to employment to recent immigrants as they would to native Canadians.
4. knew that a hotel keeper could not refuse service to East Indians but less than half agreed the innkeeper should have to provide service.

A further strategy for inducing self-insight is to present subjects with case history materials which demonstrate that people hold prejudices similar to their own for no reason or less than desirable reasons.

Empathy

Some students have difficulty recognizing situations that require empathy and some have difficulty in role exchanging with another person. In developing a measure of student ability to recognize situations in which they should feel empathy, subjects were given a description of a French Canadian in Vancouver listening to an open line program discussing the French language television station for Vancouver. Most of the discussion was against the station. When given a choice of responses twenty-eight out of thirty subjects thought "He probably thinks it's all right at this time because it is causing trouble", rather than "He probably feels hurt and perhaps angry". Literature combined with role playing can be effective in teaching students to recognize situations that require empathy and perhaps they may even have that feeling.

Similarities

Another informational approach found effective is to accentuate the similarities between their own culture and the culture of the ethnic group. Unfortunately the opposite approach is frequently the case when teachers are selecting materials for inclusion in a unit. The exotic and bizarre aspects of a culture are selected because it is expected they will be more interesting. One study (Salyachivin, 1972) found that pupils show just as much interest in similarities as they do in differences. Another study (Torney, 1977) found that children before the age of fourteen are interested both in individuals dissimilar to themselves and those who are similar. However, they tend to reject those who are seen to be culturally backward or who have strange and exotic customs. Accentuating positive similarities resulted in more positive attitudes than emphasizing differences. It may be that younger children need to see actual physical similarities. Two groups of grade six children viewed the same set of slides of India and Afghanistan. In one group verbal assertions were made emphasizing the similarities of Indian and Afghanistan and the culture of the children. The second group received verbal assertions which emphasized differences. There was no difference on a post test measure of attitude. It may be that verbal assertion of similarities is not adequate. It is possible that the visual experience in the study was perceived as not relevant or not valid. Here is a partial list of human practices found in every culture, which might be emphasized when you are comparing or studying an individual culture: athletic sports, bodily adornment, calendar, cleanliness training, community organization, cooking, cooperative labour, courtship, dancing, decorative art, etiquette, faith healing, education, ethics, family feasting, fire making, folk lore, food taboos, funeral rites, gift giving, government, greetings, hair styles, hospitality, housing, hygiene, incest taboos, inheritance rules, joking, kinship, names, language, law, luck superstitions, magic, marriage, mealtimes, medicine, modesty concerning natural functions, mourning, music, mythology, obstetrics, penal sanctions, population policy, post natal care, property rights, puberty customs, religious ritual, residence rules, sexual restrictions, soul concepts, status differentiation, surgery, tool making, trade, visiting, weaving and weather control.

Humor

Other informal approaches emphasize the use of humor and good news about ethnic groups. The use of humor is an area in need of research. It may be that ethnic jokes have a negative effect on the attitudes of high school students. If it were shown that a consequence of hearing ethnic jokes was that students perceived the ethnic group to be lower in intelligence, then people should be urged to cease telling such stories. Certain kinds of humor may be more effective in bringing about a reduction in ethnocentric behaviour. That is judging another culture as <u>wrong</u> simply because it is different from your own. It would be interesting to assess the effects of stories like the following on the ethnocentricism of subjects.

A South Asian doctor working in a Toronto hospital was standing before the wash up tubs. He turned the water on full blast, placed his finger on one side of his nose and blew the snot into the water. He did the same thing with the other side of his nose. A non-Indian doctor was standing beside him and said, "What a filthy thing to do, I can't think of anything more filthy". "You think that is bad", replied the Indian doctor, "I know a culture where they carry a little piece of white cloth around in their pocket. When they have to blow their nose, they take the piece of cloth out of their pocket and blow the snot into the cloth and then, are you ready for this, they put the piece of cloth back in their pocket, and carry it around with them!"

Good News

Placing more emphasis on good news events rather than bad news events is more likely to result in more positive attitudes and possibly more empathy for victims of discrimination. At the beginning of workshops with approximately one thousand teachers across Canada, Kehoe asked them to estimate the proportion of people in British Columbia who would agree with the statement "I wish I could speak French". The estimates consistently range from one to fifty per cent with a high proportion estimating from one to twenty-five per cent and a very few people estimating around seventy-five per cent. The actual proportion is seventy-five per cent. The reason for the significant error in estimate is the emphasis on bad news in the press. When Southam Press newspapers serialized the results of their survey, The Searching Nation (1977) headlines were consistently negative e.g., "Pessimism the prevailing mood" Ottawa Citizen, and "How do the French and English view each other darkly and suspiciously", Province. The consequences of such reporting are found in the survey itself. A high proportion of Canadians said they were not prejudiced but they knew that other people were.

When positive and negative information about a group is presented in equal amounts, the negative information dominates and is remembered longer. Holloway and Hornstein (1976) show that bad news about a group of people causes a we-they situation to develop. Bad things are happening to them rather than to me and that makes them different. Kehoe, Echols and Sakata (1978) presented historical and contemporary cases of discrimination against ethnic groups to high school students. The experimental subjects did not feel any greater empathy toward the victims but did conclude the events were frequent occurrences in Canadian history and the solution was to not let various ethnic groups come to Canada if it was going to cause trouble. Rather than presenting only negative information about an ethnic group's history and culture in Canada it is important to present good news as well. If attitudes toward South Asians are found to be negative in various parts of Canada it may be better to present a unit on the Contributions of the Indian Army to World War II rather than emphasizing contemporary cases of discrimination. A possible difficulty with the former approach is that people do not like to be confronted with information which contradicts their beliefs.

If we dislike South Asians we do not want to see them as courageous or selfless. The latter approach could lead to vicarious identification with the assailant rather than the victim.

A few other principles to keep in mind when presenting information are:

(1) The information must not be too far outside the subject's latitude of acceptance. For example, if a subject does not want a particular ethnic group to be allowed into the country little is likely to be accomplished in a discussion of close kinship by marriage.

(2) The greater the trustworthiness, the greater change towards the position advocated by the communication; the feeling of trust does not affect the learning of content but rather affects its acceptance.

(3) Similarly, the more a source is perceived to be an expert the greater the change that is likely to take place.

(4) Opinion leaders carry greater weight than papers or radio speeches.

(5) The ideal educator is a person who is a member of the group that needs to be educated.

(6) It is better to accentuate progress in the fight against prejudice and for democratic ideals, to show public agreement of the necessity and desirability of fighting prejudice. The prejudiced person needs to conform.

(7) Those who reject irrational statements against ethnic groups tend to accept irrational statements in favour of ethnic groups.

Behaviour Modification

Behaviour modification procedures are frequently considered to be unacceptable to teachers as an attitude change strategy because it is thought to be an unacceptable form of indoctrination. The strategy can be effective in coping with the specific problem of students associating negative words with a particular minority group.

Parish and Lambert (1973) used laboratory reinforcement procedures to weaken the formal black-white concept attitudes of 5-year old Caucasian subjects. Some evidence was found for a reduction in the tendency to attribute negative adjectives to pictures of Blacks and positive attitudes to pictures of Whites. A second study achieved positive attitude change when they paired positive words with pictures of Vietnamese but did not change attitudes toward Blacks when a similar treatment was used. Kehoe, Echols & Stone (1978) paired positive and neutral words with emotionally ambiguous slide photographs of East Indian Canadians. The association of positive words resulted in more positive attitudes toward East Indian Canadians.

Personal Contact

Personal contact with members of ethnic minorities does not automatically increase or reduce tension: it can do either or neither. Studies have found increased, decreased, and unchanged tolerance. For example, a brotherhood week established explicitly for the purpose of improving human relations may succeed only in making its members more self-conscious and put the more prejudiced participants on the defensive. The members of the minority may feel humiliated by the emphasis on race relations.

In situations of not very high prejudice, the introduction of personal contact between members of different ethnic groups tends to lessen prejudice. The likelihood of lessening prejudice is increased when groups meet on personal terms, on a common task with shared interests and tastes that run across ethnic lines, and on terms of economic and social equality. Equal status contact may be ineffective or have a negative effect if unequal status expectations exist on the part of one group. If Angloceltic Canadian students go to Quebec with expectations that their Quebec counterparts will be of inferior status and the Quebec students perceive themselves to be of superior status, the consequences could be the reverse of those intended. Other conditions enhancing the likelihood of success include: opportunity for frequent contact, cooperative versus competitive goals, potential for interpersonal intimacy, institutional support, the ethnic balance, and voluntary as opposed to forced contact.

It is frequently assumed that rejection of contact is based on race. Research has shown that prejudice is not based solely on race, but rather on a perceived difference in beliefs (Rokeach & Mezei, 1966). People are prepared to cross racial lines to work or associate with people who have similar belief systems. It would be very desirable if the school organized neighbourhoods to assist each other in the common task of stopping vandalism and harassment against an ethnic member of the neighbourhood. Similarly, the school could organize neighbourhood festivals or parties designed to get neighbours acquainted with each other. One strategy found effective was to ask some members to tell about their memories of autumn, of holidays, or of food they enjoyed as a child. The report reminds other participants of equally nostalgic memories and soon the group is comparing notes concerning regional and ethnic customs. The distance of the memories, their warmth and frequent humor, lead to a sense of commonality. Group customs and their meaning are seen to be remarkably alike. The results of such a meeting can be an agenda for improving community relations, or it could result in a greater willingness of neighbours to publicly disapprove of prejudicial acts.

Going Public

It is always important to answer prejudiced remarks whenever they occur. Prejudiced persons confronted with anti-prejudice remarks or propaganda become aware of the widespread opposition to their beliefs and hence more reluctant to act upon their prejudiced attitudes. Public disapproval of prejudiced remarks is comparatively easy when you are in a position of non-equal power relationships. An individual was buying a house in the South Kitsalano area of Vancouver. The salesman suggested he might not want to buy a house in the area because "the Greeks were moving across West Broadway". It sounded like a plague. When the individual challenged the salesman and told him that his remarks were in bad taste, the salesman suggested it was a great neighbourhood with a nice ethnic mix in it. It is more difficult to confront peers and friends. There are subtle ways to communicate your attitudes. For example, when an ethnic joke is being told you can indicate your embarrassment or discomfort. A more difficult situation is verbal or physical assaults on a bus or subway. People in large groups are more likely to not get involved because they are considering the reactions of observers. The following progression of strategies may be appropriate for such public discrimination. First one might go and sit beside the victim of verbal abuse. Simply introducing yourself and talking to the victim may dissuade the assailant. Second, if that is unsuccessful you should loudly and clearly (but calmly) insist the attacker stop the verbal or physical abuse. You should not threaten the assailant. A tone of righteous indignation would be helpful. Third, you should approach the bus driver and ask his assistance. Fourth, if others are present on the bus enlist their verbal support against the assailant. Appeal to patriotic or democratic motives. For example, "This kind of thing may happen in other countries but it is a sad day for Canada if it starts happening here. Let's stop it before it starts". It may be the pervasive attitude to take pride in not coming to the assistance of someone in trouble or to regard someone who came to the assistance of a person with bemused attachment. Clearly such attitudes ought to be discouraged.

Role Play and Simulations

Role-playing is a strategy which, like many others discussed, is not always successful. (Sorman (1973) found that role playing did not significantly affect the racial attitudes of White suburban fourth and sixth grade children. Verma (1977) found dramatization to be less effective than other strategies. However, role-playing or enhancing role reasoning ability seem to be important and successful strategies in some situations. Role playing a previously unacceptable position increases its acceptability. Gray and Ashmore (1975) had subjects read single paragraph descriptions of three recent newspaper articles documenting the suffering of a minority group. The subject's main task in the role play condition was to write an essay in favour of strong public and private efforts to create opportunities for minorities. The strategy was successful. Breckheiner and Breckheiner (1976) had subjects act out causes of discrimination and ways of promoting better inter-racial cooperation. They were successful in bringing about a significant reduction in prejudice. If a subject voluntarily chooses to undertake the action opposed to his beliefs, the resultant attitude change can be even greater. For example, it is possible to have subjects voluntarily role play a defense of the values of a particular ethnic group, or role play someone bearing the brunt of discrimination, or role play the part of a person torn between two value systems. The result can be that the subjects become convinced of the position as they argue to defend it, or self-insight may be induced and the subject may respond more empathetically to the plight of the ethnic group.

As we have seen with other strategies it may not be necessary or even desirable in some situations to use ethnic prejudice as a source of substantive issues. Weider (1954) had college students participate in sociodramas of the situations. Subjects were significantly less prejudiced as a result of the participation.

A particular kind of role playing activity may be more effective with a certain clientele. Pitman (1977) sets out a profile of people who perpetuated physical assaults against South Asians in Toronto. As you read the description try to devise solutions. The assailants were males in their twenties who seldom read anything but watch junk television and listen to Rock radio. Typically these men have no plans to settle down; they work irratically. When they work they will do almost anything but they do not seek anything other than a labouring job because they do not think they could do it. Most employers agree. They are the first fired and laid off. The typical assailant has no father at home and has no affection for him, but he has a great deal of affection for his mother. He is a Canadian which is something he rather doubts the French could ever be. "Pakis" never have and never will be Canadians. Pakistan people are taking over his country and taking over his jobs. He resents them but knows very little about them and won't learn about them. He considers himself more physically than intellectually inclined. He sees himself as a free spirit and happy-go-lucky. He likes to drink beer and smoke pot and had been drinking just before the assault. He doesn't spend much time thinking about why he perpetuated the assault. However, motives seem to range from simply an excess of amoral exhuberance to a fear and jealousy of perceived superior economic status and family cohesion. Pitman's description of the assailants is similar to the description of the delinquents in a study done by Chandler (1973). His subjects were enrolled in a training program which employed drama and the making of video films as vehicles for helping them to see themselves from the perspectives of others and for providing remedial training in deficient role-taking skills. The subjects were encouraged to develop, portray, and record brief skits dealing with events involving persons of their own age. The skits developed by participants had to be about persons their own age and depict real-life situations. There had to be a part for each participant and each skit was rerun until each participant had occupied every role in the plot. The videotapes were also reviewed in an effort to determine ways of improving them. The strategy was effective in enhancing the role taking ability of subjects and in an eighteen month follow-up their acts of delinquency were fifty per cent lower than the control group.

Simulations

Simulations are generally highly regarded strategies for changing attitudes. Nevertheless they are not always successful, nor in all situations. In particular studies they have been effective in changing the empathy level of secondary students (Huber, 1972) of using the 'Sunshine' simulation to improve attitudes in ethnic studies (Newman, 1974) of 'Sunshine' changing student racial attitudes (De Koch, 1969) and using 'Starpower' and discussion to change attitudes toward women and blacks (Chapman, 1974). However Kehoe, Echols and Neighbor (1978) found 'Starpower' and discussion led to grade six attitudes changing toward women but not to the poor.

Enhancing Developmental and Personality Characteristics

Moral Development

Lawrence Kohlberg (1963) has found a developmental sequence of six stages of moral reasoning. He has shown that children and adults give different and increasingly sophisticated positions for such moral issues as "reasons for obeying" and "views of human life". For example, pre-conventional children obey rules because they are afraid of being punished or because there is something in it for them. Conventional people obey rules because they are prepared to take the interests of others into consideration and believe that society would collapse if rules are not obeyed. Post conventional people perceive rules as part of a social contract which can be changed. Davidson (1975) has shown a relationship between respect for persons at each stage of development and prejudice. The lower the stage of moral development the more prejudice there is likely to exist.

At stage one disrespect and prejudice are based on either a stereotype accepted from an authority or an imputation of danger. There is little differentiation of individuals from the labeled groups to which they belong. At stage two respect for others is described as permission for peers or groups to pursue their own aims. Indifference to others is a virtue and the claim that all are equal is mere cliche. Fighting is seen to lead to further anger and fear, yet fighting is thought to be a source of justice. Both the prejudice of impulsive anger and indifference are characteristic of stage two values. At stage three the emphasis in relationships is based on pleasing one another or 'being good'. Global sympathies tend to reduce prejudice or to produce a shallow changeable evaluation of minority groups. Ethnic stereotypes are accepted because they represent the majority view. At stage four prejudice or anti-prejudice is based on conventional ideas. Claims of justice, rights, and equality are subordinated to the fixed expectations of society. If society passes laws against discrimination then one can expect stage four individuals to begin to accept anti-prejudice sentiments. However, if they believe the rules of their religion supersede the law of the country then prejudicial sentiments derived from religious beliefs may continue. At stage five and six other people are considered to have equivalent value to that of self. Universal principles of ethnical conduct are seen to be necessary and form the basis of judgment of self and others.

To date the most successful means of getting children to move from stage to stage is to make provision for the discussion of moral dilemmas. Dilemmas that challenge students to seek more mature conclusions by challenging the adequacy of their existing reasoning may include the unfairness of prejudice. The consideration of other moral dilemmas seems to produce stage change without the possibility of accusations of racism or prejudice. The most effective and efficient alternative has yet to be evaluated.

Self-Concept

Positive self-concepts are deemed important for both majority and minority students in classrooms. Majority group students with positive self-concepts have a greater tendency to have positive attitudes toward minority group students. Minority group students with positive self-concept are more likely to view themselves as worthwhile persons, and to perform accordingly.

It is argued that children who feel good about themselves will project this feeling of worth to others. If they feel good about themselves there is less likelihood of feeling threatened by the accomplishments and differences of others. Because there is constant pressure to conform, to be "like everyone else", we need to teach children to value diversity and to view being different as a positive quality.

Pamela and Chris Tiedt (1979), in their book <u>Multicultural Teaching: A Handbook of Activities, Information and Resources</u>, describe thirty-two classroom strategies for enhancing self-concept and twenty-four strategies for developing positive perceptions of others. The strategies described have face validity in that it seems that they would have the desired effect. However, no evidence is provided to show that individually or in combination the strategies achieve the goals of more positive self-concept and more positive perception of others. Nor is there any information to suggest that the strategies may be more effective with some pupils or different teachers.

Research is needed to determine whether (1) the strategies described will enhance the self-concept of pupils; (2) if self-concept is enhanced without clear effect upon attitudes toward others (i.e., if the strategies described in <u>Multicultural Teaching</u> will result in positive perceptions of others).

CONCLUSION

An examination of the literature on citizenship education indicates that to date the school is an important agent for transmitting political information to youth. It is probably fair to assume that schools would be equally effective in teaching about human rights, prejudice, and multiculturalism if they should decide knowledge of such matters were important.

The school is less influential in shaping political attitudes and behaviour. Reasons for this might be that schools are not doing appropriate things to effectively change attitudes or that the clients consider their attitudes and values as not the schools' business. It may therefore be assumed that if schools continue to function as they are presently allowed to function, no significant increase in commitment to Human Rights and Multiculturalism or decline in prejudicial attitudes can be expected.

There seems to be little reason to be optimistic about schools changing the way they presently function. As a result the strategies described above were selected because they were considered to be small modifications of what teachers now do and therefore more likely to be accepted.

NOTES

Berreman, Gerald D. "Self, Situation and Escape from Stigmatized Ethnic Identity". Paper presented at American Anthropological Association, New York, 1971.

Black, John A. "The Effects of Instruction in General Semantics on Ethnic Prejudice", Research in the Teaching of English, 7:1 (Spring 1973), 98-108.

Breckheiner, Steven E. & Rosemary Breckheiner "Group Methods for Reducing Racial Prejudice and Discrimination", Psychological Reports, 39 (1976), 1259-1268.

British Columbia The Elementary Social Studies Guide for the Province of British Columbia states, "a teacher must face the difficult task of evaluating the individual's development in attitudes and behavior".

Chandler, Michael J. "Ecocentrism and Anti-Social Behavior: The Assessment and Training of Social Perspective - Training Skills", Developmental Psychology, 9:1 (1973).

Chapman, Thomas Howard "Simulation Game Effects on Attitudes Regarding Racism and Sexism". Doctoral Dissertation, University of Maryland, 1974.

Cohen, E.G. & S.S. Roper "Modification of interracial interaction disability: An application of status characteristic theory", American Sociological Review, 37:6 (1972), 643-657.

Davidson, Florence Respect for Persons and Ethnic Prejudice in Childhood. Report of a Research Study, Harvard University, 1975.

DeKoch, Paul "Simulations and Changes in Racial Attitudes", Social Education, 33:2 (1969), 181-183.

Goldberg, S.C. "Three Situational Determinants of Conformity to Social Norms", Journal of Abnormal Social Psychology, 49 (1954).

Goldenson, Dennis R. "An Alternative View About the Role of the Secondary School in Political Socialization: A Field-Experimental Study of the Development of Civil Liberties Attitudes", Theory and Research in Social Education, 6:1 (March 1978), 44-72.

Gray, David B. & Richard D. Ashmore "Comparing the Effects of Informational, Role-Playing and Value, Discrepancy Treatments of Racial Attitude", Journal of Applied Social Psychology, 5:3 (1975), 262-281.

Henry, Francis A Study of Growth of Racism in Metropolitan Toronto. Submitted to Secretary of State, 1978.

Hess, Robert D. & David Eaton "The Role of the Elementary School in Political Socialization", The School Review, LXX (Autumn 1962), 257-267.

Hess, Robert D. & Judith Torney The Development of Political Attitudes in Children. Chicago: Aldine Publishing Co., 1967.

Huber, Harold Wesley "An Investigation of the Effects of Selected Simulated Classroom Situations of Student Teacher Attitude and Empathy". Doctoral Dissertation, Michigan State University, 1972.

Holloway, S.M. & H.A. Hornstein "How Good News Makes Us Good", Psychology Today (10 Dec. 1976), 76.

Kagan, H.E. Changing the Attitude of Christians toward Jews: A Psychological Approach through Religion. New York: Columbia University, 1953.

Kehoe, John "An Examination of Alternative Approaches to Teaching the Universal Declaration of Human Rights", International Journal of Political Education, 3:2 (1980), 193-204.

Kehoe, John & Carol-Lyn Sakata "Attitudes of Majority and Minority to Inclusion of Minority Culture in the Curriculum". Unpublished paper, University of British Columbia, 1978.

Kehoe, J., F. Echols & J. Stone "Changing Negative Attitudes toward Japanese and East Indian Canadians in Elementary School Children by Using Classical Conditioning Procedures", The Alberta Journal of Educational Research, XXIV:4 (Dec. 1978).

Kehoe, J. "Demonstrating the Relationship Between Values and Attitudes as a Means of Changing Attitudes", Alberta Journal of Educational Research, XXXI:3, (Sept. 1975).

Kehoe, J., F. Echols & C. Sakata "The Effects of Reading and Discussing Historical and Contemporary Cases of Discrimination on Student Empathy". Unpublished paper, University of British Columbia, 1978.

Kehoe, John, Frank Echols & Ted Neighbor "The Effects of the Simulation *Starpower* on Pupil Attitudes toward Women and the Poor". Unpublished paper, University of British Columbia, 1978.

Kehoe, J. & B. Hood "An Evaluation of an Anti-Prejudice Film Program". Unpublished report, University of British Columbia, 1978.

Kehoe, John "Multiculturalism and the Problems of Ethical Relativism", *The History and Social Science Teacher*, 13 (Fall 1977).

Kehoe, John & Graham Hope "Principle-Testing Discussion as a Strategy for Moving to an Ethical Universalist Position". Unpublished research, University of British Columbia, 1979.

Kehoe, John "The New Social Studies and Citizenship Education: A Critique" in Terrence Morrison & Anthony Burton (eds.) *Options: Reforms and Alternatives for Canadian Education*. Toronto: Holt, Rinehart & Winston, 1973.

Kehoe, John & Frank Echols, Jr. "A Survey of Student Attitudes toward and Knowledge of Civil Liberties and Human Rights Law", *The History and Social Science Teacher*, 15:2 (Winter 1980).

Kohlberg, Lawrence "The Development of Children's Orientation toward a Moral Order, Part One", *Vita Humana*, 6 (1963).

McDiarmid, G. & David Pratt *Teaching Prejudice*. Toronto: Ontario Institute for Studies in Education, 1971.

Metcalf, Lawrence (ed.) *Values Education*. Washington: National Council for the Social Studies, 1971.

Newman, John Joseph "Effectiveness of an Educational Simulation in Teaching Ethnic Studies to High School Students". Doctoral dissertation, Northern Illinois University, 1974.

Paris, T.S. & F. Lambert "Changing Anti-Negro and Anti-Vietnamese Attitudes in Children Using Classical Conditioning Procedures", ERIC-ED089831, April 1973.

Pitman, Walter *Now is Not Too Late*. Submitted to the Council of Metropolitan Toronto by Task Force on Human Relations, 1977.

Rokeach, Milton & Louis Mezei "Race and Shared Belief as Factors in Social Choice", *Science* (1966) 167-172.

Rosenstock, Janet & Dennis Adair Multi-racialism in the Classroom, A Survey of Interracial Attitudes in Ontario Schools. Report submitted to the Secretary of State, Ottawa, 1976.

Salyachivin, Somboon "Change in International Understanding as a Function of Perceived Similarity, Conceptual Level, and Primary Effect". Unpublished dissertation, University of Toronto, 1972.

Serow, Robert & Kenneth Strube "Students' Attitudes toward High School Governance: Implications for Social Education , Theory and Research in Social Education, 6:3 (Sept. 1978), 14-26.

Sorman, Margo "The Effects of Role Playing on the Racial Attitudes of White Suburban Fourth and Sixth Grade Students toward Blacks". Doctoral dissertation, Boston University School of Education, 1973.

Southam Press Limited The Searching Nation. Toronto: Southam Press, 1977.

Spoerl, D.J. "Some Aspects of Prejudice as Affected by Religion and Education", Journal of Social Psychology, XXXIII (1951), 69-76.

Target Canada "The Interview". Vancouver, British Columbia, 1979.

Teacher's Manual Prejudice: Toronto, Ontario Institute for Studies in Education, 1978.

Thiessen, Dennis "Education for International Understanding in the Elementary School: Toward a Re-examination". Unpublished paper, University of British Columbia, 1977.

Tiedt, Pamela & Iris Tiedt Multicultural Teaching. A Handbook of Activities, Information and Resources. Boston: Allyn & Bacon, 1979.

Torney, J.V. "The International Attitudes and Knowledge of Adolescents in Nine Countries: The IEA Civic Education Survey", International Journal of Political Education, 1 (1977), 3-20.

Ubale, Bhausahebs Equal Opportunity and Public Policy. A report on Concerns of the South Asian Canadian community regarding their place in the Canadian mosaic. Submitted to the Attorney General of Ontario, 1977.

Verma, Gajendra K. "Some Effects of Curriculum Innovation on the Racial Attitudes of Adolescents", International Journal of Intercultural Relations, 1:3 (Fall 1977).

Weider, G.S. "Group Procedures Modifying Attitudes of Prejudice in the College Classroom", Journal of Educational Psychology, 45 (1954) 332-344.

Special Education

Grant McMurray

Any discussion of children's rights in Canada must be based upon the assumption that this nation is democratic and its schools and other institutions adhere to democratic principles. Among the few educational battles to be won in recent years has been the increase in social/ educational equalities obtained by and for the handicapped. While confrontations even in education are never won without casualties, increased rights to education for children with special needs have been demonstrated overwhelmingly by the entrenchment of mandatory legislation.

The rights of both children and adults are greatly facilitated by appropriate enabling legislation. This chapter discusses some aspects of legislation as they pertain to the rights of children with special needs, especially mandatory legislation relating specifically to mainstreaming. This topic and the problems of the handicapped as they relate to the United States have been described by Reynold and Birch (1977) and Semmel, Gottlieb and Robinson (1979), as have the related problems of labelling the handicapped by MacMillan and Meyers (1979).

The enactment of PL 94-142 in the United States and, to a lesser extent, the recommendations of the Warnock Commission in England and Wales have increasingly influenced Canada in terms of changes in educational regulations and in legislation in many of the Provinces. It is dangerous to generalize about rights and, for that matter, about attitudes toward children in a country as culturally and geographically diverse as Canada. Children are frequently not thought of here in the context of "the child as citizen" (_Admittance Restricted_, 1978). This is particularly true, though by no means exclusively so, for children with special needs who are dependent and therefore uniquely vulnerable to a number of forces. It is the handicapped youngster who becomes the casualty of institutions and of systems which, when responding to the needs and demands of <u>adults</u>, assume that they actually do address the needs of children. Thus, as the authors of <u>Admittance Restricted</u> (1978) suggest, children are frequently regarded by society as pets: how else are we to interpret the growing number of housing developments that are for "adults only"?

Canadian writers, particularly if they identify with professional education in some form, equate with Canadian educational systems - which are diversely regional in nature - a degree of academic leadership and excellence that does not exist for young people. Even Ryerson, when designing and defending the public schools, glossed over the human rights justification for youngsters with special needs such as the poor, to emphasize instead the need for them to fit neatly into a well-ordered industrial society (Ryerson, 1849)

A projection of this sentiment may be found in traditional segregated programs for the handicapped. Institutions such as those euphemistically called hospital schools, special schools and/or protected settings, have traditionally held the education of their wards secondary to health care; essentially these children were segregated from the mainstream of society. Even when attending school the goal was often to keep the handicapped apart from ordinary students and teachers. This practice was rationalized, often with the very best of intentions, because of the belief that in such a segregated environment the child with a handicap could best learn and otherwise benefit from instruction. Indeed schooling was publicly provided as a right only to those deemed able "to profit from instruction". For others special provisions were sometimes provided at the discretion of local boards. In other words, the provision of special programs was permissive but not mandatory. If a child's needs corresponded to the staffing and curricular provisions of the system, he (or she) was admitted to school. If the board or provincial ministry interpreted otherwise, such children were excluded. Many such youngsters are still not receiving meaningful, publicly funded instruction in Canada.

The Exceptional Child: Compared to Whom?

"To be normal is to be different" is often stated but seldom taken seriously. The term "normal" can mean vastly different things: to a physician it most likely suggests an absence of pathology; to a psychologist or educator it may refer to a statistical majority; historically it may imply what is favoured at a particular time and to the typical citizen it probably means "like me". Except for the specific case of the gifted and talented, the exceptional youngster is one who is handicapped in one or more possible ways: physically (orthopedically, auditorally, visually, etc.), intellectually, culturally or emotionally. As well there should be added a whole array of little-understood behaviours, most often referred to as "learning disabilities" which, in part at least, relate to difficulties in "learning how to learn".

Regarded now as children with special needs, handicapped children in the last two or three decades have been, to paraphrase <u>Admittance Restricted</u> (1978), most often as not being able to participate in the regular school system, and consequently are provided with minimal facilities, staff and resources in programs external to the mainstream. The opportunity for such children to acquire the skills and abilities necessary for meaningful participation in a job in their community was seldom achieved. The development of alternative school settings for handicapping conditions such as emotional disturbance has often resulted in the removal of children from school to what is little more than some kind of holding operation, whether inside or outside of the school.

At this point it may be useful to note that the gifted (those with generally high abilities) and talented (those with superior ability in one or a few specific areas) have also been contained in some kind of "holding operation" in many school systems. All too often a gifted child is assumed to have the abilities to learn and develop on his own. Often the victim of teachers less capable and innovative than himself, such a child has to put up with a system that slowly turns him off, either through neglect or by punishing conditions which burden him with additional work under the guise of "enrichment". The gifted, it should be remembered, have rights too.

Mainstreaming: The Least Restrictive Environment

A major recent special education focus in developed nations is to provide open access to public education for all children, regardless of the nature and extent of their handicap and in the least restrictive educational environment possible. Known in the United States as "mainstreaming", this movement was prompted by legal advocates, parents and certain state legislatures and culminated in the passage of Public Law 94-142 "The Education of all Handicapped Children's Act" in 1975 (Abeson and Zittel, 1977). This federal law was based upon a number of historical events. Following the largely institutional recognition of the blind, the deaf and the retarded in the nineteenth century, it was not until after World War II that a general recognition of the field of special education became a part of general education. It was particularly through the education of the mentally retarded that a generic approach to education in all areas of disability became reflected in the structure of public school systems and in teacher training institutions. After World War II there was a heightened awareness of increasing human potential through rehabilitation and re-education. This major focus to provide <u>open access</u> to public education for all children regardless of the nature and extent of their handicap, reflected the advocacy of individual rights, court decisions, and intense concern for procedures relating to the identification and classification of the handicapped and for the provision of instruction. The problems of both over and under inclusion were recognized (particularly of cultural minorities) for children and youth who had proven difficult for schools to accommodate within traditional patterns of service. American mainstreaming emphasized the education of <u>all</u> youngsters, including the handicapped, in the least restrictive educational environment possible. In the spirit of federal intervention to protect minorities and even to compensate for their previous disadvantages, P.L. 94-142 provides federal funding and mandatory education for all children between the ages of three and twenty-one years, effective September 1980.

To consider children's rights in the context of mainstreaming, it is important to recognize what mainstreaming is and what it is not. It is not, as Meisels (1978) suggested it was, "a form of educational programming that integrates special needs and non-special needs children in regular classrooms". Rather it is or ought to be, to paraphrase Johnson and Johnson (1980), "the provision of an appropriate educational opportunity for all handicapped students in the least restrictive alternative, based on individualized education programs, with procedural safeguards and parent involvement, and aimed at providing handicapped students with access to and constructive interaction with non-handicapped peers". Mainstreaming is often a misleading term when it does not achieve each of these objectives.

American legislation such as PL 94-142 continues to have important implications for Canadian educators. Tompkins (1952) made the point that in no other country in the world is there so direct and inevitable an influence to events in the United States as there is in Canada. The estimate that 85% of the books and journals in faculty of education libraries in Canada are American in origin is evidence of such influence. Whether as a challenge to situations that exist commonly in both countries or as a defensive reaction against similar American events, Canadian educators are highly influenced by the flow of information from the United States. Mainstreaming is not a new concept. Many now living have attended schools where children with special needs, both handicapped and gifted, remained together in ordinary classrooms and all classes were open to all children. It was not until Alfred Binet was approached by the Paris school authorities to design a measure of intelligence to estimate which children could least profit from "regular" education, that psychology and education joined forces to separate slow learners from the mainstream.

The wisdom of homogeneous placement of slow learners in self-contained segregated classes was challenged first by Johnson (1962). He observed that "it is indeed paradoxical that mentally handicapped children, having teachers especially trained, having more money (per capita) spent on their education and --- designed for their unique needs, should be accomplishing the objectives of their education at the same or at a slower rate than similar --- children who have not had these advantages and have been forced to remain in the regular grades". This point of view was later developed by Dunn (1968), who felt that better educational opportunities other than special class placement were available for handicapped children, including culturally deprived children who are often labelled mentally retarded.

Programs providing a range of instructional opportunities, from the use of special instructional materials within a regular classroom to residential schooling, and hospital and home-bound instruction, have become conceptualized in the Cascade system (Reynolds, 1962). This has become a model of service provision in the public schools. Basic to Reynold's "Placement Cascade" is the idea that the child should be moved from the regular classroom only as far as necessary to obtain the necessary educational program. The child should be returned to the regular classroom or to a less restricted environment as quickly as possible. Complementing and additional to this, Reynolds (1976) developed the "Cascade of Services", suggesting that for many children services can be brought to the learner without moving the child. Intrinsic is the idea that services in many cases may be moved into the regular classroom without impairing the quality of services formally provided in a more restrictive setting. This movement of services, which recognizes the rights of the youngster to remain with his peers, facilitates a very important goal of education today: keeping the child whenever possible in the mainstream of general education. Central to the mainstreaming concept is the necessity that special education and regular education teachers (along with meaningful support personnel and materials) work together. Rather than costing less, such efforts will require the coordination of teaching materials and methods and continuing evaluation of both child and the program.

Lest mainstreaming and educational rights be thought to be equivalent, the cool caution of Cruickshank (1977) may put the current pendulum swing into perspective. Cruickshank cautioned that many exceptional children should not be integrated into regular classes: "The fact of the matter is that in terms of current educational practice, the 'least' may more often be the most restrictive place for learning-disabled children to receive their education". Cruickshank refers here to the fact that the learning characteristics of many learning-disabled pupils, such as distractibility and rigidity in conceptual thinking, may be increased in the large, relatively heterogeneous regular classroom. Thus such placement may be more restrictive than in a specialized and more segregated one. In the same year Hapeman (1977) cautioned that mainstreaming efforts have "the potential of erasing seventy-five years of gains made for visually-handicapped children and their parents". Inept mainstreaming attempts on the part of many boards may in fact mean replacing good education with poor education despite a verbalized goal of excellence. Educational treatments of the handicapped should not imply a single prescription for all, but rather appropriate education relative to the nature and extent of the handicap. Quality education takes a variety of forms in many settings. The first responsibility is not the method but the child.

A recent though less pervasive influence upon Canadian special education has been the report of the Warnock Commission in England (1978), recently amplified by the Parliamentary Report of the Secretary of State entitled Special Needs in Education (1980). Its 224 recommendations focus attention upon the child's special education needs, viewed not from the perspective of a particular handicap but in terms of the total picture: abilities and disabilities; social and cultural influences: the educational problem; the time the child may need special interventions (including those within the ordinary classroom) and particularly the manner by which education is provided. The Warnock Commission was established around the central issue of the educational needs and rights of handicapped youngsters who were not being served. Many in the developed countries of the world, particularly Great Britain, Canada and the United States, assume that what was traditionally a privilege of the few is now recognized as the right of all. There is ample recent evidence that large numbers of youngster have still been excluded from school and deprived of the educational opportunities other youngster take for granted. For example, Keeton (1978) indicated that 15,000 Ontario children were awaiting placement in special classes, and 1500 were in hospital wards, juvenile training centres and private programs removed from the immediate jurisdiction of education boards. About 130 children were simply not receiving any kind of schooling.

Recalling that most provinces of Canada have provided permissive rather than mandatory education (boards may provide special programs but are not required to do so), it is perhaps useful to look at current trends across Canada relative to the provision of special educational services for the handicapped. Recent Canadian court rulings have precipitated questions of the kind raised by Roberts (1978), who asked: "If...a school board spends...eighteen hundred dollars on every child, have equal opportunities been provided for all?"

Legislative Provisions for Exceptional Children in Canada in Perspective*

Provincial bills and regulations regarding the education of the handicapped within the public school system make little reference to the rights of children. Often one has to assume that exceptional children's rights are secondary to the religious or language rights of the parent and the restrictions against parental abuse. Children's rights within the context of special education relate to such issues as: access to educational facilities; adversarial protection in court; and uniform, definitive and fairly interpreted classifications of exceptionalities in each of the provinces. Provincial interpretations and understanding of the concept of children with special needs within the education systems are by no means uniform.

Mandatory Legislation: British Columbia

Victoria has moved more slowly than some other legislatures, although the Education Act has been reviewed and a series of public meetings have been held. Interest groups at the grass-roots level have provided feed-in from the local Council for Exceptional Children.

---

* The following comments are a resume provided by the CEC National Public Policy Committee at the 4th National Congress on Exceptional Children, Halifax, N.S., October 16, 1980.

Alberta

Legislation in Alberta states that a board must provide education for all students, though a child may still be excluded temporarily if the school system does not have the needed facilities. The word "temporarily" has come to be interpreted, due to the Duke-Alberta Supreme Court case, as some period less than one year. This time limit tends to make Alberta's Legislation mandatory, although it is not so described in the bill. Alberta provides substantial education grants for children with very special needs -- grants which may provide essentially individualized instruction where appropriate.

Saskatchewan

Legislation in Saskatchewan is described as mandatory but when updated in 1978 it did not require programs for the gifted. Saskatchewan's legislation sets down the nature of a school board's obligation to the handicapped, and has a "due process" feature. A board without services may purchase them from others, and parents must be consulted before special placements are made. Parents may also appeal the validity of diagnostic assessments made by the school system. In addition, considerable efforts have been made to make buildings physically accessible to the handicapped.

Manitoba

Manitoba's old legislation, like much of the legislation in other provinces, suggested that the schools must provide education where possible and practicable. These words have now gone from the legislation, but unfortunately the words "appropriate" education and the issue of "due process" and the "quality" of education are largely undefined.

Quebec

Some months ago the schools of Quebec were described as responsible for the education of "all children" and the money was provided by the provincial government. Recently official government policy has swung toward mainstreaming but now doubts are surfacing about covering the cost of such a program. As a consequence, boards may have to choose between those things they can do, with a local choice being possible between such provision as special education for disturbed youngsters and books in the library. The need to work out relationships between local committees of parents, the local board of education, the administrators of the school, and the provincial ministry may take longer than is acceptable to the parents of many special needs youngsters. The whole issue of linguistic rights for minority groups has eclipsed attention to other exceptional children.

New Brunswick

As a bilingual province, New Brunswick has two education programs, one in French and one in English. There are three Education Acts: (i) Auxiliary Class Act, which deals with such matters as the trainable mentally retarded; (ii) The Special Education Act, which deal with the visually and hearing impaired children (with facilities shared with the other Atlantic Provinces); and (iii) The School Act, which appears to ignore exceptional children per se, except in terms of the right of their exclusion. Protections for exceptional children are not clearly specified.

Newfoundland

Newfoundland acquired mandatory legislation by changing the permissive word "may" to the mandatory word "shall" when the new School Act was passed on December 14, 1979.

Nova Scotia

Nova Scotia has two Education Acts: (i) The Regular Education Act (1973) changed "may" to "shall" in reference to the provision of education for the mentally and physically handicapped; and (ii) The Handicapped Person's Education Act, which provides education for visually, hearing, and physically impaired youngsters from birth to age twenty-one. During the past two years there have been expressions of concern about learning disability youngsters (variously defined as those who are not achieving up to their potential) in the province, notably the high incidence of learning disabilities in juvenile offenders. One milestone in Nova Scotia is the requirement that there be mandatory courses on the nature and education of exceptional children for all beginning teachers in the province.

Ontario

An Act to amend The Education Act, 1974, known as Bill 82, was passed in the Ontario Legislature in 1980. This mandatory legislation relating specifically to the education of all exceptional children in the province is the most extensive bill of its kind in Canada. It is intended to phase its provisions into practice completely by 1985 and currently nineteen pilot boards are working through the provisions of the Bill in their own jurisdictions, with a mandatory and comprehensive adoption of the bill and accompanying regulations in all boards by 1985.*

---

* For a comprehensive discussion of Bill 82 and Ontario Regulations 554/81 see "Special Education Identification Placement and Review Committees and Appeals" cf. Case L. Bill 82: one and all - a Special Education Handbook. Toronto: The Ontario Educational Communications Authority, 1982.

Bill 82 defines an "exceptional pupil" as one considered to need placement in a special education program because of behavioral, communicational, intellectual, and physical/multiple handicaps. The bill leaves little room for vagueness in that it stipulates that a board shall ensure free and appropriate education which meets a child's unique needs. Specifically the rights of children and their parents are protected under the bill; it emphasizes the implementation of early identification procedures for children with special needs; and the diagnosis and placement of a youngster into special education programs by a board may be appealed to a Special Provincial Education Board. It is notable that appeal works both ways: boards as well as parents or their surrogates may appeal to the province. Considerable care has been taken to ensure that the definition of exceptionalities and the nature of classes and other educational facilities provided are uniform and common to the utmost extent across the province.

One of the most nobable revisions (Section 7, replacing Section 34 of the previous Act) defines the meaning of the words "appropriate special education program and services". These words are intended to imply the inclusion of:

- (i) an individual educational plan for the particular pupil,
- (ii) proper assessments of the pupil's needs,
- (iii) an opportunity for the pupil to benefit,
- (iv) implementation of a program in conformity with the pre-determined individual educational plan,
- (v) periodic evaluation,
- (vi) the suitability of the program and services equivalent to that offered pupils who are not exceptional pupils,
- (vii) a proper educational setting,
- (viii) the offering of the program and services in the least restrictive manner possible, and
- (ix) adherence to the code of procedures set out in sub-section 14.

Initially a number of boards of education wrote to the Ministry requesting deferment of the passage of Bill 82 because of the "expensive" obligations such legislation will place upon boards of education. Already there is little doubt that The Bill is providing a new era of responsibility and of far more equal rights for children with special needs, particularly for those young people of secondary school age who heretofore have been neglected and/or been provided for inadequately by the schools.

The legislation should go a long way toward ensuring that school programs fit the needs of children rather than requiring children to fit the programs offered by the school. Progress has been made in defining handicapped children, pointing up the importance of involvement by various professional groups and parents. It should maximize the achievement of children's rights and the rights of parents, and through the mechanism of the Individual Educational Plan (I.E.P.), prevent children from being lost in and to the system.

Additionally, it should be recognized that regions which have a disproportionate number of culturally and economically disadvantaged youngsters may receive subsidized assistance for special education programming. It is estimated that the passage of this bill will cost 3% (some $75,000.000) additionally to the money now spent to carry out the implications of the program. No longer will a board have the power to exclude a child from the school if he is unable to benefit from instruction by reason of mental or physical handicap. Rather the bill states that "a duty is placed on boards to provide an appropriate educational program for all children". It provides for instruction in either English or French where numbers warrant, and ensures equal services regardless of whether the child attends a public school or a separate school system.

This chapter has not attempted to discuss in detail a number of issues. For example, the issue of sexism in education usually focusses upon injustices to girls and women in western society (Ghosh, 1980). In terms of special education, however, the situation is reversed! Significantly more boys than girls are diagnosed as retarded, learning disabled, disturbed and the like. Not only is the actual incidence of these disorders higher in boys (Hingtgen and Bryson, 1972), but the number of boys enrolled in special programs is significantly beyond expectation. If ever an ombudsman were needed in education it is in the placement of boys, especially culturally different boys, in segregated and other specialized programs for the handicapped! Perhaps the rights of youngsters are most realized when their interests and needs are congruent with the program and styles of services. In our society the goal of maintaining achievement and motivation at capacity throughout education is frequently misinterpreted. Unless the concept of individual and differences is thoroughly understood, most educators, as well as parents, believe that most children can achieve academic "standards" by either working harder and longer or with remedial help. Yet, in the field of remedial reading, for example, countless authors (Spache, 1976 and MacMillan and Meyers, 1979) have suggested that neither remediation nor psychotherapy have demonstrated effectiveness with many children. MacMillan and Meyers suggest in their concluding statement that "the evidence clearly reveals that regardless of where we place mildly handicapped children, or what we call them, public education has been relatively ineffective in promoting academic achievement or social adjustment in these children".

Finally, no chapter on rights would be realistic if it were to omit comments about the rights of the teacher of children with special needs. Firstly, neither mainstreaming nor segregation will be effective for either children or their teachers unless teachers are effectively prepared for the task and supported with materials and consultative services on an ongoing basis. The untrained and unsupported regular-class teacher is especially at risk in this regard (McMurray, 1982). Of special concern is the increasing phenomenon of teacher burn-out in regular-class teachers and in other teachers of exceptional children (Weiskopf, 1980 and Bensky, et al, 1980). It is clear that work overload, lack of perceived success, continual and prolonged exposure to the handicapped, staff-child ratios, lack of structure, and the high degree of perceived responsibility experienced by those in helping professions all may infringe upon the health and the rights of teachers. While stress can be seen as either a positive or a negative reaction, when there is a perceived or real imbalance between environmental demands and one's response capability, the likelihood that the individual will experience stress as a negative reaction becomes more probable. While some administrators may regard teacher burn-out of little consequence at this time of declining enrolments and a surplus of good teachers, it is one of many variables to be considered by those who share a concern for human rights as part of their concern for the human condition.

References

Abeson, A. & J. Zittel "The end of the quiet revolution: The Education of All Handicapped Children Act of 1975", *Exceptional Children*, 44 (1977), 114-128.

Bensky, J.M., S.F. Shaw, A.S. Gouse, H. Bates, B. Dixon & W.E. Beane "Public Law 94-142 and stress: A problem for educators", *Exceptional Children*, 47 (1980), 24-29.

Canadian Council on Children and Youth *Admittance Restricted: The Child as Citizen in Canada*. Ottawa, 1978.

Canadian Teachers' Federation "Equal Opportunity to Learn" in *The Poor at School in Canada*. Ottawa, 1970.

CELDIC Report (The Commission on Emotional and Learning Disorders in Children) *One Million Children*. Toronto: Leonard Crainford Publishers, 1970.

Cruickshank, W.M. "Least-restrictive placement: Administrative wishful thinking", *Journal of Learning Disabilities*, 4 (1974), 193-194.

Dunn, L.C. "Special education for the mildly retarded -- Is much of it justifiable?", *Exceptional Children*, 35 (1968), 5-22.

Ghosh, R. "Human rights and sexism in education". Paper presented at the Comparative and International Education Society, Vancouver, B.C.: March 20, 1980.

Hapeman, L. "Reservations about the effect of P.L. 94-142 on the education of visually handicapped children", *Education of Visually Handicapped*, 9 (1979), 33-36.

Hingtgen, J.N. & C.Q. Bryson "Recent developments in the study of early childhood psychoses: Infantile autism, childhood schizophrenia, and related disorders", *Schizophrenia Bulletin*, 5 (1972) 8-54.

Johnson, D.W. and R.T. Johnson "Integrating handicapped students into the mainstream", *Exceptional Children*, 47 (1980), 90-98.

Johnson, G.O. "Special education for the mentally retarded--a paradox", Exceptional Children, 29 (1962), 62-69.

Keeton, A. "Special education: A right or a privilege?" Paper presented at the Council for Exceptional Children (Ontario). Ottawa, November, 1978.

MacMillan, D.L. & C.E. Meyers "Educational labeling of handicapped learners" in D.C. Berliner (ed.) Review of Research in Education. American Educational Research Association (1979), Vol. 7, 151-194.

McMurray, J.G. "Mainstreaming in a Canadian Context" in D. Bachor (ed.) Learning disabilities: conceptual and practical issues. London: Faculty of Education, The University of Western Ontario, 1982 (in press).

Meisels, S.J. "First steps in mainstreaming", Early Childhood, 4 (1978), 1-2.

Parliamentary Report, Special Needs in Education. London: Her Majesty's Stationery Office (Cmnd. 7996), August, 1980.

"Report of The Warnock Commission", Special Education--Forward Trends, 5:3 (1978), 10-40.

Reynolds, M.C. "A framework for considering some issues in special education", Exceptional Children, 28 (1962), 367-370.

Reynolds, M.C. "New alternatives through a new cascade". Paper presented at the Sixth Annual Invitational Conference on Leadership in Special Education Programs, November 23, 1976.

Reynolds, M.C. & J.W. Birch Teaching exceptional children in all American schools. Reston, Va.: Council for Exceptional Children, 1977.

Roberts, A. "B.C. board wants extra funds to educate handicapped", Globe and Mail (Toronto, Ontario), September 26, 1978.

Ryerson, Egerton "Canadian Mechanics and Manufacturers", Journal of Education for Upper Canada, 2 (1849), 19.

Semmel, M.I., J. Gottlieb & N.M. Robinson "Mainstreaming: perspectives on educating handicapped children in the public school" in D.C. Berliner (ed.) Review of Research in Education. American Educational Research Association (1979), Vol. 7, 223-279.

Spache, G.D. Diagnosing and correcting reading disabilities. Boston: Allyn & Bacon, 1977.

Tompkins, G.S. "Some aspects of American influence on Canadian educational thought and practice". Unpublished master's dissertation, McGill University, Montreal, 1952.

Weiskopf, P.E. "Burn-out among teachers of exceptional children", Exceptional Children, 47 (1980), 18-23.

Self and Other - The Right to a Human Education

MarySue McCarthy

We had just finished taping a radio show on 'Values and Education'. Naiomi Diamond, a writer-interviewer and I sat in the CBC cafeteria in Toronto celebrating with coffee. We were talking about another radio series she had just finished on Prejudice. Bluntly she asked me, "What causes prejudice?"

"Oh, fear!" I answered automatically. "Fear of the strange, xenophobia, fear of strangers, even fear of anything different. The weak ego or the immature egocentric person needs, I think, to have the world be a mirror-image of the self. And then I suppose there is the grandiose ego that really enjoys power". She cut into my meanderings, "What of the powerful, the privileged? Why do they show prejudice, attacking the weak?"

Realizing that she knew better than I, I still tried to answer. "We've always needed scapegoats. In extreme cases, of course, sadistic tendencies can give people stimulation, a real 'high' from hurting others. And I think the powerful want to protect their privilege. Sometimes they are ..., we are, afraid of pollution, of contamination ...".

At the word "contamination" Naiomi drew herself up with sudden intensity and energy. Her eyes went very dark and far away. "I want to tell you a story", she said. "My mother died when I was three. Each summer my dad saw to it that my little sister and I got to Loon Lake, up north, where old friends of my mother loved us, delighted in us, and nurtured us. My dad wanted us to have swimming lessons, so one day I set out with my little sister, feeling very big and responsible, taking her to the area where the lessons were given. I was about seven and she was four. The lake was roped off, a small shallow section for the very little ones and another area right next to it for those children, like myself, who were slightly bigger. I walked down the beach hand in hand with my sister and when I came to the roped-off area I saw a sign stuck in the water. It said: "NO JEWS OR DOGS". Her quiet moral outrage made her so full of dignity I sat cut to the quick, unable to breath. It had been years ago. A small personal outrage when compared to larger issues, world events. But this childhood event was a microcosm of all insults to human dignity, one which she was still struggling to understand and to document.

"So what are you doing", Naiomi said, "in your teacher training work, in your courses at York, to enlighten teachers, to prevent this fear and ignorance, the violation of respect for individuals, especially vulnerable individuals or groups? What are you really doing?"

Douglas Ray had asked me the same question a year before and I had said "Nothing and yet everything". While we believe that the need for curriculum ideas and values explorations on prejudice and human rights is urgent in the schools, our focus is on teacher education. We expect our students to question whether they as teachers, and the education processes as a whole, violate human rights and devalue or dehumanize the child. We believe education in our society is a right but we also believe that children - people - have a right to a humane, humanizing education.

Criticism of the School as a De-humanizing Institution

In the sixties 'violation' of children by parents and teachers was abundantly criticized. The assignment of 'identity labels' became a violence against the child. Compulsory education, introduced for nineteenth century reasons which had lost fashion, was criticized. So was the 'bucket theory' of education which deemed the child to be a passive receptacle of knowledge, of pre-packaged thought. Schools for the masses were run by teachers who encouraged middle-class virtues like docility, obedience, neatness, cleanliness and job-orientation or the work-ethic.

This heavily didactic and teacher-centered, traditional classroom gave too many children a failure identity. The child's right to feel equal and to become a competent and self-accepting human being seemed gravely threatened by the competitive, fact-oriented classroom. Abraham Maslow (1968, pp. 51-52) said that "never allowing children to discover" kills their imagination, their initiative, their budding facilities, their creative energy. The teacher who denies children involvement in their own education denies the child the sense of mastery and the experience of reciprocity that is needed and deserved (Plowden Report, 1968).

Not only was "ecstacy" absent from the classroom (Leonard, 1968), Richard Jones claimed that even basic feelings were not allowed. In his book, Fantasy and Feeling in Education (1968), Jones described children who had just watched a vivid, bloody sealhunt in a series of films used for a curriculum on the Inuit people. The children were overwhelmed: gorged with emotion that they were desperately needed to release and to process all that they had seen and heard and felt. But when the film was over, the teacher turned off the projector and said: "Name the tools used in the sealhunt". Phobic about feelings, most teachers stay at the basic fact level. Recognizing this, Sidney Simon (1966) appealed for "Values Clarification" in education and Lawrence Kohlberg (1970, 1975) argued for training in moral reasoning. The school was not including human relations skills or education for living in its goals.

In its own functioning the school could not be seen as a <u>just institution</u> (Stewart, 1975). Periodic physical violence, psychological injury and 'bully tactics' still branded the school as an authoritarian system which could not possibly train students for democratic living. At its worst the high school was especially repressive, dichotomizing people as well as subject areas, a process likened to a 19th century factory. The high school is accused by DeCecco (1975) of committing indignities to young adults, denying them 'due process' and/or failing to model for them and with them the democratic processes of negotiation. "I feel", says the high school student in the film "Adolescence - Crisis or Opportunity", "Like I should have left my body and my feelings at the door".

Yet when young people express their alienation in violence, vandalism, or worse, we are appalled and wonder why. We are also a little saddened, a little disillusioned at the vast numbers of high school students who, in the face of economic recession, become conformist, as conservative and sober as stockbrokers. Although we are relieved that things have 'settled down', we feel uncomfortable when Supertramp sings: "School" -

> I can see you in the morning when you go to school.
> Don't forget your books, you know you've got to learn the golden rule.
> Teacher tells you, stop your play and get on with your work
> And be like Johnnie-too-good, - well don't you know - he never shirks
> -- he's coming along.
>
> They tell you not to hang around and learn what life's about
> And grow up just like them ... won't let you work it out
> -- and yu're full of doubt.
> Don't criticize, they're old and wise
> Do as they tell you to -- you're coming along.
> School! School!
> You're bloody well right!

Reflection and Response

Teacher-training institutions responded to such criticism by a rather defensive 'back-to-basics' stance, then more intelligently with the objection that teachers are being asked to do too much. Especially now, in the face of the increasing breakdown of the family and the employment of both parents, we must not pretend to be 'all things to men'. Constant self-assessment is necessary if we are to refine, define and defend our primary goals as teachers.

We know that 'back-to-basics' does not mean that we care only about real competence, or even that we teach only how to produce some limited 'mastery'. Conversely, we know that humanistic fads, gimmicks, or enthusiasms will not necessarily produce humane educational experiences for students. Obviously we need both competence and humanism. We desperately need a synthesis, a really integrated model of education.

To educate is to 'educere', to lead out or draw out or cultivate the thinking, feeling, acting, decision-making powers of people, so that they continue learning throughout life. Since we do not attempt to force all the food a person will need for a life-time into their first twenty years, why do we try to do it with knowledge? 'Pure' academic learning need not shrivel and die if it is related to the work world or to the 'applied' aspects of knowledge. Real educational experiences involve the feelings as well as the mind; the cignitive and affective are never, in fact, dichotomized. But this is our problem. We need to distinguish but never separate; to relate but not divide; to show that reality is a web of inter-connecting events. We need a 'metaphorical mind' that will see connections: in stages of development, in modes of learning and in the human inter-action that is teaching and learning.

Challenged with this vision of a cognitive-developmental approach combined with a humanistic orientation, teacher educators often object, "But we don't have time for feelings or values or applied or inter-disciplinary stuff. We have to cover the essentials". This means that although we have the power we will not use it. Content-fixated and trained almost exclusively in didactic teaching methods, we have difficulty seeing that it is not only <u>what</u> you teach but the <u>way</u> you choose to teach which determines whether you can accomplish <u>many goals at the same time</u>, <u>at different levels</u> and <u>to different degrees</u>. The exclusively didactic approach (teacher talks, students listen) implies that it is wrong to disrupt (participate) in the lesson, to express feelings or to exhibit disinterest.

EDUCATING TEACHERS FOR RESPONSIVENESS

At York University the Faculty of Education is searching for this synthesis of theory and practice, of cognitive and affective education. Field people and University people work together to guide and contribute to the three or four year experience of the concurrent B.A. and B.Ed. programs. In our foundation course, "Communication and The Education Process", we model in seminars and lectures the integrated or 'confluent' processes that we propose. This means that faculty members who advocate being intellectually accountable and personally warm and 'congruent', find it hard to get away with being incompetent or zombies. It also means that students responsible for leading seminars must work in teams and must not do a 'presentation' (University style) but rather must 'brainstorm' with us, to plan together a seminar which highlights the key concepts of the assigned readings and films but which does so by using structured learning experiences, discussion questions, role-playing or simulated experiences or small group tasks. While the seminar leaders have a clear leadership role (like that of a teacher in the classroom) their goals are maximum involvement and participation by all seminar members. A playful approach or fun or joy in the learning process is seen as a 'plus'; but games, discussions or exercises must be well-meshed with content and a synthesis-evaluation of both content and group process must be made at the end of the class. Students say they have never been so involved in any educational experience. Moreover we learn that they carry these teaching-leadership methods into other University courses, sometimes to the despair, more often to the delight of other University faculties.

Self and Other: Education as Communication

We begin with a study of the self. We believe that by working towards a firmer self-concept in teachers (including a sense of competence based on the gradual acquisition of a repertoir of teaching skills), we are eventually working towards a more humane education for children. Student teachers find it appropriate in their first shaky days of teaching to study self-concept theory, reflecting "The teacher's main educational resource is himself". But we ask the student to keep a double focus throughout this course, for everything that applies to him also applies to the child to some degree. It becomes startingly clear that teaching is a two-way street, a mutual process: the teacher needs the child's response.

Communication is seen then as central to the knowledge process. Eli Bower (1974) calls teaching a "mediating process" between the child and the world. David Hawkins (1971) sees the education process as a triangle of relationships: "I, Thou and It". The "I - Thou" is the teacher-student relationship as they work together on the "It" of content and the outer world. The teacher who hides behind the Role of Teacher or who uses it to meet personal needs for power or for love deprives the child of a really mutual, growth-producing "I-Thou" relationship with an adult who can be authentically himself. We use theoretical viewpoints like transactional analysis (James and Jongeword, 1971; Thomas Gordon, 1974; and John Stewart, 1975) to support the importance of strong self-concept and interaction skills for the teacher.

The uniqueness of each of us, the variation in our background and our value-systems, is continually emerging. We encourage the recall of childhood body image, early sensory memories, character and value formation, experiences of power and the first recognitions of differences between ourselves and others. Going around the circle for quick childhood memories of sensory experiences, we might hear:

"I remember the special smell of my grandmother's soap"

"Sinking my teeth into the teeth marks in my Dad's pipe and wearing his big fedora"

"The feeling of my cat's fur"

"The smell in the hospital when I had my tonsils out"

"Seeing a kite in a store window"

"Finding a chestnut".

As each person speaks in the small seminar group similar memories are triggered. We discuss perceptions and sensations which have gone to make us who we are. But we are also experiencing an amazing bonding with each other in the group and with children in general, for through these brief personal examples we have entered each other's childhood worlds. Similarities and differences are clear but there are universals we can look for in this study of human formation experience. Experiences of early sensations of power, of feeling different, of memories of teachers, of punishment and pride, sprinkle and season the course content.

Building the Theoretical Base

Personal examples can be a dangerous route to trivia, but kept brief and appropriate, they can produce the 'surprise of recognition' in the group: "So we are not so different after all". Self-revelation, feedback and trust are more likely to grow in this warm climate and participatory structure. One day each week the students employ in their practicum some practical strategies from Jack Canfield and Harold Wells' book <u>One Hundred Ways to Enhance Self-Concept</u> (1976).

Everything in learning and human development goes back to the Self-Concept. Beneath all differences - personal, sexual, racial, cultural or class - lie the same human growth problems. The oceanic sense of oneness we had in the womb and early infancy gradually gives way to a sense of growing 'individuation' or 'separateness'. Separation-anxiety produces anger and fear. We long for connection, for harmony. The Self-Other polarity means that, although we have a basic need to become self-actualized, individual, autonomous; we are also constantly seeking fusion, intimacy or reciprocity with others because it nourishes us emotionally and supports us intellectually. It is impossible to grow alone.

Yet we bump up against each other. Implicit in this Self-Other polarity is the problem of freedom. While we work for all possible freedom for individual growth, there can be no <u>absolute</u> freedom (Goldstein, 1963). All human endeavours are pulled between Self and Other. We need others so much that we sometimes have to depend, even to encroach on them; alternatively we sacrifice some of our rights or pleasures occasionally when they need us. The cost to Self is offset by that necessary human contact with the Other.

"Secretly and bashfully, each man watches for a <u>Yes</u> which allows him to be. From one man to another the heavenly bread of self-being is passed" (Buber, 1965). We are growth agents for each other. This philosophy rejects the dog-eat-cat world of Hobbes, and accepts that social concern is essential for human beings who all need to contribute and 'to find a place' (Dreikurs, 1968). While our uniqueness is evident in details like the genetic structure, biological cell, or the thumbprint, the significance of such individuality and the meaning of human personality is always related to community.

Becoming human requires nurturing from 'significant others'. The teacher shares with the parent the task of reaching the child, to touch, make contact, stimulate all his senses and help him make sense of all he perceives. The film "Rock a Bye Baby" vividly illustrates the necessity of nurturing, of Stimulation of all the senses for human growth. We study the 'Human Hunger for Stroking' from <u>Born to Win</u> (James & Jongeward, 1971). The teacher is asked to look at his own formation: What significant persons or experiences formed him?

> Key questions of central importance to the beginning teacher:
>
> "What is my self-image really like?"
> "Can I <u>receive</u> positive 'strokes' or feedback and can I <u>give</u> generous support or reinforcement to others?"
> "Do I have a defensive ego or a self-accepting, even self-loving, attitude to myself?"
> "Am I <u>individuated</u> enough, that is, secure and <u>autonomous</u> enough, to accept and work with others who are <u>different</u> from myself?"
> "Can I help children (and myself) to <u>open</u> to others, to '<u>assimilate</u>' the world and then '<u>accommodate</u>' - that is, '<u>stretch</u>' to <u>meet it</u>?"

Obviously no one is expected to answer these challenges with a "yes of course" but the questions themselves are 'stretching'.

Self and Other: The Need for Self-Esteem

We all need approval. Maslow (1968) says it is one of the basic needs of human nature. Exercises of 'success-sharing' and positive support are experienced in the seminar, then weighed against the school practicum where shocking evidence of low self-concept in children abounds.

But Albert Ellis (1975) warns us of the danger of over-dependency on others, of 'the dire need for approval'. As the person develops, more and more self-validation and inner-directedness must be encouraged. Behavioural 'reinforcement' which is a consciously planned (and very effective) system of rewards for certain behaviours is distinguished from 'stroking' or 'validation' which is a 'confirmation' or deep <u>acceptance</u> of that person's <u>self</u> (Buber, 1964; Rogers, 1969).

"Discounting' another person, giving unconstructive negative feedback or having consistently low expectations of a student, is a powerful way to produce in that person a correspondingly low self-esteem. "The Eye of the Storm", a film on prejudice and stereotypical thinking, heightens awareness of the power of expectations and assumptions. Glasser (1969) graphically describes the shrinking world of 'The failure identity' person. Bonaro Overstreet (1951) lists the 'disguises of fear' in behaviour which run the gamut from extreme withdrawal or shyness to obnoxious arrogance or bullying.

The person who feels "not O.K." or "deeply discouraged" (Dreikurs & Loren, 1968) may begin to manipulate others either poassively or aggressively. Our student teachers recognize in their classrooms the attention-seeker; the power-seeker; the child who seems to want to hurt to revenge, to retaliate; and the ultimately discouraged child who displays inadequacy, helplessness, alienation or despair. In his book <u>Self-Concept and School Achievement</u> William Purkey (1970) portrays the self as a spiral, an open-ended system. When failure is experienced in any aspect of the self's performance, the whole spiral - like the whole system of self - is shaken and may take hours or even days to regain emotional equilibrium. Carrying the image of the spiral further, when the spiral of the self tightens or constricts (from threats or fears perhaps) little growth, concentration or openness to learning is possible.

Finding a way for a teacher to encourage students, to nurture their self-acceptance and self-confidence, becomes essential. But just as unrelated facts or knowledge is not enough, neither is love enough. Being sensitive to a child's ego needs, but leaving him without skills or competencies or going 'soft' on academics would be an irony indeed. High standards and warm support have always been the best combination, though it is hard to convey them in appropriate amounts and methods to each person. The child needs both the feeling of being <u>accepted</u> and the confidence of being <u>competent</u> if he is to have a flourishing and healthy self-concept. Our goal for ourselves as teachers and for our students is - <u>I am lovable and capable</u>. The teacher who does not have this "IALAC" feeling cannot give it to children.

<u>Self and Other: Values and Mutual Respect</u>

Accepting differences is easier for the person with self-confidence. Teachers who cannot respect the varying value-systems of others are often guilty of indoctrination and rigid inflexibility in their teaching. We recognize how difficult it is to listen closely and to allow for the viewpoints of others, especially when they conflict with our own. To give our students an opportunity to clarify their own position on many issues and listen with respect to their fellow students, we have designed a "Values Card Game for Teachers". This exercise leaves many teachers feeling unsettled and a little shaken. Biases, prejudices and surprising intolerance surface in all of us but we are more clarified in our own views and more aware of others. We feel it is important for teachers to recognize the inevitability of values conflicts.

Dealing with this ambiguity, this lack of dogmatic certainty in the area of values, is very hard for teachers who love to "tell" things and to have "the answers". Adorno's classic <u>The Authoritarian Personality</u> (1950) describes both the home and the school system in which many of us have been reared. It is a world of black and white absolutes, rigid rules and stereotypical thinking. In a time of radically shifting values teachers need tools such as the moral reasoning approaches of Lawrence Kohlberg (1970, 1975) and Edward Sullivan (1975) and the Values Clarification work of Raths (1978) if they are to integrate into all curriculum areas the kinds of questions which might lead students beyond rigid, thoughtless dogmatism, or to its opposite of moral apathy or helplessness of the will. Gordon Allport's definition (1978, p. 75) of the goal of education is apt: We should strive to educate students so that they would be "emotionally secure or stable" but at the same time "intellectually tentative".

Self and Other: Sexuality

Sexual differences are accepted by the child and sexual identity is achieved, according to Kohlberg (1974), when the child comes to terms with his own self-concept and has come to know the constancy of objects so that he can accept his body as a permanent endowment. Although accepting physical differences comes fairly easily, at the interpersonal level we have a long history of fear and mistrust between male and female.

What is the role of the teacher in consolidating the child's sexual identity and self-image? Sears and Feldman (1974) find raw bias and preferential treatment, damaging to both sexes. What is the teacher's attitude to the body and to those embarrassing questions which children and adolescents ask? In our faculty, we put our students on the spot by a role-play experience, in which we play a small child asking very pointed questions. Our students, if they choose to answer, must reply as a parent in very simple, very direct words which a pre-schooler would understand. "Go and ask your mother" is unacceptable. The follow-up discussion about basic concepts, acceptable vocabulary and values helps our student-teachers assess their personal comfort-level with their own sexuality. We also confront the thorny problems of honouring sexual orientations and sexual values differing from our own.

Even teachers who never teach sex education *per se* may blush at the mention of the reproduction of bread-mold, display rigidly stereotypical attitudes to men or women, or make 'fag' jokes, are sending powerful and very influential educational messages. The need for respect and friendship between the sexes is depicted by the film "Free to Be You and Me" which our students enjoy for themselves and then use and process in the classrooms. The exposure to inspiring literature, including great myths and stories which feature strong women and sensitive men, becomes crucial for the child. Cultural differences and family values regarding sex-roles must be respected and handled delicately. Teachers have to reflect the maxim by Dorothy Baruch (1959): "Every child has the right to feel whole and beautifully made".

Self and Other: Competition and Cooperation

How the school handles competition will deeply affect the child's self-concept and his attitude to cooperation with others. Johnson and Johnson (1975) maintain that every classroom needs individual learning strategies, competitive processes and cooperative approaches with a predominance of cooperation in order to prepare children for our society. Eliot Aronson's <u>Jig Saw Learning</u> (1975) strategy showed that when teachers replaced constant didactic in-put with the same content in a learning process which required peer cooperation, they found not only content mastery but more involvement, more excitement in learning and more friendship among previously alienated students.

Glasser's Schools Without Failure (1969) and William Hedges' ideas for evaluation in the elementary school (1969) provide alternatives to the usual obsession with grades. The erosion of human dignity which our grading systems produce with their quantitative emphasis have little to do with the quality of education or the value or meaning of learning.

Yet some evaluation process is necessary. Albert Ellis (1975) maintains that the person with a healthy self-concept will not have this "dire fear of failure" or this "dire need for approval" but will handle competition well and will be a self-directing, self-loving person. Terry Orlick (1978) stresses communty, Winning Through Co-operation, but any healthy, balanced approach to the Self-Other polarity is not easy to master. Although children in school have not chosen to be measured against each other, our very questioning techniques, our relentless control of the classroom, and our grading systems encourage competition for our favours. This is the dilemma: we must push and challenge our students enough to produce excellence, yet at the same time we must honour individual differences, encourage self-acceptance, cooperation and friendship among students.

The school which values only academic achievement or athletic prowess produces alienation. Douglas Heath (1971) says schools are plagued with "boredom", belonginglessness", "meaninglessness". Melville Seeman (1971) has cited six signs of alienation that occur in society as a whole and also in some schools: a sense of helplessness or a 'victim' mentality, a sense of meaninglessness, normlessness, cultural isolation, social loneliness and, sometimes, personal fragmentation.

Vandalism in schools in the United States has assumed epidemic proportions and we see it fast-increasing in Canada's large urban centres. Larger social problems obviously underlie much of this anger and alienation but schools must face the fact that students in our society have rarely been educated for involvement, responsible decision-making, cooperation or negotiation.

As an antidote for these problems DeCecco (1975) pleads for more "due process" and negotiation with students; Eddie Edmonds (1980) emphasizes the need for small scale in schools; James Coleman (1974) pleads for more relevance to the work world by giving students "work credits" for skills learned in the community; Maurice Gibbon (1974) describes "Walkabout", a Vancouver program which gives high school students credit and recognition for work that is practical, creative, adventurous, of service to others, and which requires some logical inquiry on their part. John Stewart (1975) calls for a more "organismic-holistic" or humane educational environment. He quotes Kohlberg: "Much of what kids learn comes not from books and materials but from the moral environment and atmosphere that you establish in your classroom - your hidden curriculum".

Self and Other: Rules and Relationships

It is useless to talk about the school as "a just community" in a Values Class and then use control-methods which are punitive and humiliating. Teachers need democratic leadership skills as children move from rules to relationships. Teachers have an obligation to lead, to be sensitive and to care does not preclude their own needs and rights. Like the family and indeed all society, the school and the classroom are networks of interdependent relationships with a mutual give and take, a flow of reciprocal knowledge and feelings.

> For me to live a full human life my neighbours must be just as free as I am. Their freedom is my freedom, their equality is my equality, their dignity is my dignity. Freedom is indivisible, human rights are universal.
>
> (Gordon Fairweather).

Skills are needed to accomplish this. Dreikurs' (1968) concepts of 'encouragement' and 'logical consequences' permit strong, democratic leadership. Glasser's Classroom Meetings (1969) may lead to group responsibility for problems. Thomas Gordon's Teacher Effectiveness Training (1974) develops in the teacher a sensitivity to interpersonal cues and an ability to respond with flexibility.

His "12 Roadblocks to Communication" include the most familiar and handy power methods of putting down, imposing solutions or denying the problem. Even tough these negative reactions come very naturally to teachers, in a sensitive situation they can sabotage any democratic solution of a problem.

Active Listening is a Counselling skill but it also enhances teaching when group discussion is being used. In order to handle conflict situations or values collisions effectively, the teacher needs self-assertiveness, confronting skills and mutual problem-solving or negotiation tactics. Students who are respected grow in responsibility through group discussions or peer-teaching experiences; they tend to approach conflict-of-needs situations with a problem-solving attitude. Most of our students and the children they teach have not experienced group problem-solving, creative brainstorming nor negotiating to consensus. Yet these are skills which are needed by all thinking, critical and creative members of a democratic society. This eclectic mix of approaches to human interaction or 'discipline' in the classroom seems to be more humane than old power methods. Although these approaches are ego-enhancing, they lead the student gently from egocentrism to more of what Douglas Heath (1971) calls "allocentrism" - the awareness of others, the ability to live with others.

Self and Other: The Education Process

We can support students' identity development by good student-teacher relationships and we can use the classroom and community environment to help them develop life skills. But our teaching, our actual educational planning and work to develop professional faculties is the central core of our vocational focus.

This may employ a vast array of teaching models. Most important are Piaget's (1968) stages of cognitive development, Erikson's (1968) developmental tasks, Bloom's (1964) taxonomy of thinking skills and questioning techniques

and so many of the learning strategies that make Joyce and Weil's book
<u>Models of Teaching</u> (1972) a Bible for educators. We believe that when
students are confronted with intellectual vigour in teachers they begin to
smell the possibility of excellence for themselves and they become excited.
We believe that there is a natural drive for competence but only good teachers
and good life experiences make it happen.

Intellectual development means that we escape the narrow world of opinion
and egocentrism, that we check out assumptions, listen to the other side, wait
for the data to come in. The study of perception is a basic place to check out
subjective bias. Visual cues and perspectives yield such varied responses that
students can graphically see that we come at the world from different spaces
and places. Our values biases emerge from our individual interpretations of
the visual ones in, for example, newspaper pictures or ads. To make children
aware of this subjective bias we can use the well-known poem about the <u>Five Men
Who Saw an Elephant</u> or the short film "Up Is Down".

Intellectual movement from the global generalization or the opinionated
stance does not mean that subjectivity is abandoned so that we become fact-
machines or objective robot-computers. Rather, it means that our <u>subjectivity
is acknowledged</u> and only then can we begin to move toward any kind of objectivity
(Lowen, 1970). We become conscious of the Self as a filter on reality. Those
who are acknowledging their own subjective views or feelings of anger, hurt or
fear are less likely to project this dark shadow on other persons or things.
They are less likely to scapegoat or fear 'contamination'. They are able to
open themselves to the vastness and the inter-connectedness of knowledge.

To provide the stimulus and aliment for this kind of continuing development,
we need to know what to teach and how. Kieran Egan (1979) outlines four stages:

the mythic, the romantic, the philosophic and the ironic. His work is new, but it will help to close the gaps in educational thought between the cognitive and the affective, and those between the psychological operative stage theories and the educationally relevant or meaningful. In both the human interaction in the life of the school and in the thrust and organization and interaction of ideas, the teacher can, then, work for the intellectual maturity of his students but in an integrated and humane way.

Strong words. Powerful convictions. A few small steps towards implementation.

I just received a phonecall from a teacher who is participating in a Ministry of Education program to develop responsibility and leadership skills in students. She phoned to ask me to do a two-hour 'listening skills workshop' for twelve students who had taken a summer Ministry course on leadership. "These students are", she said, "organizers, movers; they act like leaven in the student community". Together with a few teachers, these students try to keep planning ahead to meet students' needs, to try to make the school "a more humane environment".

"You have a really diverse racial mix there", I said. "Do you ever do any work on prejudice or racial tension?"

"No", she said. "We haven't really mentioned race or prejudice. We've been emphasizing <u>meeting students' needs</u>, both educationally and for social human living. That seems to be 'it' - meeting student needs".

A dervish was sitting by the roadside when a haughty courtier with his retinue, riding past, struck him with a cane, shouting: "Out of the way, you miserable wretch!"

When they had swept past, the dervish rose and called after them: "May you attain all that you desire in the world, even up to its highest ranks!"

A bystander, much impressed by this scene, approached the devout man and said to him: "Please tell me whether your words were motivated by generosity of spirit, or because the desires of the world will undoubtedly corrupt that man even more?"

"O man of bright countenance", said the dervish, "has it not occurred to you that I said what I did because people who attain their real desires would not need to ride about striking dervishes?"

REFERENCES

Adorno, T.W. *The Authoritarian Personality*. New York: Harper, 1950.

Allport, Gordon *The Person in Psychology*. Boston: Beacon Press, 1968.

Aronson, Eliot "The Jig-saw Route to Learning and Liking", *Psychology Today*, Feb. 1975.

Baruch, Dorothy *New Ways in Sex Education*. New York: McGraw-Hill, 1959.

Bloom, Benjamin J. *Taxonomy of Educational Objectives Book 1 Cognitive Domain. Book 2 Affective Domain*. New York: Longman, 1964.

Bower, Eli "Education as a Humanizing Process and Its Relationship to Other Humanizing Processes", *American Journal of Orthopsychology*, 44(4) July 1974.

Bowlby, John *Separation*. New York: Penguin, 1973.

Brown, George Isaac *Human Teaching for Human Learning*. New York: Penguin, 1977.

Buber, Martin *The Knowledge of Man*. New York: Harper & Row, 1965.

Bremer, John *A Matrix of Modern Education*. Toronto: McClelland & Stewart, 1975.

Canfield, Jack & Wells, H. *One Hundred Ways to Enhance Self-Concept*. Englewood Cliffs, N.J.: Prentice-Hall, 1976.

Coleman, James *Youth: Transition to Adulthood*. Chicago: University of Chicago Press, 1974.

DeCecco, John P. & Richards, Arlene K. "Civil War in the High Schools", *Psychology Today*, Nov. 1975.

Dreikurs, Rudolph & Loren, Grey *A New Approach to Discipline: Logical Consequences*. New York: Hawthorn, 1968.

Edmonds, Edward "Small Schools: An Argument Continued", *Can. Ed. Ass. Newsletter* Mar/Apr. 1980.

Egan, Kieran *Educational Development*. New York: Oxford University Press, 1979.

Ellis, Albert *A New Guide to Rational Living*. California: Wishire Book Co., 1975.

Erickson, Eric H. *Identity, Youth and Crisis*. New York: Norton, 1968.

Fairweather, Gordon *Statement on Human Rights*. Ottawa: Office of the Chief Commissioner for Human Rights, n.d.

Farnham, Diggory-Sylvia *Cognitive Processes in Education*. Esp. chapter on Processing Pictorial Information. New York: Harper & Row, 1972.

Furth, Hans G. *Thinking Goes to School*. New York: Oxford University Press, 1975.

Gibbon, Maurice "Walkabout" *Phi Delta Kappan*, Vol. 55 (May 1974), 596-602.

Glasser, William *Schools Without Failure*. New York: Harper Colophon, 1969.

Goldstein, Kurt *Human Nature*. New York: Schocken Books, 1963.

Gordon, Thomas *Teacher Effectiveness Training*. New York: Peter Wyden, 1974.

Hamachek, Donald *Encounters with Self*. New York: Holt, Rinehart & Winston, 1978.

Hawkins, David "I-Thou-It" from *Open Education* (ed.) Charles Rathbone. New York: Citation Press, 1971.

Heath, Douglas *Humanizing Schools*. New York: Hayden Book Co., 1971.

Hedges, William *Evaluation in The Elementary School*. New York: Holt, Rinehart & Winston, 1969.

James, M. & Jongeward D. *Born to Win*. Phillipines: Adison-Wesley, 1971.

Johnson, D.W. & Johnson, R.T. *Learning Together and Alone*. New Jersey: Prentice-Hall, 1975.

Jones, Richard M. *Fantasy and Feeling Education*. New York: Harper Colophon Books, 1968.

Joyce, Bruce & Weil, Marsha *Models of Teaching*. New Jersey: Prentice-Hall, 1972.

Kohlberg, Lawrence "The Cognitive-Developmental Approach to Moral Education", *Phi Delta Kappan* (June 1975) pp. 670-677.

-----.   "Development of Sex Concepts" from *Intimacy, Family and Society* (eds.) A. & J. Skolnick. Boston, Mass.: Little, Brown & Co., 1974.

-----.   "Education for Justice: A Modern Statement of the Platonic View" from *Five Lectures on Moral Education* (eds.) Nancy F. & Theodore R. Sizer. Cambridge, Mass.: Harvard University Press, 1970.

Leonard, George *Education and Ecstacy*. New York: Delacorte Press, 1968.

Lowen, Alexander *Pleasure*. New York: Penguin Books, 1970.

Maslow, Abraham *Toward a Psychology of Being*. New York: Van Nostrand Reinhold, 1968, pp. 51 and 52.

May, Rollo *Man's Search for Himself*. Esp. chapter "The Experience of Becoming a Person". New York: Norton, 1953.

Orlick, Terry *Winning Through Co-operation*. Washington, D.C.: Acropolis, 1978.

Overstreet, Bonaro *Understanding Fear*. New York: Harper, 1951.

Piaget, Jean *Judgment and Reasoning in The Child*. Totowa, N.J.: Littlefield, 1968.

Plowden Report *Children and their Primary Schools: A Report to the Central Advisory Council for Education*. London: Her Majesty's Stationery Office, 1966.

Purkey, William *Self-Concept and School Achievement*. Englewood Cliffs, N.J.: Prentice-Hall, 1970.

Quarter, Jack "The Teacher's Role in the Classroom" from *Must Schools Fail?* (eds.) Neill Byrne & Jack Quarter. Toronto: McClelland & Stewart, 1972.

Raths, Louis Edward *Values and Teaching: Working With Values in the Classroom*. Toronto: C.E. Merrill, 1978 (2nd. edition).

Rogers, Carl *Freedom To Learn*. Columbus: Merrill, 1969.

Rosenthal, Robert & Jacobson, Lenore *Pygmalion in the Classroom*. New York: Holt, Rinehart & Winston, 1968.

Sears, Pauline & Feldman, David H. "Teacher Interaction with Boys and Girls" from *And Jill Came Tumbling After* (ed.) J. Stacey. New York: Dell, 1974.

Seeman, Melville "Alienation", *Psychology Today*, Aug. 1971.

Shah, Idries The Magic Monastery. New York: E.P. Dutton & Co., 1972. Reprinted, permission by Collins-Knowlton Wing Inc. and Jonathan Cape Ltd.

Simon, Sidney, Raths, L. & Harmin, M. *Values and Teaching*. Columbus, Ohio: Charles E. Merrill Pub. Co., 1966.

Stewart, John "The School as Just Community: Transactional-Developmental Moral Education" from *Values Education* (eds.) John Meyer, Brian Burnham & John Cholvat. Waterloo: Wilfrid Laurier University Press, 1975.

Sullivan, Edmund V. *Moral Learning, Some Findings, Issues and Questions*. New York: Paulist Press, 1975.

White, Robert "Competence" from *The Study of Lives*. New York: Atherton Press, 1966.

Films

Adolescence: Crisis or Opportunity. Studio City, Col.: Filmfair
    Communications, 1973. 13 min., sound, colour, 16 mm.

Eye of the Storm. New York: American Broadcasting Co., 1970.
    28 min., sound colour, 16 mm. (The Now Series).

Free To Be You and Me. N.S. Foundation, 1974.
    42 min., sound, colour, 16 mm.

Rock-a-bye-Baby. New York: Time-Life, 1971.
    30 min., sound, colour, 16 mm. (The Life Around Us Series).

Up is Down. Northfield, Illinois: Morton Goldsholl Design Assoc., 1970.
    6 min., sound, colour, 16 mm.

GROUP RIGHTS AFFECTING EDUCATION

RACISM IN EDUCATION: OLD AND NEW
Michel Laferrière

Racism can be defined as the use of ascriptive, or quasi-ascriptive characteristics, and particularly of race, for the inferiorization of and discrimination against certain categories of people. Racist ideologies and practices are not new to North American education. Race relations have been a major component of U.S. history. Racial segregation was confirmed or established on firm legal grounds in 1896, and it was not until 1954 that segregation was pronounced illegal in primary and secondary schools, and not until the 1960s in other domains of social life. Racist laws and behaviours have been less documented in Canada but have persisted up to the 1960s, especially in the Ontario and Nova Scotia school systems (Winks, 1971). In the last two decades, however, a number of declarations of principles and of Human Rights legislations have been established at the Canadian federal level and in the provinces to fight discriminatory practices in most areas of social life and on several grounds such as race, sex, national origin, language, etc.[1] Human rights codes and commissions now attempt to prevent overt discriminatory behaviour: thus they limit the damages which could be done to individuals or groups, and they may also in the long run change attitudes. But they are also often difficult to apply, and they also may be an easy way to appease liberal consciences through token gestures. Moreover, Human Rights legislation does not always eradicate

---

[1] One should mention that the extension of protection is not the same in different parts of Canada. Quebec has the most recent, but the most progressive Human Rights Charter, including sexual orientation and social and economic backgrounds, besides more traditional areas for protection.

traditional practices of individuals, or practices which may be linked to the nature and functioning of institutions and not to the actions of individuals themselves. Such institutional racism may stem from the past; it may also be linked to new practices which were not themselves intended to discriminate against specific groups but in their favour, and it may find its origins in the demands of such groups. Finally, in the last decade, racism has sometimes found its ideological justification in recent research which attempts to show that differences between groups are genetic in their origins.

This chapter will examine how irrelevant ascriptive status is often used in education to discriminate against individuals or groups. As there is no term in English to designate this process, we shall use the term "racism", though rather inappropriately, since we shall not limit our remarks to discrimination based on race only, be it biologically or socially defined, but to many other types of ascriptive status as well. The first part examines some of the ways through which racist stereotypes and attitudes are transmitted and perpetuated in the schools, whether in a conscious and intentional manner, or in an unconscious one. This first part will principally focus on processes at the interpersonal level, and in the classroom. A second part will stress some aspects of institutional racism, due to the functioning of education as a social institution more than to the intent and will of specific individuals, and sometimes in spite of good and generous intents. A third part will look at recent work in education and in the social sciences which could eventually be used to justify discriminatory and racist practices under the guise of science.

I. EDUCATION MAY PERPETUATE RACIST STEREOTYPES AND ATTITUDES

Whether in Canada or the U.S., schools are no longer legally segregated by race with the exception of Indian and Inuit schools. Although de facto segregation persists, due to geographical reasons, political choice or historical influences, it appears that one of the dangers of perpetuation of racism in the schools comes from the everyday functioning of the classroom itself. Teachers and students may transmit detrimental stereotypes of minority groups, consciously or not. We shall review here some of the racist sins by commission and omission perpetuated in the schools, and some of the difficulties in trying to absolve them.

Racism by commission: Teachers and students may transmit, repeat, and sometimes create racism, even if they are not conscious of it and they do not consider themselves racist. Racism may permeate everyday thoughts and language: in our society, and in others, a negative connotation is associated with darkness and the word black. What is black is dirty, impure, and should be avoided. Some blacks object to the use of words such as blackmail, which contain the word black and have a negative connotation. Women have stressed that language itself was often sexist, and did not include appropriate qualifications to describe women in what have been traditionally male positions. They urge the use of neutral instead of masculine terms to qualify positions of authority (chairman) or to qualify everyday actions (workmanship) in order to avoid assuming that all humans are men only, and to avoid using the "universal He". Racism by commission is often reflected in school material and especially in textbooks which present a negative image of minority groups (Katz, 1970) and often teach prejudice

(McDiarmid and Pratt, 1971). Special efforts have been made to avoid blatant stereotypes, but these efforts are recent and deal mostly with those nearby. For example, Indians are no longer "les sauvages" in French schools, and Inuit and Indian songs and literature are now part of the curriculum of many Quebec schools. But racist attitudes may be transmitted by the way that people in other countries are considered. Tales of "little black Sambo" are still to be found. Moreover, presentation of other cultures without explanation may in fact create negative attitudes, for children may not understand the reasons for differences between other societies and their own, and consider their own as superior. An emphasis on the fate of the "boat people" may create pity and compassion on the one hand, but also contempt for the "uncivilized Vietnamese rulers" on the other, perhaps extending to all or most non-whites. Similarly, emphasis placed upon the _problems_ of underdeveloped countries may help children imagine that Canada and similar societies are inherently better. In many cases, underdevelopment is seen as due to the geographical position or the history of the country, with few studies of other causes of underdevelopment, such as the exploitation by foreign powers or/and by indigenous elites. Underdevelopment becomes an unfortunate historical or geographic accident and not the result of voluntary human actions.

Racism by omission: In many cases, racial and other minorities are simply absent from the schools, with the exception of the children from these groups themselves. Few teachers come from minority groups, and thus minority group children cannot immediately identify with most of the adults with whom they spend their time in schools. In textbooks and curriculum materials, minority group members are rarely present, and if they are, it is in what are considered to be inferior social positions. Blacks are porters; Chinese are laundry workers or waiters; Indians are hunters; and French-Canadians, peasants. Minority group members are rarely seen in prestigious positions. Moreover, the history of minority groups is presented in a detrimental way; within the perspective of the majority, when it is presented at all. Omissions create an impression that nearly all the great artists, writers, politicians, and valuable heroes were white men: there has been a process of "occultation", so that minorities are mentioned only in their relationship with the majority group. Whether conscious or not, a process of occultation is never socially neutral (Castel, 1973). The fact that something or some people are left out eliminates them as important and worthwhile.

Recent efforts have attempted to overcome this situation: racial minorities or women are now often mentioned on a more equal basis. This creates problems, for it is sometimes quite hard to find minority group members who can be compared with the majority. There are fewer women or black painters, or surgeons, or scientists. Rediscovering a few may only emphasize their paucity, and the differential achievements of different groups. There are only a few fields where the achievements of women or of blacks can be compared with those of majority men, even if one takes into account the occultation process.

Several solutions seem at hand, however. First, one could explain why there are so few minority group members in some positions, by giving historical and sociological accounts of the extent and causes of racism and discrimination. One could also show the limitations of the traditional conceptions of a "hero", for our society sometimes rewards morally dubious individuals. It may be harder, and more respectable to be a minority welfare mother than to be a space physicist, if one takes into account some of the qualities required and some of the performances of these two individuals. Unfortunately, our society rewards physicists more than welfare mothers. Changing the conceptions of heroism held in our society may eventually change the basic values held by people and lead to question the reward and stratification system in which we live. While this may be the political philosophy of some or perhaps many, it would go against the conservative function of the school system, which is often to reproduce inequalities (Bourdieu et Passeron, 1970). Racism by omission or by commission has detrimental consequences for both minority and majority group children. Minorities learn that they cannot achieve certain things in life, for no member of their own group has achieved them. Majority children learn that minority group members are not as respectable as the members of their own group. This is a form of racism.

II. INSTITUTIONAL RACISM: OLD AND NEW FORMS

Institutional racism may be defined as racism coming from some of the requirements of the institution itself, without specific discrimination by individuals or policies. We shall examine here two common types of institutional racism: one prevalent in the workings of schools and educational agencies, the other linked to the organization of schooling itself and the philosophy underlying the process of education.

Schools have to select and evaluate students, as well as teach them. In order to do so, a number of procedures have been established, the goals of which were originally to help students. Thus students are often tested on I.Q. or other types of "objective" tests, i.e., tests where teachers' biases are eliminated. It is well known that blacks and those from most other minority groups in the U.S. do not succeed as well as majority students on standardized tests. Several types of explanations of this well-known result have been offered. Some stress the social class of most minority students, others the failure of teachers and the schools; others consider that the tests themselves, the testing situation, or the standardization process of the tests discriminate against minority students and lower class individuals in general (Samuda, 1975; Senna, 1973; Richardson and Spears, 1972). Testing is an obvious way of discriminating against minority students, and for that reason has been opposed in many parts of the United States. Although I.Q. testing has been forbidden in several school districts, there are other ways of labeling and directing minority students (Rist, 1977). Placing students in tracks or streams "adapted to their abilities" has often meant that minority students were placed in the less prestigious tracks. In Quebec the Black Education Task Force Report on Education (1978), concerned writers (Déjean, 1978) and school officials (Commission des Ecoles Catholiques de Montréal, 1975) all noted that a very high percentage of the black students of English West Indian and Haitian origins were in the "short professional" programs in secondary schools, i.e., programs which do not permit access to short or long higher education. The rationale for this placement is that those students do not succeed in school, either because they are recent immigrants who have had a different and often inferior schooling, or because of their different cultural and social class backgrounds, but "short term professional" (read vocational) education will allow them to be productive members of society by getting a job after high school. Placement in these sections confers upon students an inferior label, of which they are often aware.[2]

Testing and placement in vocational education were originally seen as ways of better serving different student populations; they are now routine practices in many schools and reflect a certain type of discrimination based upon social class and race. What was thought of as a well-intentioned purposeful policy has had unintended consequences: we find here an example of institutional racism and of what Merton (1949) has called the "unanticipated consequences of purposive social action", or Boudon (1977) an "effet pervers".[3]

We may presently be witnessing another example (not yet documented) of "effet pervers", where good intentions may have detrimental consequences that belie their original goals. In many societies where ethnic and racial minorities are found, recent policies have been implemented in order to stress and boost the cultures of those groups. In education, the rationale for these policies has been that they would enhance the image of the minority groups concerned, and that the children of these groups would have better self-concepts. Schools, by mentioning these groups and stressing their cultures and achievements, would end the previously mentioned occultation process, and education would be made more relevant for both minority and majority children.

---

2. This is not always the case, however. As Goode has noticed, secrecy or unawareness often fulfil specific social functions. As for minority group students, many may not be totally aware that they are in "slow learners" or vocational programs. In a study we conducted in a Montreal French catholic school, we found that a very high percentage of our Haitian respondents had very high educational aspirations, which, given the fact that they were in vocational tracks, would usually prove to be unattainable.

3. This notion may even be traced to the writings of Condorcet and other thinkers, as Boudon recognizes.

These programs have taken different forms and received different names. In Canada they have been strongly influenced by the federal policy of multiculturalism. This policy, adopted in 1971, has attempted to go beyond the traditional "mosaic" ideology, an ideology which stressed the fact that many different groups could live side by side without forming a new entity, contrasted with the "melting pot" of U.S. ideology. The mosaic had been criticized for being a "vertical" mosaic (Porter, 1965), where groups from British, or white anglo-saxon origins were at the top and the hyphenated-Canadians at the bottom. Multiculturalism is both an ideology and a policy (Burnet, 1979) and several programs have been created. Many educational programs, both in and out of schools, have been funded by the Canadian Multiculturalism Program, in order to promote research or training in the cultures of many Canadian ethnic groups. Provincial and local educational authorities have also created their own programs (McLeod, 1979). Ontario has numerous heritage programs and most of the other Canadian provinces, or at least their major multi-ethnic cities, have recently created programs aimed at preserving and enhancing the different cultures of origin of their inhabitants. It is somewhat ironical that many of these programs are carried out in the schools, which were often the major agency of anglo-canadianization. Quebec has been one of the latecomers in this area: only since the fall of 1979 - and in an experimental manner - has the Ministry of Education started language programs to teach children of ancestry other than French and English the languages of their forebears in the *Projet d'enseignement des langues d'origine* (PELO). However, the Quebec Ministry of Immigration has been granting different ethnic groups funds to serve the needs of their respective communities, including education and media-broadcasting, and the Quebec Minister of State for Cultural Development has also given funds.

Similar programs are carried out in Western Europe for the children of immigrant workers (Rist, 1978, or *International Review of Education*, 1975). They often consist of weekend or after school-hours classes, given by teachers from the country of origin, and aimed at preventing too radical a rupture with the family and the homeland. American bilingual education programs, although originally conceived as means of promoting equality of educational opportunities (U.S. Office of Education, 1974), have now taken a bicultural aspect and often go beyond the mere teaching in a mother tongue other than English to include the teaching of the culture of origin. Specific study programs are also aimed at specific ethnic groups or other minority groups, such as the Black, Native, Puerto-Rican, Women's, and Mexican-American study programs.

All of these programs may have an unintended consequence of increased racism which has not been investigated yet. On the one hand, these programs may be seen as segregating minority group children in special classes or schools: they stress their difference as valuable, but by doing so may reinforce or even create these differences. They also rarely reach majority children, who will often not understand the separate treatment of their school mates and who may not come to appreciate more minority cultures if they do not learn to know and understand them. Minority cultures - because they are the cultures of inferiorized groups - are usually seen as inferior.

Another example of institutional segregation which may lead to some kind of racism is the confessional structure which characterizes several educational systems. In the case of Quebec, for instance, even the public school system in the major urban areas is divided into catholic and protestant boards. This system has been inherited from traditional religious divisions, but in these same boards there has often been a linguistic difference. Three systems? There remained an important discrimination against non-catholics and non-protestants. Jews were very reluctantly admitted and recognized in the English protestant system of Montreal (Kage, 1975) and have thus been anglicized; one had to wait until the last decade for the admittance of French speaking Jewish or non-catholic immigrants by the French sector of the *Commission des Ecoles Catholiques de Montréal*. This institutional segregation along religious lines has now been attenuated in the public school system, but has extended to private schools. Since 1967 Quebec has had a rather liberal policy concerning the funding of private schools: under certain conditions, the Quebec Ministry of Education pays up to 80% of the cost of each child's education. The conditions are that the schools sign an agreement and are recognized by the Ministry, that they follow the Quebec Ministry of Education core curriculum, teach 40% of this curriculum in French, and that the teachers teaching this part of the curriculum are certified to teach in Quebec. The Ministry thus has a certain control on both the content and the quality of education in these private schools, which in return receive subsidies computed on the basis of the cost per child in the public sector. Moreover, Quebec tax laws allow private schools to be considered charitable organizations, so the parental share of the private school costs is considered a charitable donation. Many ethnic schools have taken advantage of these opportunities: well established middle-class Jewish schools, both English and French[4],

---

4. There are now about 25,000 French speaking Jews in Montreal, coming usually from ex-French colonies and protectorates in North Africa and the Middle East, such as Morocco, Tunisia and Lebanon. They are Sefarad and their mother tongue is usually French and/or Arabic.

Armenian and Greek schools are now government-aided private schools. All these schools supplement the required curriculum with courses related to the culture of origin of the children: courses on Greece and Greek history and literature are taught in Greek in the Greek school; courses on Israel and on the Jewish culture and religion are taught in Hebrew in the Jewish schools.[5] This part of the curriculum is not financed by the Quebec Ministry of Education, nor are these teachers necessarily certified in Quebec; they are often from Greece in Greek schools and Israel in the Jewish schools.[6]

Among the consequences of this organization in Quebec is that private religious or ethnic schools have been encouraged, and parents sending their children to those schools have been less at a disadvantage than is traditional in Canada. [Newfoundland, Alberta and British Columbia have programs with some similar benefits (Editor)] Only very religious Jewish schools, usually Yeshivas, and one private English school, which call themselves "independent schools" have not accepted these conditions by the Quebec Ministry of Education. Thus, besides the segregation of the public school system along religious and linguistic lines,[7] Quebec education is now more and more divided along religious and ethnic lines. The origins of this segregation lay both in the intolerance of the denominational publicly supported school system (where catholics refused non-catholics, and protestants only recently accepted

---

5. Some present Jewish schools started as Yiddish schools, but it seems that Yiddish is now nearly completely abandoned and that most of the teaching is in French, English and Hebrew.

6. Originally I wrote "teachers from the country of origin", but this is not true for most of the Jewish or Armenian children, whose parents are often Canadian born.

7. It should be mentioned that only religious separation is identified in the British North America Act in matters of education. The linguistic separation of the Quebec school systems is an historical fact, without much constitutional basis.

non-protestants as equals) and the more recent attempts at liberalization and acceptance of others which characterized the Quiet Revolution of the 1960s in Quebec.

One of the unintended consequences of this liberalism, however, may be that ethnic and religious groups are now more segregated than before. Recent events seem to confirm this interpretation: a group of parents asked that the Notre-Dame-des-Neiges school (a French school of the Montreal catholic commission) be made "pluralistic", i.e., a religiously neutral school where no "Christian project" would be mentioned in the curriculum, and where religion would only be mentioned in religion classes. Children of different faiths would only be separated during religion classes, and agnostic or atheist children would be sent to classes in philosophy and moral education. While it is possible in catholic schools to be exempted from religious instruction today, the proposed pluralist school would have meant a complete recognition of religious pluralism in the catholic public schools and would have brought together children of different faiths. Although the Notre-Dame-des-Neiges School Committee[8], a majority of all the parents of the school polled in June 1979 by the School Committee, left-wing and liberal Catholics, different community groups[9], the Catholic Committee of the Superior Council of Education[10], and the Ministry of Education itself

---

8. The School Committee is a legal entity in Quebec representing parents of the school. It is not an Ad Hoc, or a political group.

9. Such as, for instance, the AQADER or Association Québecoise pour l'Application du Droit à l'Exemption de l'Enseignement Religieux, a French group aiming to create a religiously neutral French educational system in Quebec and which is the inheritor of the Mouvement Laïc de Langue Française of the 1960s.

10. This Committee, along with the Protestant Committee for protestant schools, decides upon moral and religious education in the Quebec public schools.

supported the proposal, it was not implemented by the Catholic school commission, apparently under pressures of conservative catholics and of the Archbishop of Montreal.

Racially segregated schools within Quebec have always existed under Federal legislation for Indians. Provincial policies make no racial distinctions. That is why Blacks or other racial minorities, although concentrated in some areas, always live in predominantly white neighbourhoods. Thus, although some schools have an enrolment which is nearly 50% black, the de facto segregation found in many U.S. cities is unknown in Montreal, where most Quebec Blacks are concentrated. Attempts at creating a special institute of primary education which would have been geared towards the adjustment of black students from the English West Indies have been defeated by the Protestant School Board of Greater Montreal as leading to racial segregation (Laferrière, 1978).[11]

But if racial segregation is not an issue in Quebec education, religious and ethnic divisions in both public and private schools seem to be becoming one. The unintended consequences of liberal educational policies, i.e., the creation of several systems and the social segregation along ascriptive or quasi-ascriptive ethnic and religious status, beg questions similar to those by Marcuse (1965) in his critique of pure liberal tolerance: are there background limitations to tolerance? Are there not dangers in benevolent laissez-faire tolerance? Marcuse calls "This non-partisan tolerance 'abstract' or

---

11. French Creole speaking black children of Haitian origin are dispersed in many French schools of the catholic school commission, if they are lower or middle class, or in private French schools if they are from intellectual or upper middle class families (Laferrière, 1978; Déjean, 1978).

'pure' inasmuch as it refrains from taking sides -- but in doing so, it actually protects the already established machinery of discrimination" (Marcuse, 1965: 85). One can wonder if the acceptance of de facto discrimination on the basis of religious or ethnic diversity may not lead in the long run to the estrangement of the different groups coexisting in society.

Even if a truly multiracial and multicultural educational system could be devised, one would not escape the general problem of the normative content of the curriculum used in that system. For the education of children of the majority (or of different minorities in the cultures of other groups than their own) requires the definition of what these cultures are made of. In order to avoid philosophical or political controversies, the material cultures and the folklores of different groups are usually emphasized in multicultural programs. A certain fiction is thus created according to which minority groups are unified, and several differences, particularly class differences, are occulted. By promoting ethnic and racial differences, one may often negate internal group particularities and arrive at an abstract stereotypical concept of "the Jew" or "the Black" or "the Chinese". Such a concept often approximates the standards of the middle or of the upper class in the minority group concerned. To paraphrase Marx, the dominant ideology is the ideology of the dominant group, even in minority communities, and standards of normalcy may be used to make occult and oppress parts of the minority groups themselves.[12]

Ideological segregation and oppression stemming from liberalizing policies may be monitored and made conscious. In the last decade, however, other types of inferiorization and separation of different groups have been created or recreated by experts in education and the social sciences.

---

12. One of our student-researchers, Francoise LeBrun, is now examining some of the strifes concerning educational issues within the Montreal Greek community.

III. THE EDUCATIONAL CONSEQUENCES OF THE NEW SCIENTIFIC RACISM

In the beginning of 1969 the Harvard Educational Review published an article by Arthur Jensen entitled "How Much Can We Boost I.Q. and Scholastic Achievement?" (Jensen, 1969). In this article Jensen presented the view that compensatory education in the U.S. had failed, and offered a genetic perspective to explain this failure. He examined several studies dealing with I.Q. differences between individuals varying in genetic closeness and/or environmental conditions (such as studies of identical twins reared apart or together, siblings, parents and children, and adoptive parents and adopted children) in order to establish the heritability of I.Q.

Jensen came to the conclusion that the heritability of intelligence was 0,80. He also distinguished between two types of intelligence, level I corresponding to rote learning or associative ability and level II or conceptual ability. According to him, culturally deprived children do quite well on level I type tasks, while education is geared towards and privileges level II type of abilities, and thus turns off many children. Jensen's conclusion is that - because of different endowments - schools should provide different types of education for different types of children. Subsequent articles and books by Jensen (Jensen, 1972, 1973 a and b, and 1979) refine a number of points included in the 1969 article: definitions of intelligence, calculations of heritability, and different points dealing with population genetics, cultural deprivation, etc.

Two other American writers have been forcefully presenting views of the same vein as Jensen. In an article published in 1971, and republished in 1973 in a book, Harvard psychology professor Richard Herrnstein attempts to show that, because American society stresses achievement (and especially educational achievements) for mobility and position within the stratification system, America is moving towards a meritocratic society where the stratification system will be more and more rigid, since it is based nearly exclusively on education and intelligence, and since intelligence is genetically determined. Neither Jensen nor Herrnstein deal directly with the question of racial differences in intelligence in their initial work, but this point was taken up by Nobel laureate William Shockley, a physicist turned eugenist. Started from the well-known fact that blacks as a group score one standard deviation below the white norm on I.Q. tests, and adopting an hereditarian paradigm like Jensen, Shockley mentions that the average intelligence level of the American population will decrease, since the poor and the blacks, all lower I.Q. groups, have more children. Shockley (1973) offers as a solution eugenic programs in order to limit the number of children in low I.Q. groups.

Similarly, in England, E.J. Eysenck, in a book published at the same time in the United States (Eysenck, 1971) stresses that blacks may be less intelligent than whites for genetic reasons. In a subsequent book, Eysenck (1975) also used an hereditarian genetic paradigm to attempt to show that sex differences, criminality and schizophrenia, besides intelligence, were predominantly inherited.

Several books and hundreds of articles have been written to oppose the views of these writers, and to criticize their conceptions of intelligence, race, and population genetics (or more rarely, to defend them).[13]

---

13. We cannot start enumerating even the most significant books and articles, the list would be too long. We can only refer the reader to the bibliographies included in the articles on the controversy itself that we cite.

Articles have attempted a sociological explanation of the controversy, (e.g., Harwood, 1976 and 1977; Laferrière, 1980). The four "heredity" authors have been subjected to censorship, harassment, and even physical threats (Herrnstein, 1973 preface or Jensen, 1972 preface). It could also be mentioned that these authors have written policy statements of a racist and/or classist nature, and have attempted (especially in the case of Shockley) to publicize them widely. In this, they have gone beyond standard academic practices and have had to suffer the fate of unpopular polemicists. What is of interest here is not the social aspect or the scholarly content of the controversy, but some of its educational implications. The genetic hereditarian paradigm is not new in American social sciences (Kamin, 1974; Chase, 1977, for instance) but environmentalist views have been dominant, especially since the end of World War II, although it started before in some fields like anthropology (Harris, 1968). A return to this hereditarian paradigm may mean that oppressed racial and social groups once more will be stigmatized. This stigmatization had started with the use of some environmental ideas, as for instance the Baratzes (Baratz and Baratz, 1970) have shown: compensatory education was an institutional way to treat differently the different racial and social groups. Other environmentalists' views, such as the idea of culture of poverty and of cultural deprivation have also been criticized (Valentine, 1968; Leacock, 1971) as means of "blaming the victim" (Ryan, 1971). What is different in the hereditarian paradigm is the view that institutional segregation can be justified because of "natural" causes, and that it could be permanently established. While the ideas of cultural deprivation and compensatory education could lead to temporary segregation for helping purposes, the policies stemming from hereditarian genetic views imply a system segregated not on the basis of changeable cultural traits, but of supposedly immutable genetic characteristics. "Nature", often used to justify inequalities between social groups in the past, has been used again in the last decade to justify oppression. Several ethologists as well as a few evolutionists have in their recent writings justified the inferior position of women (for one analysis see Reed, 1978). What we have in the new hereditarian writings on intelligence is similar: the justification of the unequal treatment of blacks, the lower classes, and other groups by the "intrinsic" genetic attributes of these groups.

In the case of the hereditarian writings, as in the previous case of discriminatory educational ideologies and policies, the original intent was not to hurt or destroy specific groups, but to better their education. But in the process, these writings have been inferiorizing those groups, whether that was unconsciously intended or not, and this inferorization has had the prestigious label of science, the ideological importance of which cannot be underestimated in our society. Although it is still unfashionable to adopt hereditarian views, social and political unrest could lead to their greater acceptance in the future.

This chapter has stressed some of the discriminatory policies and ideologies presently found in several educational systems. Education should not be blamed for what may be larger societal problems. Racism and discrimination are prevalent in many societies. Canada offers privileges that are vital. At least there is still no open hunting of people, as is the case for the Indians of the Amazone, and children do not disappear because of their parents' ethnic backgrounds or political opinions, as is the case in certain South American countries: Argentina, Uruguay and Chile (Amnesty International,

1979). But Blacks, Indians, and many non-white minorities complain of police harassment and of frequent popular discrimination either open or disguised. Unfortunately, very few empirical studies of racism in Canada are available. A recent psychological study (Henry, 1977) describes racism in Toronto, but deals more with perceptions and attitudes than with behaviour.

It seems that education has a specific role to play, since it may work both on the attitudinal and the behavioral levels to promote or lessen separation among different groups. One of the major problems, however, may be that the powers of education to eradicate racism are limited, since racism may have social functions at different times. Thus formal education may only partly act upon the causes of racism and answer the "why" question. To eliminate racism may require political actions and social and cultural changes much beyond the scope of the school and its participants.

REFERENCES

Baratz, Stephen & Joan "Early Childhood Intervention: The Social Science Base of Institutional Racism", *Harvard Educational Review*, 40(1) 1970, 29-50.

Black Community Education Task Force *Report prepared for the Superior Council of Education*. Montreal: mimeographed, 1978.

Boudon, Raymond *Effets pervers et ordre social*. Paris: Presses Universitaires de France, 1977.

Bourdieu, Pierre & Passeron, Jean-Claude *La Reproduction*. Paris: Editions de Minuit, 1970.

Burnet, Jean "Myths and Multiculturalism", *Canadian Journal of Education-Revue Canadienne de l'Education*, 4:4 (1979), 42-58.

Castel, Robert *Le psychanalysme*. Paris: Francois Maspero, 1973.

Chase, Allan *The Legacy of Malthus. The Social Costs of the New Scientific Racism*. New York: Alfred A. Knopf, 1977.

Dejean, Paul *Les Haïtiens au Québec*. Montréal: Les Presses de l'université du Québec, 1978.

Eysenck, H.J. *The Inequality of Man*. Londres: Fontana-Collings, 1975 (original 1973).

Harris, Marvin *The Rise of Anthropological Theory*. New York: Thomas Y. Crowell Co., 1968.

Harwood, Jonathan "The Race-Intelligence Controversy: A Sociological Approach - I Professional Factors", *Social Studies of Science*, 6, (1976), 369-394.

-----. "The Race-Intelligence Controversy: A Sociological Approach - II 'External' Factors". *Social Studies of Science*, 7, (1977), 1-30.

Henry, Frances *Racism in Toronto: A Research Report*. Toronto: York University, 1977, mimeographed.

Herrnstein, Richard J. *I.Q. in the Meritocracy*. Boston: Little, Brown and Co., 1973.

International Review of Education *Volume XXI. Immigrant Children Education in Western Europe*, 1975.

Jensen, Arthur R. Genetics and Education. New York: Harper & Row, 1972.

-----. A) Educability and Group Differences. New York: Harper & Row, 1973.

-----. B) Educational Differences. London: Methuen & Co., 1973.

Kage, Joseph "The Education of a Minority: Jewish Children of Greater Montreal" in Mingus, Pau (ed.) Sounds Canadian. Language and Culture in Multi-Ethnic Society. Toronto: Peter Martin Associates, 1975, 93-104.

Kamin, Leon J. The Science and Politics of I.Q. Potomac, Maryland: Lawrence Erlbaun Associates, distr. by John Wiley, 1974.

Katz, Michael B. Minorities in Textbooks: A Study of Their Treatment In Social Studies Texts. New York: Watts, Franklin, Inc. 1970.

Laferrière, Michel "The 'Jensen's thesis': Sociological Perspectives on a Controversy". A Paper presented at the Annual Meetings of the American Educational Research Association, Bosson, Mass., 1980.

Leacock, Eleanor Burke (ed.) The Culture of Poverty: A Critique. New York: Simon & Schuster, 1971.

Marcuse, Herbert "Repressive Tolerance" in Robert Wolff, Barrington Moore Jr. & Herbert Marcuse, A Critique of Pure Tolerance. Boston: Beacon Press, 1965, 81-123.

McDiarmid, Garnet & Pratt, David Teaching Prejudice. A Content Analysis of Social Studies Textbooks Authorized for Use in Ontario. Toronto: The Ontario Institute for Studies in Education, 1971.

McLeod, Keith A. (ed.) Intercultural Education and Community Development. Toronto: Guidance Centre, University of Toronto, 1980.

Merton, Robert K. Social Theory and Social Structure. Glencoe, Ill.: The Free Press, 1949.

Porter, John The Vertical Mosaic. Toronto: The University of Toronto Press, 1965.

Reed, Evelyn Sexism and Science. New York and Toronto: Pathfinder Press, 1978.

Richardson, Ken & Spears, David (eds.) Race and Intelligence. The Fallacies behind the Race-I.Q. Controversy. Baltimore, Maryland: Penguin Books, 1972.

Rist, Ray C. "On Understanding the Processes of Schooling: The Contribution of Labeling Theory" in Karabel, Jerome & Halsey, A.H. (eds.) Power and Ideology in Education. New York: Oxford University Press, 1977, 282-292.

-----. Guestworkers in Germany. The Prospects for Pluralism. New York: Praeger Publishers, 1978.

Ryan, William Blaming the Victim. New York: Pantheon Books, 1971.

Samuda, Ronald J. Psychological Testing of American Minorities. Issues and Consequences. New York: The Third Press, 1975.

Senna, Carl (ed.) The Fallacy of I.Q. New York: The Third Press, 1973.

Shockley, William "Dysegenics, Geneticity, Raceology: A Challenge to the Intellectual Responsibility of Educators", Phi Delta Kappan, January 1972, 297-307.

Valentine, Charles A. Culture and Poverty. Critique and Counter-Proposals. Chicago and London: The University of Chicago Press, 1968.

Winks, Robin W. The Blacks in Canada. A History. New Haven and London: Yale University Press, with McGill-Queen's University Press, Montreal, 1971.

MINORITY OFFICIAL LANGUAGE EDUCATION: WHERE CAN IT BE SECURE?

Jacques Lamontagne.

Not so long ago, it would have seemed strange to discuss the educational rights of anglophones (English speakers) in Canada as a minority group. Since Confederation, the English language has occupied a prominent place in Canadian society, including the Province of Quebec. The English minority of Quebec has always had control over its school system, and the average number of years of schooling of the anglophone Quebecker surpasses that of the francophone Quebecker. With the advent of the language laws in Quebec (Bill 63 in 1969, Bill 22 in 1974, and Bill 101 in 1977), the anglophones and the would-be anglophones (i.e. those whose mother tongue is not English, but who wish to integrate to the anglophone community) have voiced their claim that, as a minority group, part of their educational rights were being withdrawn. There is now a widespread sense of minority-group belonging among the non-francophones in Quebec.

On the other hand, since Confederation the francophones of Quebec have considered themselves to be a minority group within Canada, and even as a dominated majority group in Quebec. The domination of the anglophone majority over the francophone majority in Quebec is mainly to be seen in the economic sphere. Since education is within the jurisdiction of the provinces, the francophone majority in Quebec secured for itself a complete system of education.

Such has not been the case for the francophone minorities in the nine other Canadian provinces. The various educational rights of francophones in these other provinces have been only those specified (even worse, they may not be acknowledged) by each province. On the whole limitations have historically been imposed on the teaching in French and the teaching of French in the non-francophone provinces. But important decisions have been taken recently to promote the educational rights of the francophone minorities in the non-francophone provinces. Of course, "where numbers warrant" remains a determining factor in the remedial steps to be taken: there has to be a minimal number of students to justify teaching in French or of French.

It is significant to note that the present tendency to promote the educational rights of francophones outside Quebec coincides with new limitations to the educational rights of non-francophones (including anglophones) in Quebec. Among the landmarks of the recent evolution of minority language education are the Quiet Revolution in Quebec, the Official Languages Act of Canada, and the expression of the aspirations of minority language groups. The cultural rights of minority language groups have been fostered by national multiculturalism initiatives, although educational matters are within the jurisdiction of the provinces.

At their 18th Annual Conference in St. Andrews, New Brunswick, on August 18 and 19, 1977, the provincial Premiers expressed their concern for the educational rights of the language minorities in Canada. They agreed that they would "make their best efforts to provide instruction in English and French wherever numbers warrant" (State, 1978, p. 1) and they decided to "direct the Council of Education Ministers to meet as soon as possible to review the state minority language education in each province". The premiers also agreed that "each Province would undertake to ensure such provision of Canadian minority language education, and would then make a declaration of the policy plan and program to be adopted by the Government of that Province, in this respect".

The Education Ministers' Report minority language section centered on education in French for French-speaking students outside Quebec, and on education in English for English-speaking students in Quebec. It describes for each province the size and geographical distribution of the minority language population, the legislative provisions governing minority language education, and the educational services available to the minority language population. In all these respects, there are large differences between the ten provinces. Too much space would be required to summarize this information here, so this chapter will compare the education of anglophones in Quebec and of francophones in Ontario, which has the largest francophone population: 462,075 or 5.6% of the Ontario population, in 1976. The second largest concentration of francophones outside Quebec is New Brunswick: 223,785 or 33% of the New Brunswick population, in 1976. Because of the size and concentration of the francophones of Ontario and New Brunswick they are considered to be the two non-francophone provinces where the improvement of the educational rights and educational practices for francophones is the most feasible.

Comparing Francophones in Ontario and Anglophones in Quebec

In an article on the educational rights of Franco-Ontarians, Stacy Churchill (1978-79) has ably explained the educational situation of Franco-Ontarians, and concluded that contrary to the perception of many Anglo-Canadians, Franco-Ontarians are not a privileged group. Moreover, circumstances are unfavourable, notably because of declining enrolments and ensuing cutbacks in school facilities and services. Political tensions between the anglophone and the francophone views are therefore expected to continue to rise. Churchill suggests that Franco-Ontarians should base their demands on the notion of "special needs" rather than that of "special status", in order to avoid being the target of anti-Quebec or anti-separatist opinion.

By contrast, the FFHQ (Fédération des francophones hors-Québec) argues that (a) the disparity in the treatment of the two minority groups (anglophones in Quebec and francophones outside Quebec) is not in line with their legally recognized place in Canada, and (b) these disparities are socially unjust (<u>Deux poids, deux mesures</u>, 1978).

It appears that the hour is very late to attempt to stop what could be the ineluctable assimilation of Franco-Ontarians into the English community.

Demographic data suggest the rapid linguistic transfers of Franco-Ontarians, which provides an index of this process of assimilation.

According to Churchill, the outcome will largely depend on the attitudes of the anglophone majority, but the case should be presented to the anglophone community by the Franco-Ontarians, along with the use of political pressure. Although this political pressure need not hinge upon the ethnic majority-minority relations in Quebec as a basis of comparison, it is doubtful that recent socio-political and cultural developments in Quebec can be ignored.

Our comparative analysis will be based on three postulates:

a) French is recognized as one of the two official languages in Canada. All francophones in Canada speak a language that has an identical status throughout Canada, as recognized for federal purposes by the Official Languages Act of 1969. However, French and English do no have equal status in the educational laws of either Ontario or Quebec.

b) Franco-Ontarians are comparable to French-speaking Quebeckers in that both groups belong to a country in which they constitute a minority group, the difference being that Franco-Ontarians are also a minority in Ontario, whereas French-speaking Quebeckers are a majority in Quebec.

c) Franco-Ontarians are comparable with anglophone Quebeckers in that they both constitute a linguistic minority group in their respective province.

We shall analyze salient characteristics of the battle for survival of Franco-Ontarians as an ethnic group, particularly in securing appropriate educational rights and services. In particular, stress will be laid on the rate of assimilation of Franco-Ontarians to the anglophone community and the chances of survival and/or development of the French language in Ontario, notwithstanding steps which may be taken to alter the course of events.

But the linguistic situation in Ontario and in Quebec does not fully explain the dynamics of the relationships between the anglophone and francophone majorities and minorities in these two provinces. One must also look to the unequal distribution of socio-economic resources between the interacting language groups. A two-way and self-reinforcing relationship will be found to exist between the possession of socio-economic resources and educational achievement.

Demographic Trends in Ontario and Quebec

French Canadians have always been preoccupied with their cultural and linguistic survival in North America and particularly in Canada. This explains the importance they give to their demographic composition in Canada with relation to the other ethnic and linguistic groups, especially the British and the anglophones.

Arès (1975) has drawn attention to the recently increasing rate of population growth in Ontario. From 1961 to 1971, the increase of the Ontarian population has been 23.5% in comparison with 14.6% in Quebec. In 1971, the respective populations were: Ontario 7,703,105, Quebec 6,027,725. Preliminary 1981 data suggest that the trend continues.

The proportion of Ontarians in Canada has consistently increased from 1936 to 1971 (from 32.1% to 36%) while that of Quebeckers has been relatively stable (from 27.6% to 27.9%).

As explained by Charbonneau and Maheu (1973):

> Between 1936 and 1951, a period during which there was practically no immigration, the high fertility rate in Quebec has resulted in the increase from 27.6 to 29% of Quebeckers in the total population of Canada. From 1951 to 1966, immigration was strong, and Quebec's new immigrants constituted at least 20% of the net Canadian positive migration... However, since 1967, the rate of natural growth is a little lower in Quebec, as compared with Canada: the net migration has become the most important factor; and since the net migration has become negative, Quebec's share has dropped from 28.9% to 27.9% between 1966 and 1971. In Ontario, the rate of natural growth has always been lower than in the rest of Canada (except in 1970). However its share has continually increased because of its strong net migration.

Ontario's magnetic effect over the province of Quebec is manifested by the inter-provincial migrations of recent years. From 1966 to 1971, 48,370 Ontario residents have migrated to Quebec, in comparison with 99,430 Quebec residents who have migrated to Ontario (Dossiers, 1976, p. 33). Preliminary data show even more disparity subsequently (<u>Perspectives Canada II</u>, 1980, p. 16).

In Canada as a whole from 1901 to 1971, the proportion of Canadians of French origin has dropped from 30.7% to 28.7%. The drop of Canadians of British origin is more substantial: from 57% to 44.6%. Thus, the other ethnic groups in Canada have become proportionately more important: from 12.3% to 26.7% (Report, 1967, Vol. IV, p. 248).

In Ontario, the percentage of Franco-Ontarians rose from 4.7% in 1871 to 10.4% in 1961, but has declined to 9.6% in 1971 (FFHQ, Vol. 1, p. 22). In comparison, the percentage of the British-origin population of Ontario has decreased steadily since Confederation: 82.4% in 1871 to 59.4% in 1971 (Arès, 1975, p. 45). This decrease corresponds to an increasing number and proportion of immigrants in Ontario. But a relatively small proportion of those immigrants are of French origin. Between 1968 and 1972, the annual percentage of immigrants in Ontario who knew French varied from 3.2% to 4.2%, but 54% to 66% of immigrants knew English (FFHQ, 1977, Vol. 2, p. 18).

In Quebec, the proportion of people of French origin has decreased very slightly from 1901 to 1971 (from 80.1% to 79%), but there is a sharp decrease in the proportion of people of British origin (from 17.7% to 10.6%) The increase of the "other ethnic groups" is from 2.2% to 10.5% (Dossiers, p. 31). Between 1968 and 1970, immigrants in Quebec from French-language countries varied from 19.9% to 27.7%, whereas immigrants from English-language countries varied from 24.5% to 34.1% (Rapport 1972 Vol. 3, pp. 214-215). The largest group (collectively) was neither English nor French.

The Assimilation of Franco-Ontarians

We define the assimilation of French Canadians as the process by which they cease to use the French language and increasingly use the English language. This process may take place by the adoption of English as the means of communication at work, at school, and/or at home.

This process of assimilation can be traced through three statistics: (a) ethnic origin; (b) mother tongue; and (c) language spoken at home. They record a two-step process of assimilation of francophones to the anglophone community, a process which is initiated when one ceases to use one's mother tongue and which is furthered when one's mother tongue is not transmitted to one's offspring (Figure 1).

FIGURE 1

Language Classifications of French Canadians and Franco-Ontarians
(1971)

Canadians of French origin	Franco-Ontarians
(6,180,120)	(737,360)
89.3% had French as their mother tongue	60.1%
85.4% spoke French at home	44.6%
14.5% spoke English at home	55.1%
10.4% had English as their mother tongue	39.3%
8.2% knew English and did not know French	32.5%

(Arès, pp. 103, 137).

To give some idea of the rate at which this assimilation has been taking place, let us look at the evolution of the linguistic transfers of Franco-Ontarians since 1941.

FIGURE 2

LINGUISTIC TRANSFERS OF FRANCO-ONTARIANS

	1971	1961	1951	1941
French, mother tongue	60.1%	61.4%	68.2%	74.4%
English, mother tongue	39.3%	37.7%	31.3%	25.1%
Know English only	32.5%	33.6%	27.8%	24.0%

(Arès, p. 138)

Although the rate of anglicization of Franco-Ontarians is obviously very high, only in Quebec and New Brunswick have they a better chance of resisting linguistic assimilation (see Figure 3).

FIGURE 3   (Statistics for 1971)   LINGUISTIC ASSIMILATION OF FRENCH CANADIANS

Province	English spoken at home	English mother tongue	Know English and do not know French
Newfoundland	86.9%	80.3%	74.1%
British Columbia	89.8	65.4	59.7
Alberta	77.4	54.1	49.9
Nova Scotia	67.7	53.8	48.2
Prince Edward Island	72.5	54.6	47.9
Saskatchewan	73.4	47.3	43.3
Manitoba	56.9	35.5	33.0
Ontario	55.1	39.3	32.5
New Brunswick	18.3	12.3	9.2
Quebec	2.5	1.9	0.6

(Arès, pp. 111, 144)

Exogamy is possibly instrumental in the assimilation of francophones. In Ontario, in 1971, 28.9% of French-Canadian men and 30.4% of women were wed to a person of a different linguistic group. As would be expected, the language spoken in the home of these couples or families is largely English (92.0%), rather than French (FFHQ.1977, Vol. 1, p. 33).

The Assimilation to the Anglophone Community in Quebec

Although the ethnic origin figures show that a nearly constant proportion of French Canadians exists outside Quebec (22% in 1941, 24% in 1961, 23% in 1971) use of French in the home, as mother tongue and language of preference, all show that outside Quebec the language disappears. In Canada and also in Quebec the proportion of French Canadians has been decreasing (30.3% and 80.9% in 1941; 28.3% and 79% in 1971). This decrease of French Canadians in Quebec is accompanied by a decrease of Quebeckers of British origin (13.6% in 1941 and 10.6% in 1971) and with an increase of other ethnic groups (5.5% in 1941 and 10.4% in 1971) (Arès, 35). In 1971, only 72% of anglophones (i.e. those who spoke English at home) in Quebec were of British origin; the remaining 28% were mainly immigrants who had chosen to adopt the English language. In the same year, 11% of anglophones in Quebec did not have English as their mother tongue. The non-French ethnic groups are concentrated, especially in Montreal (Figures 4 and 5).

FIGURE 4   ETHNIC GROUPS IN QUEBEC

Ethnic group origin	1971 Quebec (province)	1971 Montreal
French	79%	58.9%
British	10.6%	17%
Other	10.4%	24.1%
	100%	100%

(Arès, p. 37)

FIGURE 5   LANGUAGE(S) OF FRENCH CANADIANS IN MONTREAL

Of the 1,762,695 French Canadians (i.e. Canadians of French origin) in Montreal in 1971

    96.7% had French as their mother tongue

    95.8% spoke French at home

    37.7% were bilingual (Quebec, province: 24.4%)

    4.1% spoke English at home

    3.0% had English as their mother tongue

    1.1% knew English only (Quebec, province: 0.7%).

(Arès, pp. 106, 117, 121).

Arès has used the notion of "assimilating power" to compare the official language spoken at home for New Quebeckers in Montreal. Figure 6 shows two examples.

FIGURE 6   ASSIMILATION OF JEWISH AND ITALIAN MIGRANTS IN MONTREAL (1971)

Ethnic origin	English spoken at home	French spoken at home	Ratio of Assimilating Power
Jewish	76.8%	7.1%	10 to 1
Italian	15.7%	18.5%	1 to 1.25
Mean	41.1%	16.1%	2.50 to 1

Arès, p. 130.

Although the assimilating power of the English language varied greatly among the Neo-Quebeckers, in all cases except for the Italians, the English language had a stronger assimilating power.

The Education of Franco-Ontarians

The B & B Commission reported in 1967 that

> French language education outside Quebec has suffered principally from two weaknesses. First, it has been largely achieved through the struggles of French-speaking Canadians despite the resistance of the English-speaking majority. The toll in efficiency and vitality is readily appreciated. Second, it has not constituted a 'system'. There have been serious gaps and dislocations in the sequence from one educational level to another; essentials such as teacher-training, guidance, and so on, have left a great deal to be desired; a technical or scientific education has been largely unavailable. As a consequence, even where conditions have been most favourable, French-speaking children have been seriously handicapped in their education, with the result that often they were deficient in both languages.
> (Report, Vol. 1, p. 122).

In Ontario, French holds the status of an official language of schooling, but the right to receive schooling in French is conditional upon regulations which hinder access to education in the French language. The "Education Act" in Ontario guarantees the right of Franco-Ontarians to be educated in French at the elementary and secondary levels where there are sufficient numbers:

> (2) Where ten or more French-speaking ratepayers of a school division, school section or separate school zone apply in writing to the board thereof for the use of the French language in instruction of French-speaking pupils, and,
>
> (a) the parents or guardians of thirty or more French-speaking pupils in the primary, junior or intermediate division elect to have such pupils taught in the French language, and such pupils can be assembled for this purpose in a class or classes as part of a school, the board shall provide for the use of the French language in instruction in such class or classes, and
>
> (b) in the opinion of the board the number of such French-speaking pupils so warrants, the board shall provide for the use of the French language in instruction in a French-language elementary school (FFHQ. 1977, Vol. 1, p. 65).

Such promises are relatively new and perhaps imperfectly availed. The FFHQ reports that Franco-Ontarians have less schooling than Anglo-Ontarians: in 1971, 53.6% of Anglo-Ontarians in the 15-24 age group were still in school in comparison with 48.2% for the francophones (FFHQ. 1977, Vol 2, p. 22). Also, 71% of Franco-Ontarians have reached less than grade eleven, in comparison with 56% for the total population of Ontario. The resulting deficiency appears in university graduates: 7% for Franco-Ontarians and 10% for all Ontarians (FFHQ. 1977, Vol. 1, p. 38)

According to S. Churchill,

> The primary cause of this imbalance situation was the policies of the period before 1967. Refusal to allow the use of French as a language of instruction in secondary school meant that Franco-Ontarians left the elementary system where they were taught in French and entered a totally English environment where many could not cope; thus the great majority dropped out by the end of grade 10. (...) The creation of French language secondary schools and the enlargement of French language course offerings in mixed secondary schools suddenly changed this trend from 1968 onward (...). (pp. 62-63).

Franco-Ontarians still get a lower level of service, despite the fact that theoretically they now have an education "system" from kindergarten to grade 13, with possibilities of university education in French. Churchill's study has identified major areas of need:

> The only real problem at the elementary level was in service for newly-created schools. Migration of francophones to the more urbanized southern areas of the province has led in recent years to the creation of elementary schools where none existed before. Our study of a group of these schools (usually only one existed per school board) revealed major inadequacies in support services, access to cultural facilities, transportation for pupils from a distance, and so on. (...)
>
> In a more general sense, the whole spectrum of cultural resources for schools at both elementary and secondary levels was considered deficient. (...)

> The second major area of service need applied to mixed secondary schools as a group. The most important educational deficiency was the very low number of French language courses available in the schools. (...)
>
> The final area covered in the study was that of special services (...). Secondary principals gave very low ratings (...) to almost all the special services affecting students (...). (pp. 63-64).

The Education of Anglophones and Francophones in Quebec

A study on educational aspirations and career orientations of secondary and college students in Quebec reveals that parents of students in the English system have a higher socioeconomic status than those in the French system: 45% of fathers in the English system but only 26% of fathers in the French system have twelve years or more of schooling. For the occupational categories "manager, administrator, executive, and professional" combined, we find 42% of fathers in the English system and only 16% of fathers in the French system. Similarly, unequal proportions of parents in the English and in the French system would like their son (or daughter) to get a university education (English: 73%; French: 61%) (ASOPE, 1974, Vol. 2, pp. 62, 117).

In the sixties and early seventies, the population attending the French system of schools on the Island of Montreal was approximately the proportion of children whose mother tongue is French. In 1971, this proportion was 63%. In other words, the French system of schools on the Island of Montreal catered solely to students whose mother tongue was French. Thus, students whose mother tongue was neither French nor English went to the English schools. In 1971, 12% of students were in this category. Added to the 25% of students whose mother tongue was English, we find that 37% of all students on the Island of Montreal attended an English school (Amyot et Dufour, 1975, p. 12).

At the provincial level, the education of children of immigrants was also by and large in the English rather than in the French schools of Quebec, as is shown by the following statistics for the academic year 1972-73 (FFHQ. 1978, p. 43):

	Children of immigrants
English schools	52,280 (86.3%)
French schools	8,323 (13.7%)

Vaillancourt has found that, in 1971, unilingual francophones of Quebec were underrepresented in the administrative occupations and overrepresented in the category "production employees". The situation was the opposite for bilingual francophones. However, both unilingual and bilingual anglophones of Quebec were overrepresented in the administrative occupations and underrepresented in the category "production employees" (p. 34). Moreover, unilingual francophones in the administrative positions had a lower annual income than bilingual francophones. The latter's annual income was, in turn, lower than the annual income of anglophones, be they unilingual or bilingual. In the category "production employees", unilingual francophones, who were overrepresented, had the lowest income. And, here again, the bilingual francophones had a lower income than unilingual or bilingual anglophones (p. 3).

To what extent do these differences reflect the inequalities in education that we have earlier observed? Vaillancourt's computations give an answer to this question. Controlling for education, sex, age, employment status (full-time or part-time) and economic sector, Vaillancourt has found that francophones, unilingual or bilingual, have a lower annual income than anglophones, unilingual or bilingual, in the economic sectors of "manufacturing" and "transport and communication". A somewhat different result was found in the "government" sector where the lowest income was for unilingual francophones and the highest income for bilingual francophones (Vaillancourt, p. 5).

It is then quite understandable that the <u>Charte de la langue française</u> (Bill 101) would have a significant impact on the language of education chosen by the newcomers in Quebec. Articles 72 and 73 of the <u>Charte</u> read as follows:

> "Article 72
> L'enseignement se donne en français dans les classes maternelles, dans les écoles primaires et secondaires sous réverse des exceptions prévues au présent chapitre.
>
> Cette disposition vaut pour les organismes scolaires au sens de l'Annexe et s'applique aussi aux enseignements subventionnés dispensés par les institutions déclarées d'intérêt public ou reconnues pour fins de subventions en vertu de la Loi de l'enseignement privé (1968, chapitre 67).
>
> Article 73
> Par dérogation à l'article, peuvent recevoir l'enseignement en anglais, à la demande de leur père et de leur mère,
>
> a) les enfants dont le père ou la mère a reçu au Québec, l'enseignement primaire en anglais,
>
> b) les enfants dont le père ou la mère est, à la date d'entrée en vigueur de la présente loi, domicilié au Québec et a reçu, hors du Québec, l'enseignement primaire en anglais,
>
> c) les enfants qui, lors de leur dernière année de scolarité au Québec avant l'entrée en vigueur de la présente loi, recevaient légalement l'enseignement en anglais dans une classe maternelle publique ou à l'école primaire ou secondaire,
>
> d) les frères et soeurs cadets des enfants visés au paragraphe c".

The "French-immersion-class" phenomenon also contributes to the francization of Quebec. While the English educational system used to cater to practically all English children plus a large majority of children of non-francophone immigrants, we now witness the development of French immersion classes in English schools. In September 1976, 11% of the students of The Protestant School Board of Greater Montreal were in French immersion classes (PSBGM. 1976, pp. 1-7). More recent data show that the "immersion" movement has become even more widespread in Montreal. Indeed, in just two years, the share of French immersion classes has increased to 22%.*

Conclusion: The Future of Francophone Education

We have compared minority language education in Ontario and Quebec. Stress was laid on demographic data showing the relative importance of the French Canadian population in these two provinces and the rate of assimilation of French Canadians to the anglophone community. There are signs in Quebec of the magnetic power of the English language. This problem has led to the successive adoption of language laws, the last one being the Charte de la langue française (Bill 101), in order to preserve the French character of Quebec. In Ontario, the French Canadian problem is

---

*Data obtained through the courtesy of the Communication Services of the Protestant School Board of Greater Montreal, May 24, 1979. In addition to enrolment in French immersion classes, 3.5% were in French language classes, and 1.8% were in welcoming classes.

acute because French Canadians are very rapidly being assimilated into the anglophone community. Despite this trend, the Franco-Ontarian community still wages its battle to obtain educational services that would ensure their linguistic and cultural survival.

In its Strategy, the FFHQ has recently compared the treatment of the minority anglophones of Quebec with the minority French Canadians outside Quebec. In educational matters, it is clear that the anglophones in Quebec do not as yet, and despite Bill 101, suffer from the linguistic transfers and the assimilation which are characteristic of Franco-Ontarians. Anglophones in Quebec control their own system of education at all levels, and their educational achievement and socio-economic status are superior to those of the francophones in Quebec.

Bill 101 does not deprive anglophones now in Quebec of their right to be educated in English. The aim of Bill 101 is for the newcomers to integrate into the francophone community and to stop the massive assimilation of the immigrants of Quebec to the anglophone community.

Bill 101 limits the freedom of language of anglophone Canadians coming to reside in Quebec: these anglophones are submitted to the same obligation to francization as the other newcomers. However, the Quebec government has proposed special reciprocal arrangements with other provincial governments. In this way, the Quebec government would try to obtain from the other provincial governments the assurance that they will extend the educational rights of French Canadians and that they will develop and improve the present educational facilities of this minority group outside

Quebec. The offer of reciprocity made by Quebec is for all Canadian provinces, but it is addressed most specifically to Ontario and New Brunswick, the two provinces outside Quebec where the largest concentrations of French Canadians are to be found. New Brunswick responded with full constitutional guarantees to its large francophone minority. Ontario refused to make such guarantees.

In Ontario, Franco-Ontarians are represented by ACFO (L'Association canadienne-française de l'Ontario) which was created in 1910 as l'ACFEO (l'Association canadienne-française d'éducation de l'Ontario). Originally, emphasis was laid on educational problems for Franco-Ontarians, as related to faith and language. With the eventual creation of a number of provincial associations specialized in education, ACFEO has turned its attention to other areas. In 1969, the name of the association was changed from ACFEO to ACFO. But ACFO retains a coordinating role among Franco-Ontarian associations.

The problems that ACFO and the educational associations for Franco-Ontarians are now trying to solve are:

> ... mise sur pied de cours concernant l'histoire des Franco-Ontariens, répartition des crédits pour l'étude de la langue française au niveau secondaire, problèmes causés par l'autonomie des Conseils scolaires récalcitrants à appliquer les lois scolaires, problèmes des francophones "noyés" dans des écoles ou des Conseils scolaires à majorité anglophone, problèmes dûs à la présence d'anglophones dans les classes et les écoles de langue française, utilisation de l'institution scolaire comme outil de promotion de la fierté franco-ontarienne, expansion de l'éducation en langue française au niveau post-secondaire. (FFHQ. 1977, Vol. 2, p. 10).

The courage and determination manifested by ACFO leaders in the defense of their language are commendable. They display a struggle for cultural survival not unlike that of their forbears who have resisted assimilation to the anglophone community of Ontario, despite their demographic, political and economic minority status. Perhaps in the context of a more explicit recognition of human rights, the Franco-Ontarians will be better able to resist assimilation forces.

REFERENCES

Amyot, Michel et Dufour, Richard Evolution de la clientèle étudiante suivant le niveau et le degré d'enseignement, par territoire de commission scolaire et région administrative, réseau public, Québec 1965-66 à 1973-74. Documents Démographie scolaire, 9-31. Québec: Ministère de l'Education, Direction générale de la Planification, janvier 1975.

Arès, Richard Les positions - ethniques, linguistiques et religieuses - des Canadiens français à la suite du recensement de 1971. Montréal: Editions Bellarmin, 1975.

Aspirations scolaires et orientations professionnelles des étudiants (ASOPE). Analyse descriptive des données de la première cueillette. Trois volumes (Les étudiants; Les parents; Les enseignants). Québec: Faculté des sciences de l'éducation, Université Laval, 1974.

Charbonneau, Hubert et Maheu, Robert Les aspects démographiques de la question linguistique. Québec: Editeur officiel du Québec, 1973.

Churchill, Stacy "So why aren't the French ever Satisfied? - Educational Rights for Franco-Ontarians", Interchange, Vol. 9, No. 4, 1978-79, pp. 59-66.

Les Dossiers du Devoir: Population et fait français au Canada. Montréal: Le Devoir, novembre 1976.

Editeur officiel, Québec. Charte de la langue française. Sanctionnée le 26 août 1977. Québec, août 1978, pp. 68-9.

Fédération des francophones hors-Québec. Les héritiers de Lord Durham. 2 volumes. Ottawa: FFHQ, 1977.

Fédération des francophones hors-Québec. Deux poids, deux mesures. Ottawa: FFHQ, 1978.

Perspectives Canada II. Ottawa: Supply and Services, 1977.

Rapport de la Commission d'enquête sur la situation de la langue française et sur les droits linguistiques au Québec. Volume 3: Les groupes ethniques. Québec" Gouvernement du Québec, 1972.

Report of the Royal Commission on Bilingualism and Biculturalism. Books I and IV. Ottawa, 1967.

The Protestant School Board of Greater Montreal. Deputy Director General's Summary of Enrolment as at September 30th, 1976. Montreal: PSBGM, 1976.

<u>The State of Minority Language Education in the Ten Provinces of Canada</u>.
A Report by the Council of Ministers of Education, Canada, January, 1978.

Vaillancourt, François <u>La situation des francophones sur le marché du travail québecois et le Livre blanc sur la langue</u>. Montréal: Université de Montréal, miméo., 19 avril 1977.

CONTESTED OR NON ASSURED EDUCATIONAL RIGHTS

Vincent D'Oyley

The confidence that Canadian society operates fairly and equitably is shattered by comparing the quality of development of the native peoples with the operations of the Anglophone-Francophone communities. The native peoples are a distinct racial group with well-demarcated cultural histories and aboriginal linguistic patterns. Their different life styles, languages, religions and their virtual exclusion from national and regional affairs have frustrated many attempts at acquiring balanced access to the fruits of citizenship.

For many Indians, their major relationships with federal and provincial governments and as a consequence with many municipal governments have been conditioned by the series of nineteenth century treaties and by the 1921 Treaty 11. These treaties regulated their lot, and made them essentially wards of the state; and only within the past two decades has there been the emergence of autonomy in some native development and transactions (Canada, Indian Treaties and Surrenders, 1971).

Native peoples themselves had long questioned whether the treaties under which they live were fairly negotiated (Hawthorn, 1966, 1967). In those places where no treaties were signed, their aboriginal rights were not well respected (Berger, 1981). Pressure for fair settlements led to recognition by both federal and provincial governments during the 1970s that aboriginal rights to land and natural resources have been inadequately compensated, and that new and "aboriginal settlements" must be made before the resources of Canada's unopened frontiers, especially the North and Northwest, can be aggressively tapped. This pressure for recognition has continued through several federal ministries without being fully resolved. Several provinces are also confronted. The re-negotiation of the treaties with native peoples and clarification of these peoples' main socio-economic and political rights has become more important.

A major pressure in both the earlier settlements and in the current renegotiations is the need for access to the land, to strategic locations, and to the natural resources. One new feature is the higher quality and more publicized articulations of the native peoples. They now comprehend how Canada, and particularly its bureaucracies, have affected their participation and growth.

Walter Stewart summarized the modern mood of the aborigine population when he wrote:

> Red Power has this overwhelming similarity to Black Power: A minority people is held down, despised and oppressed, on racial grounds, and that minority has decided not to take it any more.... (Stewart 1974)

The struggle of the Nishgas for aboriginal rights illustrates the difficulties for native peoples in obtaining or re-negotiating settlements. In 1973 the final vote of the Supreme Court on the Nishga claim to the Nass Valley (which they have occupied for centuries and claim under aboriginal right) was, 3 for the claim, 3 against, and 1 rejection "for procedural reasons... (with) no comment on the aboriginal rights question" (Sanders, 1973; Berger, 1981). This near success was a signal that native peoples need not lose in their main struggles for re-transactions. The success of Indians in the USA gave them similar hope for success through the courts.

The Berger reports on the Mackenzie Valley Pipeline inquiry propose a new basis for human rights development for native peoples.

> If we build the pipeline, it will seem strange, years from now, that we refused to do justice to the native people merely to continue ourselves with a range of consumer goods and comforts.... the pipeline if it were built now...would stand in the way of a just settlement of native claims...it would leave a legacy of bitterness throughout a region in which the native people have protested, with virtual unanimity... in the end, the Dene, Inuit, and Metis will follow those of their leaders who refuse to turn their backs on their own history...and who articulate the values that lie at the heart of native identity (Berger, 1977).

Berger has pressed for humane settlements on the aboriginal rights claims before further industrial advances are unleashed. His reports and subsequent speeches highlight that it is in the national interest for Dene, Inuit and Metis to gain a measure of control over their lives and over the political institutions that shape their lives.

Human rights for Indians, Inuit, and Metis require at least federal and provincial legal rearrangements that will provide both groups and individuals more land and resources, enlarged political rights and autonomies, and more comprehensive access to the nation's institutions. This stage has been entered by some groups like the Quebec Cree on James Bay and by some Inuit and Slavey Indians. It is still the first step envisaged by most others. It was demanded at the conference on "Human Rights for British Columbians" in Vancouver in December, 1979. That seminar concluded that "issues revolving around legal questions...(are) of paramount importance to the dignity of Native People" (Human Rights Commission of B.C. 1980, p. 27). The resolution of the four main land and resources' treaties that were discussed in March-April 1980 by Federal Minister John Munro in his tour to Canada's Northland and the understanding that the Dene will negotiate on behalf of the Metis would be major breakthroughs to providing social justice to Canada's aborigines.

Such progress would make it easier for the federal Department of Indian Affairs and Northern Development to move progressively from mere special status based on race for the registered Indians of Canada, the Inuits and the Metis, towards full citizenship participation with equal group and (individual) rights both on reservations or autonomous territories and in the urban areas to which increasing numbers are attracted. Without firm promises, the Indians will resist changes in their existing treaties. For example, efforts by the federal government to shift responsibility for Indian affairs to provincial governments (Canada, 1968) stirred native anger and a demand for native control: the Alberta Indian Chiefs responded with a "Red Paper" which was a concise demand for that control and a notice that Canadian Indians were resolved to remove the stigma of lesser rights. Native rights refined since then include: title in perpetuity for extensive tracts; pre-specified shares in natural resources; agreements about conservation measures; the control and development of adequate schooling; a better balancing of the rights of men, of women, and of children; autonomous management of a group's fiscal and social development affairs, and inclusion of special recognition of Indian rights in the Canadian constitution.

Later Visible Minorities

Although they came to Canada quite recently, those from Africa and Asia have been like the Canadian Indians and Inuit, in that they have enjoyed fewer human rights than those of European background. Both groups came mostly because of Canadian labour needs; in a few instances their numbers were increased because of Canadian humanitarian gestures. In the 18th century there were slaves in the Atlantic provinces, but escaped or freed slaves were the ancestors of most of the Blacks in Nova Scotia and Ontario until recently (Winks, 1971).

Chinese and Japanese were denied many business, familial, political, legal and mobility rights (Berger, 1981, Ashworth, 1979) in British Columbia and the Prairies, a national blot that is infrequently analysed in our schools. While attacks on the Chinese of Vancouver between 1880 and 1910 (a period of high unemployment) is one example of public racist expression; another is the excessive and prolonged withdrawal of rights from Canadian-born Japanese during the Second World War and the inadequacies of compensation thereafter (Adachi, 1976).

Keith Henry outlines how

> ...the hostile external environment and the scarcity of community resources led to repeated defeats and cumulative frustration.

The human rights of both Asians and Africans remain threatened today, partly because of their racial origin. A recent example was the CTV public affairs program "Campus Giveaway" which falsely presented the Chinese in Canada as usually foreign born and non-Canadian. CTV eventually apologized for the misrepresentation and anguish, admitting "distorted statistics combined with...visual presentation [that were] racist in tone and effect" (<u>Vancouver Sun</u>, 1980, p. A12).

The relationships between the majority race and Afro-Asians in Toronto deteriorated to the point where these minorities doubted police to be impartial. To improve racial harmony, Toronto's Metropolitan Council established the Carter Commission in 1979 and began to dialogue with the Urban Alliance on Race Relations and with other groups alarmed by the growth of racism. The type of human rights legislation that will require fair access to services and socio-economic opportunities and prevent race from remaining a key basis for discrimination will go far to creating the harmony needed in cities like Toronto, Saskatoon, Winnipeg and Halifax.

Language

A focus of aboriginals' discontent has been the lack of respect by the larger society for their languages. Some native languages have disappeared: only a few social occasions center on native orators. A few small grants have been awarded for recording the linguistic structures of some native languages, and in preparing teachers of them. Some basic linguistic work has been done on Cree, Athabascan and Algonguian languages for instance. Thus Aert H. Kuipers, <u>The Shuswap Language, Grammar, Texts, Dictionary</u> (1974), a type of standard study of native language, is of fundamental importance to both native readers and speakers from the Shuswap area between the Fraser River and the Rocky Mountains.

Native children increasingly speak only English or French, although many of them understand their own native speakers. The written native language enables some who "read" and do not speak the tribal tongue to draw upon the treasure house of their heritage; this reading is an important activity for many who plan to acquire and teach their language. Formal schools in some places now promote the speaking of native languages.* For example the Chilcotin children already speak their language, they now learn to read and write it in school (K-9 in Nehemiah Valley, 1-8 on the Stone Reserve and on the Alexis Creek Indian Band Reserve; and two levels of literacy at the Junior High in Williams Lake). Since the Shaswap children do not yet speak their ancestral language, their classes are the "second language" occasions where they learn to speak Shaswap (Alkali Lake K-8; Sugar Cane 1-7; Canam Lake Junior Secondary levels; and Ann Stevens Secondary in Williams Lake). The Carriers are already native speakers who have only to learn to read and write at Anahim Lake. Since 1980-81 both Chilcotin and Shuswap have received native languages' instruction at the senior secondary levels in Williams Lake.

− − − − −

* Based on discussions with Mr. Allan Haig Brown of school district #27.

The Nishgas, by taking control in 1975 of British Columbia School District #92 in New Aiyansh, have promoted the importance of their own language for improving the level of school achievement in their youth. They argue that their use of Nishga with language assistants and daily classes is to be credited with raising academic performance by about two grades for pupils by the junior high school level in the New Aiyansh school system.

It is important to note that the central struggle between English and French over language rights and other features of sovereignty, and the continuing requests by native peoples are not the only sources of language demands. Two other groups have been the later Europeans (non English and non French) and the later visible minorities (Africans and Asians). However, neither Asian nor African populations are homogeneous; for some the language is of very great significance, most speak fluently (and sometimes only) Canada's official languages, and for others the cultural aspects of language are maintained through private instruction. Some later Europeans such as the Ukrainians and Italians have been able to negotiate for limited third language rights in some parts of Canada (Lupul, 1982). Most small groups have had to opt for linguistic assimilation in spite of the socio-psychological consequences of that route. In Ontario school programs began in the 1970s to offer a heritage language emphasis for some of these groups. Some boards offer more than fifty such programs.

Yet linguistic rights, including the right to receive even a narrow range of social services in one's mother tongue, have not been guaranteed. Not even English or French are perfectly protected, Native language rights are not yet defined and the more disadvantaged African and Asian sectors have no specified language rights enshrined constitutionally.

TABLE 1

LANGUAGE IN THE HOME, WORK PLACE AND SCHOOL 1975

	ENGLISH	FRENCH	OTHER
HOME	60%	27%	13%
WORK PLACE:			
In mother tongue	98%	80%	N.A.
Of all workers	76%	21%	3%
EDUCATION:			
In mother tongue	98%	80%	N.A.

	ALL OTHER PROVINCES ENGLISH	QUEBEC FRENCH
In second language programs:		
elementary	37%	37%
secondary	42%	100%
In second language schools:		
elementary	5%	16%
secondary	4%	15%

Perspective Canada II, 1977.

The compelling issue is that language is the carrier of the cultural heritage and of the native religion. To forbid Canadian youth to study in their native language is to deny them access to a fundamental right, and thereby to stultify their chances of attaining their individual and group potential, and any viability as a people. No other Canadian group has a more urgent need for legislation that will guarantee the development and utilization of their mother tongue than do the native peoples, for many of whom only a few orators yet survive. The guarantee of mother tongue should hold for some areas of formal public schooling and also in highly stressful situations such as dealing with the courts and health care delivery (Lane et al., 1978, Starr, 1978). It should also promote their unique religious persuasion and spirituality, and their own expressive arts. It must do so very soon to avert the imminent impact of southern imagery (television programming and delivery to native communities) and the potential for further erosion of their language and culture unless they soon acquire more autonomy over aspects of media development and implementation.

Religion

Religion, according to its Latin roots religio, serves the purpose of binding. The forms of man's religious experiences are varied; so also are the revelations and manifestoes which the spiritual innovators of the world's larger religions (Hinduism, Buddhism and Confusianism, Judaism, Islam and Christianity) have employed to spread their doctrines. Not all peoples follow these main religions; countless others have adopted methods of worship comparable to or different from the six huge religions referred to here. In varying degrees religious practices bind their adherents to particular concepts of God, His relationship to man, and to certain moral codes, methods of living and discipline.

The relationship between religion and human rights in Canada is the focus of Peter Jones' "Theology and Ethnicity". He summarized the issue as

> a significant historical and theretical link between the cultural development of ethnic groups in Canada and the presence of religious forces both within and outside those groups which sometimes support a person's sense of cultural identity, and sometimes...demolish it. Judaism and the flourishing Jewish cultural life in Canada could not have survived without the supports of the Jewish faith and communal religious life. On the other hand, ...certain segments of main-line Christian churches have...so identified themselves with the cultural lifestyle of middle class Anglo society that joining them meant simultaneously to opt to some degree out of one's cultural past (Jones, 1979, pp. 53-54).

There can be little doubt that Judaic-Christian traditions pervade the operations of the main Canadian bureaucracies. For Canadians of other backgrounds, normal operations of society are likely to infringe upon their individual and sometimes their group rights.

The exclusive use of Christian worship in particular public situations, the irreverent treatment of non Judaeo-Christian 'maxi and mini' religions in some social studies and other school materials, and public anger in some cities at the emergence of non-Christian places of worship, cause anxiety on the part of non-Christians in many parts of Canada. Public hostility expressed through slogans to the establishment of a Sikh Temple in the Toronto East area in 1976-77 was one such circumstance, which stirred the "watchfulness" of many ethnic groups, and reminded main bureaucracies of the society's low level of tolerance for modes of worship that are non-Christian. Within the last fifty years, not even Jews have escaped Canadian public wrath; in this connection the anti-semitic riot at Christie Pitts in Toronto in August 1933 looms as a sobering reminder that Canada has been brutal (Betcherman, 1975).

Canadian religious intolerance has sometimes received the support of the government- for example against Jehovah Witnesses in Quebec or against Hutterites in Alberta until comparatively recently (Berger, 1981). The smouldering discontent of the 'Sons of Freedom' sect in British Columbia, the reported community pressures against Saskatchewan Hutterites, the imposition of "sanitary practices" that threatened to force Ontario Mennonites to abandon dairy farming or even leave the country, suggest hostility extends to the official level.

The native peoples have suffered more than any other group from a negative public attitude to their forms of worship. Yet there are small signs of tolerance towards the native mode of worship within education. One of the apparently successful education systems to be developed by Indians and for Indians is that of the Stoney Indians. It was carefully designed around native traditions, including religion (Snow, 1977).

Some Resolutions of Denials Based on Race, Language and Religion

Two main types of resolutions are appropriate for these denials. The first and most important was the substantial, albeit not universal, support for the Canada Act 1981 with its entrenched rights. The second will be the defence of rights on the basis of its promises. The third will require extensions into areas that were left uncharted by the Canada Act.

Human rights legislation is an operational resolution of the dilemma. Removing racial, linguistic, and religious disadvantages from our society can be promoted by the type of constitutional reform which will state equality for these groups and provide speedy equity as in the case of the aboriginal rights issues. The preoccupation of the law makers can no longer be with the competing levels of sovereignty of the "official duality" -- anglophones and francophones.

The rights of native peoples, the later visible minorities or Afro-Asians, and of the later European groups with traditions distinct from the Anglophone and Francophone communities cry out for attention. Only through a constitution that honours these five main presences in the Canadian society can we hope for the type of human rights' understanding that will be progressive and long lasting. Canadian unity itself is at stake!

Another type of resolution of current human rights inadequacies is one in which the schools may assist. Both core issues or plans for their school use were well outlined in Wes Knapp (1979) "Notes on Racism" and Gary Onstad (1979) "Working with Racism" in <u>Working Teacher</u>. Onstad outlines six centers of concerns: teachers, students, community/home-parents, information/materials, native education; and other. One may begin with his list, extend it and plan in-school strategies: one could be guided by the excellent outline of "Core of Knowledge available in most Native Indian communities in B.C. (or elsewhere)" (King, 1978, pp. 72-73). The suggestions below are adaptations from Onstad.

- where teacher colleagues openly express prejudice, we can persuade them to the contrary of the stated opinion.

- where we identify impact of media racism on our students we should delete that program or promote discussion on the issue. If our school system has built-in failure for native and immigrant children, we should identify this and suggest alternations.

- where our community lack meaningful school-community multicultural programs suggest some small beginnings. Promote respect for other languages and religions, and cooperate with ESL/ESD programs.

- remove biased materials, stimulate the development and analysis of the facts of Canadian multiethnicity in appropriate activities; and present, wherever possible, positive news about other countries and peoples.

- seek to counter high drop-out rate and also over-representation of native peoples and blacks in occupational type programs.

- avoid ethnic jokes and racist hmour.

The promotion of bilingualism -- official language and students' mother tongue -- whenever feasible, and the development of the type of music, social studies and art programs that respect the traditions of the five main Canadian groups (native people, Anglophones, Francophones, later Europeans, later visible minorities) will in its own small way serve the ends of salutary human rights concerns of a just Canada.

NOTES

Adachi, Ken, *The Enemy That Never Was*. Toronto: McClelland & Stewart, 1976.

Ashworth, Mary A., *The Forces Which Shaped Them*. Vancouver: New Star, 1979.

Berger, Thomas R., *Fragile Freedoms: Human Rights and Dissent in Canada*. Toronto: Clarke, Irwin, 1981.

-----. *Northern Frontier, Northern Homeland*. Toronto: James Lorimer, 1977.

Betcherman, Lita-Rose, *The Swastika and the Maple Leaf: Fascist Movements in Canada in the Thirties*. Toronto: Fitzhenry & Whiteside, 1975.

Canada, Indian Treaties and Surrenders. Toronto: Coles, Fascimile Editions, 1971.

Canada. *Statement of the Government of Canada on Indian Policy*. Ottawa: Queen's Printer, 1969.

Hawthorn, H.B., *A Survey of the Indians of Canada*. (2 Vol.) Ottawa: Queen's Printer, 1966, 1967.

Henry, Keith, "The Internal Conditions of Black Political Efforts in Toronto in the Half Century Following World War I". Toronto: mimeographed, n.d.

Human Rights Commission of B.C., *Proceedings of the Conference on Human Rights for British Columbians*. Victoria, February 1980.

Jones, Peter, "Theology and Ethnicity" in Keith McLeod (ed.) *Multiculturalism, Bilingualism and Canadian Institutions*. Toronto: University of Toronto, Faculty of Education, Guidance Center, 1979, pp. 53-60.

King, A. Richard, *Native Indians and Schooling in British Columbia*. Victoria: University of Victoria, Faculty of Education, 1978.

Knapp, Wes, "Notes on Racism", *Working Teacher*, Vol. 1, No. 3 (Winter 1979), pp. 11-13.

Notes cont'd.

Lane, E.B., H.W. Daniels, J.D. Blyan & R. Royer, "The Incarcerated Native", *Canadian Journal of Criminology*, Vo. 20, No. 3 (July 1978) pp. 308-316.

Lupul, Manoly R., "Multiculturalism and Canadian National Identity - The Alberta Experience" in E. Brian Titley & Peter J. Miller (eds.) *Education in Canada: An Interpretation*. Calgary: Detselig, 1982, pp. 209-218.

Onstad, Gary, "Working With Racism", *Working Teacher*, Vol. 1, No. 3 (Winter 1979), pp. 13-15.

Snow, Chief John, *These Mountains Are Our Sacred Places*. Toronto: Samuel Stevens, 1977.

Starr, Fred M., "Indians and the Criminal Justice System", *Canadian Journal of Criminology*, Vol. 20, No. 3 (July 1978) pp. 317-323.

Stewart, Walter, "Red Power" in J.S. Frideres (ed.) *Contemporary Conflicts*. Scarborough: Prentice-Hall, 1974, pp. 192-193.

Winks, Robin, *The Blacks in Canada*. New Haven: Yale, 1971

HUMAN RIGHTS IN CANADIAN EDUCATION
Douglas Ray

Questions that touch human rights are now being asked at every level of Canadian society. They involve decisions for individuals, voluntary organizations like Amnesty International, the churches and service clubs, and governments at every level. Many of these questions concern human rights for those in only the immediate community but some involve persons in other countries. Although very few Canadians are well informed on the details of such questions, many of which are highly controversial, more widespread interest suggests that human rights lie at the heart of decisions concerning society.

This chapter considers present debates that touch education and human rights in Canada. Official information was gained through correspondence, interviews, recent regulations, legislation and legal decisions. Popular opinion was deduced from editorials, letters to the editor, and submissions to appropriate decision makers. In all cases emphasis is upon processes of change, particularly identifying those which seem to be priorities.

Political Influences

Human rights may be respected in principle by all Canadians, but the means of promoting these are debated along political lines. Conservative governments have been in power both in Ottawa (recently) and in seven provinces (eight if the British Columbia government were classified as conservative). The Liberal, New Democratic and Parti Quebecois present the alternative in all cases. Minor parties take up more extreme positions:

the Western Canada Federalists and Libertarians as ultra-conservative, the Communist and Marxist-Leninist as ultra-radical. What happens to human rights when the electorate swings left or right for a combination of reasons? How much does it matter which party is governing?

Most of the arguments in previous chapters assume that the government (local, provincial or national) will provide or protect in order that human rights may be extended. These principles have been most closely reflected in the programs of the Liberal and New Democratic parties, and by the Parti-Quebecois. Conservatives propose a different view of how to promote human rights, one which stresses private sector involvement and responsibility. Although conservatives prefer to respond to initiatives, they may assist individuals or groups by providing help like expert advice to define or plan means of achieving their perceived goals. Conservatives will be criticized for ignoring problems that are not locally championed or forcing self-reliance upon those least competitive but not for pushing into private concerns.

This conservative philosophy is consistent with expansion of Human Rights Commissions, Ombudsmen and similar responsive agencies, while reducing the size and numbers of affirmative action programs.

It is also consistent with the monetarist view that inflation should be controlled by minimizing public spending, maintaining only the ultimate protection of social security for the jobless. On the whole, conservative philosophy would rely on the private sector to increase employment rather than to stimulate the economy with heavy government spending. On occasion Conservative governments have ignored this dogma, for example by Diefenbaker's aid to technical and vocational education which transformed education in most provinces. Similarly, Clark retained public sector official language instruction for unilingual federal civil servants. Although conservativism would imply that such instruction be left with the private sector, this would have resulted in the largest number of privately qualified bilingual civil servants having French as a mother tongue. English families and those speaking any other language would probably have been disadvantaged. Several provincial Conservative governments, including the long established Ontario regime, have very large public sectors justified in part by their concern for human rights.

Conservatives expect that government involvement in many expensive but socially justified activities will decline or increase more slowly. Although they seek an overall reduction in government costs and services, the priority among cutbacks is not yet firmly established. Services will survive if they are thought to enjoy broad popular support or moral justification. <u>Popular support</u> might be reflected for education that is free, available to all, and competitive with the best in other countries. In other words, slashing educational grants by provinces to universities, colleges, and school boards might prove politically unpopular despite the general demand for tax restraint or the need of other sectors for a larger share. <u>Moral justification</u> would result in extension of certain educational services, despite their possible high per student costs, to various disadvantaged groups: the physically handicapped, Indian schools, retraining the unemployed, single parents with no employment, etc. Although all these examples are strengthened by the human capital argument, even if education were not a good investment, society would expect many programs to continue, albeit sometimes in new formats.

Conservative philosophy stresses freedom _from_ government power. A significant early bill of the Clark government reflected this emphasis on open information concerning such government activities as police, immigration, and cabinet commissioned secret studies. The Trudeau government approved an amended version of this bill on its reelection. Human rights in education is involved in more than a nominal sense: if freedom of access is to be meaningful, citizens and non-government agencies must exercise and defend it. Adult education, probably through a media campaign, would be necessary to implement such a program; public education would be important to retain it. For youth, a school-based program would be a normal approach.

Model Institutions

Schools, colleges and universities do not yet model the ideal means of promoting human rights in all possible ways. For example, power too frequently replaces reason or participation in decision making. Information about what could be accomplished is not easily accessible to parents or pupils. The quality of programs or of teaching is sometimes shrouded in mystery, with intruders being repelled. Although educational institutions are among the most influential of all government agencies in the money required or the duration of their impact on every person, there are some aspects not closely studied and popularized. For example, educational spending has never been investigated by a dramatic public auditor like Maxwell Henderson. (Do we really have 500 years supply of inkwells?) More serious debates concern both the cost/benefit of programs and the adequacy of graduates' qualifications to earn a living or to participate as effective citizens.

The role of education in demonstrating or modelling human rights has been underutilized. The teaching force and school administrators are not a cross section of the population. Handicapped persons are still rare in these positions; even Indian schools cannot get enough Indian teachers; sexism is still general; age and seniority rather than competence determine most teachers' status and income. Although changes in these areas would be desirable, schools should not be expected to model the society desired by a political party that wishes to use government control or funding to promote its particular interest. Canadian teachers or professors have rarely officially endorsed or condemned the government of the day. Although relatively few have ever joined a political party, those who run for office rarely find their professional security thereby threatened. Provided the profession retains its present degree of academic freedom, party membership or activity will not be a factor in a teaching career.

Constitutional Problems

The Canada Act (1867) limits the areas where the Federal government can legally affect education. However, national influences are felt through general grants to provinces, regional equality, retraining, language opportunities, multiculturalism and cultural expression, Native peoples, and foreign students. Certain forms of reductions in family allowance, student loans and similar programs or increases in direct student costs like tuition fees would appear to violate Canada's international commitments for the progressive introduction of free education at the secondary and higher level [Internatioal Covenant on Economic, Social and Cultural Rights, 1966, par. 13(2)]. Changes in regulations concerning health care or in prosecution for certain offenses (like child abuse or sex crimes) will affect human rights and education indirectly.

Each province has its own urgent problems so common ground is hard to find. Nevertheless, certain causes appear to be widely promoted, linked at least potentially to both human rights and education, and in principle capable of being protected by legislation or government regulations. One widely shared provincial priority is that responsibility for education, including that promoted by radio or television, should remain a provincial matter. But provinces may need to cooperate more closely in order to serve needs like ethnic education more effectively and economically (Ray 1978). They are already cooperating in many programs for higher education and education at a distance.

Practices and regulations for the business and social worlds must be linked to those of schools before provinces are adequately serving human rights. For example job opportunities are not equally available to certain groups. Normally provinces have the necessary constitutional authority to require the private sector to improve its practices. In the long run education will advise the public of rights and responsibilities to make such programs work better.

Physical Disabilities

Most provinces have concluded that all government buildings, including schools and colleges, and stipulated other public buildings and certain apartments shall provide for physically handicapped persons. Timetables for conversion of old vacilities vary. Transportation problems often remain. Progress can be gauged by the appearance of wheelchair ramps or elevators, accessible toilet facilities, light switches and elevator controls, phones with adjustable volume, and labels which are clear to impaired vision. Food services are sometimes involved, particularly as institutions try to maintain profitable food services to a small number of users through the use of dispensers and the inevitably restricted menu. Although policy and physical changes may extend access at the official level, the ultimate objective is that all citizens must voluntarily admit handicapped persons into a wider circle of activities, and that the handicapped must learn to cope with many problems while exercising their rights.

Employment reforms now being discussed progressively require that those with handicaps may have preferred access to suitable work. Such changes, involving both changes of regulations and safeguards against violation, would transform the world for handicapped persons. The possibility of living in sheltered environments will give way to a nearly universal expectation of self-reliance and competitive vocational skills. There are already successful blind mechanics, paraplegic computer programmers, deaf mill workers, moronic process operators.... Many of them became productive, profitable workers; certainly requiring fewer concessions and less financial assistance than they would if structurally unemployed.

Such changes in society involve education in several important ways. There must be changes to permit students with special needs to attend and to learn effectively. This involves subsidies, transportation and special equipment, changes in schedules, special curricula, instructional materials and evaluation procedures. It is very important that teachers learn how they can ensure the best results from such changes.

Most provinces have changed or are changing regulations so that local school boards shall (instead of may) provide for education of all children, and therefore all pupils are required to attend. Previously those "not able to profit from instruction" was interpreted very broadly to save trouble and money. The proposed changes will mean that all children will learn how to adjust to special needs of their handicapped classmates, an ability that may enable future society to accept differences in more situations. (See for example McMurray's analysis).

Social Disadvantages

Although one need not equate physical with social or cultural disadvantages, the latter remain substantial barriers to equal participation in education, employment and other benefits of society. Important aspects of disadvantage are those of illegitimacy, poverty, language, sex - women usually are disadvantaged, but this may not always be true (Laferrière, 1975) - and race, especially Indians, Inuit and Métis, but also visible minority persons from Africa or Asia. For some purposes additional hurdles are legal status within Canada, with a progressive decline from native born, naturalized citizen, landed immigrant, visitor's or student visa, to illegal status. For still other purposes, age or the employer of one's parents (usually father) determines access to grants or other privileges. In some cases rights have been withheld -- perhaps illegally -- because of minor transgressions or personal relationships that violate community norms, such as religion, drinking customs or sexual orientation. This type of taboo may affect students, teachers or administrators.

Entitlement to Education is profoundly affected by social status but only some provinces have recognized the problem to be essentially structural, therefore justifying programs that would progressively reduce barriers. Such affirmative action programs are permitted under the Canada Act (15.2). For example, Saskatchewan Métis and non-status Indians are obviously disadvantaged. Among the programs designed to counter the problem are adult training courses which offer free tuition, free texts and course materials, training allowances and direct support to the sponsoring institutions. In 1977, daily support varied from $13.50 to $20.00, according to the number of dependents. Usually such programs are criticized for having too many white employees - especially those making decisions. The right blend of intervention is hard to establish (Moore-Eyman, 1977). Preventing Abuse (Notably of children, students, teachers, mothers and others who may require protection) is easily accepted in principle, but Canadian traditions almost sanctify the rights of certain persons to abuse under the guise of protection. Parents, husbands, teachers and principals are sometimes excessively cruel. Ontario illustrates how these traditions may be challenged. Mary Van Stolk's persuasive argument in The Battered Child in Canada (1972) was followed by a tragic, politically compelling and thoroughly reported case of child battering where child welfare safeguards were heavily criticized. In this interval of popular preparedness for reform, a determined Attorney General strengthened the previous guidelines for teachers and other public servants likely to become aware of child abuse. Like the police, teachers had previously been reluctant to become involved in domestic disputes, a delay that sometimes led to tragedy. Now there are obligations for teachers to learn their new responsibilities of detecting reasonable grounds for suspecting abuse and they are legally protected against retaliation if the suspicions prove to be unfounded.

Violence against adults may be lessened by two kinds of changes: in regulations and in technology. Although regulations against carrying weapons are traditionally opposed by well organized and financially influential gun owners and users, schools could if necessary be screened by devices like those for detecting illegal removal of library books or merchandise. Throughout Canadian history there have been occasional incidents where weapons in schools have caused death or injury, although these occasions have been infrequent when compared with the violence in bars, brothels and bank lobbies. Although the frequency or at least the seriousness of attacks in schools will be reduced as a result of gun control legislations, Canadian principals, teachers or pupils have no real assurance that the planned attack can be averted. It is doubtful whether any Canadian schools could justify the use of a security force. There has been no serious attempt to educate youth to accept a society forbidding the owning and use of firearms or the regular carrying of other weapons like knives. Campaigns to the population as a whole are sometimes viewed as state control.

Promoting security rather than dealing with abuse has led to several new regulations affecting education. Examples include closer attention to school bus inspections, restriction of passenger behaviour, training and testing of drivers. There are periodic upgradings of comparable standards of educational premises and procedures: physical education, shops, and laboratories. One recent example involved the precautionary removal from all school laboratories of a potentially explosive chemical. However, the building materials (asbestos) or dangers from a school's landsite (radon gas) may be involved. One of the values of periodic reviews and changes is the opportunity thereby presented for professional development, civic education and participatory democracy. Occasionally precautions are not introduced until a tragedy alerts authorities to their importance.

Educational Management

It is difficult to recognize when procedures once thought to safeguard human rights acquire the appearance of threats. That seems to have happened with compulsory attendance, originally introduced to prevent child labour and promote the child's right to education. A similar misalignment may have happened with the reversal of the expansion of enrolments, accessibility, resources and programs that characterized Canadian education since confederation. Contraction has meant that long established policies sometimes exacerbate the problems - for example pitting seniority or class size arguments against those for quality of instruction and diversity of faculty (Ray, 1980). These problems have been clarified for Ontario by the multi-volume Jackson Report (1978) with its supporting monographs, but there are still relatively unexamined problems like the reasons for stopping out from voluntary attendance (i.e. from colleges and universities) or the differences among participation rates for different segments of the population.

Even worse are the failures to recognize the seriousness of the human rights questions involved in establishing priorities (Ray 1981). Who shall retain jobs when cuts are made? How will the highly qualified unemployed or underemployed be treated? How will the poorly qualified be dealt with? Will school closings bear principally on minority groups?

After a very long struggle to obtain entry and to build demand for educational opportunity for minority groups (e.g., the sexual, racial, religious, economic and linguistic disadvantaged) <u>mismanagement</u> of decline would remove many of the gains made and possibly result in bitter recriminations. It must be recognized that even with equal educational qualifications such minorities are sometimes disadvantaged in the market place despite the continual efforts of provincial human rights commissions. If educational equality becomes more difficult to achieve, their futures and that for social justice in Canada become bleak indeed.

<u>Monitoring Outputs</u>. For many years Canadian education was helped by financial equalization systems. There is little prospect of a poor municipal government closing schools because teachers cannot be paid (like Chicago, Detroit or New York). Nor have sparcely populated regions with a low tax base been unable to provide quality education.

But financial measures that help provide facilities and qualified teachers do not ensure opportunity. When drop-out rates remain very high, when pupils are habitually absent, when graduates prove unable to compete in further education or in the work force, there is an indication of a problem that is very serious. To be properly advised about such conditions and their possible corrections requires new research and management practices that are not yet adequate in many provinces.

<u>Responsibility</u>

It may be convenient to think that governments, employers or some other authorities are responsible for the many remaining imperfections in society. To a degree this may be so. But individuals can assume a greater role if they choose to do so, perhaps by making effective use of existing systems.

An example is the fairly large number of inequalities between women and men in education: pay scales, fringe benefits, promotion opportunities. If a collective agreement exists (as is normally the case for teachers in tax supported schools) the federation or union of employees share with the employer responsibility for its contents. If in negotiating many contracts, the teachers have bargained for more money but neglected injustices or imperfections in the conditions of their work, they should share the blame. If part of the membership has not tried to influence their negotiating team nor tried to gain office themselves, that diffidence is partly responsible for collective bargaining that addressed the wrong issues. It is easy for any reader to find examples of local importance. Different rates of salary deductions for men and women who will receive the same pension, recognition of experience in only certain fields (veterans for example) as a basis for seniority or promotion, and the expectation that the wife will follow her husband when he is transferred or seeks a job in a distant place, illustrate both the usual local and provincial practices. The issues involved are not unique to education, but they are among those that could be addressed quite effectively within education.

It may be well to conclude with the emphasis upon responsibility. Clearly the governments have shown some leadership, with all but Quebec agreeing on a new Constitution that emphasizes human rights. Quebec has its own Charter of Rights that is both comprehensive and generous. Educational practices are already enlightened for the most part and compare favorably with those in most other nations. The images of despair are confined to a relatively small number of Canadians so it should be possible to deal with them if an acceptable way can be found.

The acceptability of various reforms is crucial. In the past certain proposals have led to bitter opposition from some of the supposed beneficiaries. A noted example was the 1969 White Paper which proposed to end federal responsibility for Indian education (Weaver 1981). In the long run a series of alternatives was worked out with the bands participating more fully. Similar dialogues are advocated everywhere if good intentions are to be transformed into good programs.

NOTES

Commission on Declining School Enrolments in Ontario (The Jackson Report) The Challenge of Declining Enrolments. Toronto: Ministry of Education, 1978.

Commission on Declining School Enrolments in Ontario (The Jackson Report) The Missing Pupils in the Schools of Ontario Today and Tomorrow - A Statement of Conditions, Causes and Issues. Toronto: Ministry of Education, 1978.

Commission on Declining School Enrolments in Ontario (The Jackson Report) Implications of Declining Enrolment for the Schools of Ontario - A Statement of Effects and Solutions. Toronto: Ministry of Education, 1978.

Laferrière, Michel "Les Femmes, Les Noirs et Les Homosexuels", McGill Journal of Education, X:1 (Spring 1975), 70, 76.

Moore-Eyman, Evelyn "A University's Search for a System of Delivering Basic Skills to Canadian Native Peoples - A concurrent approach" in Vincent D'Oyley (ed.) The Impact of Multi-Ethnicity on Canadian Education. Toronto: Urban Alliance on Race Relations, 1977, 120-146.

Ray, Douglas "Alternative Scenarios for Managing Educational Contraction", Canadian Journal of Education, 6:1 (1981), 65-72.

Ray, Douglas "The Canadian Educational Take-Off: An Account, Some Comparisons, and Conjectures", Canadian and International Education, 3:2 (Dec. 1974), 1-23.

Ray, Douglas "Ethnicity and Reorientation of the Curriculum in Canada", Comparative Education, 14:1 (March 1978), 19-32.

Ray, Douglas "The Management of Educational Collapse" in Robin Farquhar & Ian Housego (eds.) Proceedings and Selected Papers from the I.I.P. '78 Conference for Educational Administrators. Vancouver: University of British Columbia, 1980, 297-304.

Van Stolk, Mary The Battered Child in Canada. Toronto: McClelland & Stewart, 1972.

Weaver, Sally M. Making Canadian Indian Policy. The Hidden Agenda 1968-1970. Toronto: University of Toronto Press, 1981.

BIBLIOGRAPHY

- compiled by Douglas Ray and
Danny Zawadsky.

This bibliography emphasizes recent studies, Canadian themes, and Canadian authors. It includes several studies, some popular sources, some visual materials and a few frequently cited 'classic' studies that extend the themes of Human Rights in Canadian Education.

ABBOT, Sylvia "Gifted Children, Our Wasted Resource", B.C. Teacher (Nov./Dec. 1979), 64, 65, 71.

ADACHI, Ken The Enemy That Never Was. Toronto: McClelland & Stewart, 1976.

ADAMS, G.R. & A.S. Cohen "Examination of Cumulative Folder Information Used by Teachers in Making Differential Judgments of Children's Abilities", Alberta Journal of Educational Research, 22:3 (Sept. 1976), 216-225.

ADAMS, Howard The Education of Canadians 1800-1867. The Roots of Separatism. Montreal: Harvest House, 1968.

ADAMS, Ian et al. The Real Poverty Report. Edmonton: Hurtig, 1971.

ANDERSON, D. "The Failure of Paternalism, Aboriginal Education in Victoria", Dialogue, 7:3 (Dec. 13, 1974), 57-62.

ANDERSON, J.T.M. The Education of the New Canadian. London and Toronto: J.M. Ent & Sons Limited, 1918.

ANSELMO, S. "Parent Involvement in the Schools", Clearing House, 50 (March 1977), 297-299.

AOKI, T., J. Dahlie & W. Werner (eds.) Canadian Ethnicity: The Politics of Meaning. Vancouver: Center for the Study of Curriculum and Instruction, University of British Columbia, 1978.

AOKI, Ted T. "Curriculum Approaches to Canadian Ethnic Histories in the Context of Citizenship Education", History and Social Science Teacher, 13:2 (Winter 1978), 95-99.

ARMSTRONG, D. A Selective Bibliography on Human and Civil Rights. Toronto: Ministry of Labour, 1973.

ARNOLD, A.J. "How Far Do We Go With Multi-Culturalism?", Canadian Ethnic Studies, 2:2 (Dec. 1970), 7-14.

ASHWORTH, Mary The Forces Which Shaped Them. A History of the Education of Minority Group Children in British Columbia. Vancouver: New Star Books Limited, 1979.

ASHWORTH, M. *Immigrant Children and Canadian Schools*. Toronto: McClelland & Stewart Limited, 1975.

AYIM, M. "School as a Mixed Blessing: The Female Perspective", *Teacher Education* (Apr. 1978), 60-74.

BANE, Mary J. "Marital Disruption and the Lives of Children", *Journal of Social Issues*, 32:1, (1976).

BANKS, J.A. "Ethnic Studies as a Process of Curricular Reform", *Social Education*, 40 (Feb. 1976), 76-80.

BANTON, Michael *The Idea of Race*. London: Tavistock, 1977.

BARGEN, Peter *The Legal Status of the Canadian Public School Pupil*. Toronto: Macmillan, 1961.

BASSETT, I. *The Parlour Rebellion: Profiles in the Struggle for Women's Rights*. Toronto: McClelland & Stewart, 1975.

BAUREISS, G. "The Chinese Community of Calgary", *Canadian Ethnic Studies*, 3:1 (June 1971), 43-55.

BEAUCHAMP, Tom L. *Ethnics and Public Policy*. Toronto: Prentice Hall, 1975.

BELOK, Michael V., Shoub, Ralph (eds.) *Sex, Race, Ethnicity and Education*. Meerut, India: Anu Prakashan, 1976.

BERGEN, J. "A Decision that Shook Education in Alberta", *Challenge in Educational Administration*, XVIII:1 (1979), 32-42.

BERGER, Thomas R. *Fragile Freedoms: Human Rights and Dissent in Canada*. Toronto: Clarke, Irwin, 1981.

BERKLEY, H., C. Guffield & G. West "Children's Rights in a Canadian Context", *Interchange*, 8:1-2 (1977-78), 1-4.

BERKLEY, H., Chad Guffield & W. Gordon West *Children's Rights: Legal and Educational Issues*. Toronto: Ontario Institute for Studies in Education, 1978.

BERNSTEIN, B. *Class, Codes and Control: Theoretical Studies Toward a Sociology of Language*. Don Mills: Paperjacks, 1974 (2nd edition).

BERNSTEIN, M. & F. DiVesta "The Formation and Reversal of an Attitude as Functions of Assumed Self-Concept, Race, and Socio Economic Class", *Child Development*, 42 (1971) 1417-1431.

BERNSTEIN, N. *Diminished People: Problems and Care of the Mentally Retarded*. Boston: Little, Brown, 1970.

BERRY, W. John, et al. *Multiculturalism and Ethnic Attitudes in Canada*. Ottawa: Dept. of Supply and Services, 1977.

BEZEAU, L.M. "Equality of Education: Opportunity and Inequality of Per Pupil Expenditures", *Alberta Journal of Educational Research*, XXIII (3 Sept. 1977), 218-225.

BOGGS, Theodore H. "The Oriental on the Pacific Coast", *Queen's Quarterly* (Jan./March 1926), 311-324.

BRETT, Joyce "What's That Honey? Sex Role Stereotyping", *Challenge in Educational Administration*, XVIII:1 (1978), 10-15.

BRIDGES, S. *Problems of the Gifted Child*. New York: Crane Russak, 1973.

BROOKS, J.R. "Teaching Native Children: Lessons from Cognitive Society", *Journal of Educational Thought*, 12:1 (Apr. 1978), 56-67.

BROPHY, J. & Thomas L. Good *Teacher-Student Relationships: Causes and Consequences*. Toronto: Holt-Rinehart (1974), 400.

BROUDY, H.S. "Cultural Pluralism, New Wine in Old Bottles", *Educational Leadership*, 33 (Dec. 1975), 173-175.

BROWN, James A. "Intercultural Understanding", *McGill Journal of Education*, X:2 (Fall 1976), 270-278.

BROWNLIE, I. *Basic Documents on Human Rights*. Oxford: Clarendon, 1971.

BULLIED, George J. *The People Of The Valley*. Wardsville: Twin Valley Press, 1976.

BUNDY, McGeorge "Beyond Bakke: What Future for Affirmative Action?" *Atlantic*, 242:5 (Nov. 1978), 69-73.

BURNET, J. "Myths and Multiculturalism", *Canadian Journal of Education*, 4:4 (1979), 43-58.

BURTON, Anthony *The Horn and the Beanstalk*. Toronto: Holt Rinehart & Winston, 1972.

BUSKIN, Martin *Parent Power*. New York: Walker & Co., 1975.

CAIRNS, Kathleen V. "Women and School Administration", *Journal of Educational Thought*, 9:3 (Dec. 1975), 165-175.

Canada: Department of Labour *Human Rights in Canada*. Ottawa: Ministry of Supply and Services, 1978.

Canada *Indian Conditions - A Survey*. Ottawa: Indian and Northern Affairs, 1980.

Canadian Consultative Council on Multi-Culturalism Multi-Culturalism as
     State Policy. Ottawa: C C C on M, 1976.

Canadian Consultative Council on Multi-Culturalism First Annual Report
     of the Canadian Consultative Council on Multiculturalism.
     Ottawa: C C C on M, 1975.

Canadian Council for Children and Youth Admittance Restricted: The
     Child as Citizen in Canada. Ottawa: C.C.C.Y., 1978.

CARD, Brigham Young The Emerging Role of the Community Education
     Coordinator in Alberta. Edmonton: University of Alberta, 1975.

CARDINAL, Harold The Rebirth of Canada's Indians. Edmonton: Hurtig, 1977.

CARLTON, Richard A., Louise A. Colley & Neil J. MacKinnon Education,
     Change and Society: A Sociology of Canadian Education. Toronto:
     Gage, 1977.

Center for the Study of Democratic Institutions "Child Abuse and Neglect
     in the American Society", The Center Magazine (March/Apr. 1978) 70-77.

CHARTRAND, Luc "Une Enclave Inuit à Dorval", Education Québec, 9:5
     (Feb./March 1979) 19-21.

Children's Rights: Educational and Legal Issues, Interchange, Special
     Issue, 8:1,2 (1977-78).

CHURCHILL, Stacy "International Education and Education on Human Rights
     The Canadian Experience", Canadian and International Education, 9:1
     (1980), 6-32.

CHURCHILL, Stacy "National Linguistic Minorities: The Franco-Ontarian
     Educational Renaissance", Prospects, VI:3 (1976), 439-450.

CIPYWNYK, Sonia "Multiculturalism and the Child in Western Canada: Then
     and Now". Western Regional Conference of the Canadian Association
     for Curriculum Studies, Saskatoon, Feb. 1978.

CLARKE, Austin & Hank Clarke "Caribbean Canadians Adapting to the Metropolis".
     Toronto: Ontario Institute for Studies in Education, 1977.

CLAUDE, Richard P. Comparative Human Rights. Baltimore: John Hopkins, 1976.

COELHO, Elizabeth "Curriculum Change for a Multicultural Society",
     Teacher Education (Apr. 1978), 74-80.

COIGNEY, Virginia Children are People Too. New York: Wm. Morrow & Co., 1975.

Commission on Declining School Enrolments in Ontario (The Jackson Report)
     The Challenge of Declining Enrolments. Toronto: Ministry of
     Education, 1978.

Commission on Declining School Enrolments in Ontario (The Jackson Report) *Implications of Declining Enrolment for the Schools of Ontario A Statement of Effects and Solutions*. Toronto: Ministry of Education, 1978.

Commission on Declining School Enrolments in Ontario (The Jackson Report) *The Missing Pupils in the Schools of Ontario Today and Tomorrow: A Statement of Conditions, Causes and Issues*. Toronto: Ministry of Education, 1978.

Community Relations Commission "Recruiting Minority Group Teachers", *Teacher Education and Community Relations*, II:2 (Spring 1974), 1.

Community Relations Commission and the Association of Teachers in Colleges and Departments of Education *Teacher Education for a Multi-Cultural Society*. London: Community Relations Commission, 1974.

CORRY, James Alexander *The Power of the Law*. Toronto: CBC, 1971, 746-751 (The Massey Lectures, 1971).

COULTER, Karen "Like Talking to a Horse", *B.C. Teacher* (May/June 1978), 187-188.

Council of Ministers of Education *The State of Minority Language Education in The Ten Provinces of Canada*. Toronto: Council of Ministers of Education, Toronto, Canada, 1978.

CRITTENDEN, Brian "Ethnic Pluralism and Moral Education in the Public Schools" in Terance Morrison & Anthony Burton (eds.) *Options: Reforms and Alternatives for Canadian Education*. Toronto: Holt, Rinehart & Winston, 1973, 171-180.

CUMMING, Peter A., Neil H. Mickenberg *Native Rights in Canada*. Toronto: Indian-Eskimo Association of Canada, 1972, 2nd edition.

CURLE, Adam "Reflections on Working in a University", *Studies in Higher Education*, 2:1 (1977), 9-13.

CURTIS, James E. & Ronald D. Lambert "Educational Status and Reactions to Social and Political Heterogeneity", *Canadian Review of Sociology and Anthropology*, 13:2 (May 1976), 189-203.

CURWIN, Richard L. & Fuhrmann, Barbara Schneider *Discovering Your Teaching Self, Humanistic Approaches to Effective Teaching*. Englewood Cliffs, N.J.: Prentice Hall Inc., 1975.

DENNIS, Wayne & Margaret Dennis *The Intellectually Gifted: An Overview*. New York: Grune & Stratton, 1976.

Department of Indian and Northern Affairs "Indian Control of Indian Education", *Indian Education*, III:5 (June 1973).

Department of Indian and Northern Affairs *Statement of the Government of Canada on Indian Policy, 1969*. Ottawa: Government of Canada, 1969.

D'OYLEY, Vincent *Black Presence in Multi-Ethnic Canada*. Vancouver: Center for the Study of Curriculum and Instruction, University of British Columbia, and Toronto: Ontario Institute for Studies in Education, 1978.

D'OYLEY, Vincent "Comments on Whether Multi-Culturalism Should Have An Impact on Testing and Counselling", *School Guidance*, 30 (March/Apr. 1975), 9-13.

D'OYLEY, Vincent *The Impact of Multi-Ethnicity on Canadian Education*. Toronto: Urban Alliance on Race Relations, 1977.

D'OYLEY, Vincent R. "Schooling and Ethnic Rights", *Interchange*, 8:1-2 (1977-78), 101-108.

DUCKWORTH, Eleanor "Assessing the Canadian Studies Foundation Phase 1: An Approach to National Evaluation", *Canadian Journal of Education*, 2:1 (1977), 27-34.

DYLWARD, Gunnar "Basic Legal Aspects in Providing Medical, Educational, Social and Vocational Help to the Mentally Retarded", *Journal of Special Education*, 7:1 (1973), 39-50.

ECKSTEIN, M. "Ultimate Deterrents: Punishment and Control in English and American Schools", *Comparative Education Review*, 10:3 (Oct. 1966), 433-441.

EDEN, D. *Mental Handicap, an Introduction*. Toronto: Wiley, 1975.

EDGENTON, D. *The Physically Handicapped Child in Your Classroom*. Springfield, Ill.: Charles Thomas, 1976.

EDWARDS, R. "Language Politics and Ethnicity as Educational Variables: The Quebec Case", *Compare*, 8:1 (1978), 15-30.

EASTABROOK, Glenn "School Change and the Implications for Students' Rights", *Interchange*, 8:1-2 (1977-78), 128-142.

ELLIOTT, J.L. *Minority Canadians Vol. II, Immigrant Groups*. Scarborough: Prentice Hall, 1971.

ELLIOTT, J.L. *Minority Canadians Vol. I, Native Peoples*. Scarborough: Prentice Hall, 1971.

ELLIOTT, J.L. *Two Nations, Many Cultures: Ethnic Groups in Canada*. Scarborough: Prentice Hall, 1979.

EMERSON, Goldwin J. "The Egalitarian Paradox in Public Education", *Canadian Journal of Education*, 4:3 (1979), 53-59.

EPP, Frank H. The Mennonites in Canada 1786-1920. The History of a Separate People. Toronto: Macmillan, 1974.

FAURE, Edgar et al. Learning To Be: The World of Education Today and Tomorrow. Paris: UNESCO, 1972.

FINCHER, Cameron I. "Institutional Practice and Threats to Individual Privacy", New Directions in Institutional Research, 14 (Summer 1977), 17-31.

FISCHER, L., & J.A. Cheyne Sex Roles: Biological and Cultural Interactions As Found in Social Science Research and Ontario Educational Media. Toronto: The Ministry of Education, 1977.

FISHMAN, Joshua A. Bilingual Education: An International Sociological Perspective. Rowley, Ma.: Newberry Publishing House, 1976.

FLATHAM, Richard E. The Practice of Rights. Cambridge, England: Cambridge University Press, 1976.

FLEMING, W.G. Educational Opportunity. Scarborough: Prentice-Hall, 1974.

FLYGARE, Thomas "The Legal Rights of Teachers", Bloomington, Indiana: Phi Delta Kappan, 1976.

FONTANA, Vincent J. Somewhere A Child is Crying. New York: Macmillan, 1973.

FORCESE, Dennis The Canadian Class Structure. Toronto: McGraw-Hill, 1975.

FOUNTAINE, M. "Responsiveness and the Multi-cultural Society". Education Canada, 15 (Winter 1975), 49-52.

FRAENKEL, Jack R. et al. The Struggle for Human Rights: A Question of Values. New York: Random House, 1975.

FRETZ, J. Winfield The Mennonites in Ontario. Waterloo: Mennonite Society of Ontario, 1967.

FRIDERES, James S. "Termination or Migration: The Hutterites - A Case Study", Canadian Ethnic Studies, 3:1 (June 1973), 17-24.

FRIEDENBERG, Edgar Z. "The Limits to Growth: Adolescence in Canada", McGill Journal of Education, XV:2 (1980), 131-138.

FRIESEN, J.W. "Mennonites and Hutterites in Twentieth Century Alberta Literature with Special Reference to Educational Implications", Alberta Journal of Educational Research, XXII:2 (June 1976), 106-128.

GALLAGHER, James J. Teaching the Gifted Child. Boston: Allyn & Bacon, 1975.

GARCIA, Ricardo L. "Fostering a Pluralistic Society Through Multi-Ethnic Education", *Phi Delta Kappan*, 1978.

GASTILL, Raymond D. "The Relationship of Regional Cultures to Educational Performance", *Sociology of Education*, 45 (Fall 1972), 408-425.

GENESEE, Fred "The Suitability of Immersion Programs for All Children", *Canadian Modern Language Review*, 32:5 (May 1976), 494-515.

GEZI, Kalil "Education, Race, Ethnicity and Integration" in Kalil Gezi (ed.) *Education in Comparative and International Perspectives*. Toronto: Holt, Rinehart & Winston, 1971, 373-379.

GIBBON, John Murray *The Canadian Mosaic: The Making of a Northern Nation*. Toronto: McClelland & Stewart, 1938.

GIBSON, Joy & Prue Chennells *Gifted Children: Looking to their Future*. London: Latimer, 1976.

GILBERT, Sid & Hugh A. McRoberts "Differentiation and Stratification: The Issue of Inequality" in Dennis Forcese & Stephen Richer (eds.) *Issues in Canadian Society: An Introduction to Sociology*. Scarborough: Prentice-Hall, 1975, 91-136.

GILCHRIST, Robert S. & Bernice R. Roberts *Curriculum Development, A Humanized Systems Approach*. Belmont, California: Lear Siegler, Inc., Fearon Publishers, 1974.

GINSBURG, Morris *On Justice in Society*. Harmondsworth, Middlesex: Penguin, 1971, 1965.

GLAZER, Nathan & Daniel P. Moynihan *Beyond the Melting Pot*. Cambridge, Mass.: Harvard University Press, 1963, 1970.

GLAZER, Nathan & Daniel P. Moynihan *Ethnicity, Theory and Experience*. Cambridge, Mass.: Harvard University Press, 1975.

GOLDENBERG, Ronald & Bruce McNair "The Child No One Knows", *The Journal of Educational Thought*, XI:1 (April 1977), 28-32.

GOTLIEB, Allan Ezra *Human Rights, Federalism and Minorities*. Toronto: Canadian Institute for International Affairs, 1970.

GREENFIELD, T. Barr "Bilingualism, Multiculturalism and the Crisis of Purpose" in Merrill Swain, *Bilingualism in Canadian Education: Issues and Research*, 3rd Yearbook of CSSE, 1976, 107-136.

GULUTSAN, Metro "Language Learning in Culturally Diverse Contexts: Some Psychological Considerations", *Compare*, 8:1 (1978), 69-80.

GWYN, S. "Multiculturalism: A Threat and a Promise", *Saturday Night* (Feb. 1974), 15-18.

HALEY, Alex *Roots: The Saga of an American Family*. New York (Garden City): Doubleday, 1976.

HALLAHAN, Daniel B. & James M. Kauffman *Exceptional Children: An Introduction to Special Education*. Scarborough: Prentice-Hall, 1978.

HARNEY, R. & Harold Troper *Immigrants, Portrait of the Urban Experience, 1890-1930*. Toronto: Van Nostrand Limited, 1975.

HARRIS, John J. "The Culturally Different: An Analysis of Factors Influencing Educational Success", *Clearing House*, 50:1 (Sept. 1976), 39-43.

HATT, Fred K. "The Canadian Metis: Recent Interpretations", *Canadian Ethnic Studies*, 3:1 (June 1971), 1-16.

HAWKINS, Freda *Canada and Immigration: Public Policy and Public Concern*. Montreal: McGill-Queen's University Press, 1972.

HAYWARD, Gordon "What Do Parents Expect of Education?", *Challenge in Educational Administration*, XIII:2 (1974), 8-19.

HENRY, Francis *Forgotten Canadians: The Blacks of Nova Scotia*. Don Mills: Longman Canada Ltd., 1973.

HERSCH, Jeanne *Birthright of Man*. Paris: UNESCO, 1969.

HERSOM, Naomi "The Recentralization of B.C. Curriculum" in Robin Farguhar & Ian Housego (eds.) *Canadian and Comparative Educational Administration*. Vancouver: University of British Columbia, 1980.

HEYMAN, Richard D. "A Political Economy of Minority Group Knowledge Demands", *Compare*, 8:1 (1978), 3-14.

HILL, Daniel G. *Human Rights in Canada: A Focus on Racism*. Toronto: Canadian Labour Congress, 1977.

HODGETTS, A. Birnie & Paul Gallagher *Teaching Canada for the '80s*. Toronto: Ontario Institute for Studies in Education, 1978.

HOROWITZ, Irving Louis "On Human Rights and Social Obligations", *Society* (Nov./Dec. 1977), 26-27.

HOWARD, Joseph Kinsey *The Strange Empire of Louis Riel*. Toronto: Swan Publishing, 1970.

HUGHES, David R. & Evelyn Kallen *The Anatomy of Racism: Canadian Dimensions*. Montreal: Harvest House, 1974.

HUGHES, John F. & Anne O. Hughes Equal Education: A New National Strategy. Bloomington: Indiana University Press, 1972.

Human Rights in Canada 1976: Legislation. Ottawa: Canada Department of Labour, 1976

Human Rights in Canada 1975: Legislation and Decisions. Ottawa: Department of Labour, 1974.

Human Rights Research in Canada. Ottawa: Queen's Printer, Department of Labour, 1974.

Human Rights Review. Ottawa: Citizenship Branch, Department of the Secretary of State, 1970.

Human Rights Studies in Universities. Paris: UNESCO, 1973.

HUMPHREY, J. "The Role of Canada in the U.N. Program for the Promotion of Human Rights", Canadian Perspectives on International Law and Organization (1974), 612-619.

HUNKA, Steve "Prospectives in Educational Research", McGill Journal of Education, XIV:2 (Spring 1979), 149-162.

JACKSON, R. "Canada: Decline and Fall", CSSE News, 3:9 (May 1977), 10-12.

JAENEN, Cornelius J. "An Introduction to Education and Ethnicity", Canadian Ethnic Studies, 8:1 (1976), 3-8.

JAENEN, Cornelius J. "Minority Group Schooling and Canadian National Unity", Journal of Educational Thought, 7:2 (Aug. 1973), 81-93.

JAMIESON, Kathleen Indian Women and the Law in Canada. Ottawa: Ministry of Supply and Services, 1978.

JANKOWSKI, Paul & Frances Jankowski Accelerated Programs for the Gifted Music Student. West Nyack, New York: Parker, 1976.

JANNE, Henri "Educational Needs of the 16-19 Age Group: A Sociological Perspective", International Review of Education, XXI:2 (1975), 127-148.

JENCKS, Christopher et al. Inequality: A Reassessment of the Effect of Family and Schooling in America. London: Allen Lane, 1973.

JENKINS, E.C. "Multi-ethnic Literature: Promise and Problems", Education Digest, 39 (Oct. 1973), 55-58.

JONES, Richard A. "Freedom and Discrimination in Canada", Quarterly of Canadian Studies, II:3 (1973), 144-154.

JOHNSON, F.L. et al. "Teachers' Attitudes Affect Their Work With Minorities", *Educational Leadership*, 32 (Dec. 1974), 193-198.

JURY, Mark & Dan Jury *Gramp*. New York: Viking, 1976.

KALLEN, Evelyn *Ethnicity and Human Rights in Canada*. Toronto: Gage, 1982.

KARNES, M.B. & R.R. Zehrback "Parental Attitudes and Education in the Culture of Poverty", *Journal of Research and Development in Education*, 8 (Winter 1975), 44-53.

KEHOE, John "Ethnic Prejudice and the Role of the School", *Perspectives*, 12:1 (Winter 1977), 11-14.

KEHOE, John "Group Understanding and Human Rights". Vancouver: University of British Columbia, 1977.

KEHOE, John "We Need More Good News", *Multiculturalism* II:1 (1978), 17-19.

KELNER, Merrijoy "Ethnic Penetration into Toronto's Elite Structure", *Canadian Review of Sociology and Anthropology*, 7:2 (1970) and *Critical Issues in Canadian Society*. Toronto: Holt, Rinehart & Winston, 1971, 329-336.

KENNETH, Keniston *All Our Children*. New York: Harcourt, Brace, Jovanovich, 1977.

KEREKES, Andrew Z. & Ian J. Collins "Government Action to Secure Human Rights", *The Quarterly of Canadian Studies*, II:4 (1973), 224-229.

KINDRACHUK, M.J. "Some Thoughts on Multiculturalism", *Education Canada*, 15 (Winter 1975), 59-61.

KOLMES, Jo-Ann "Spare the Rod and Spoil the Child", *ATA* (March/Apr. 1975), 6-11.

KOSTASH, Myrna *All of Baba's Children*. Edmonton: Hurtig, 1977.

KOSTASH, Myrna "Questions About Ethnics: An Open Letter From Edmonton", *This Magazine*, 11 (Jan./Feb. 1977), 10-11.

KOVAKS, L. Martin *Ethnic Canadians: Culture and Education*. Regina: Canadian Plains Research Centre, 1978.

LAFERRIERE, Michel "Les Femmes, Les Noires et les Homosexuels", *McGill Journal of Education*, X:1 (Spring 1975), 70-76.

LAPATI, Americo D. "Education: Privilege, Claim or Right?, *Education Theory*, 26:1 (Winter 1976), 19-28.

LAWRENCE, Charles "The Bakke Case: Are Racial Quotas Defensible?", *Saturday Review* (Oct. 15, 1977), 10-16.

LAWSON, Robert F. "On the Ideological Conditions of Canadian Independence", British Journal of Educational Studies, XXIII (Feb. 1975), 24-48.

LAYCOCK, Samuel Ralph Gifted Children: A Handbook for the Classroom Teacher. Vancouver: Copp Clark, 1957.

LAYCOCK, Samuel Ralph Special Education in Canada (Quance Lectures of 1963). Toronto: Gage, 1963.

LAYCOCK, Samuel Ralph Study of Educational Provisions For and Needs of Emotionally Disturbed Children in the Elementary and Secondary Schools of British Columbia. Vancouver: Educational Research Institute of British Columbia, 1969.

"Legal Aspects of Corporal Punishment in Canada", Saskatchewan Administrator, 10:1 (July 1977), 24-36.

LESSARD, Claude "The Montreal School Reorganization Process: Why or Why Not?", Canadian and International Education, 9:1 (1980), 33-47.

LEVIN, Malcolm & Christine Sylvester Rights of Youth. Toronto: General Publishing, 1972.

LEVITAN, Sar A., William B. Johnston & Robert Taggart Minorities in the United States: Problems, Progress and Prospect. Washington, D.C.: Public Affairs Press, 1975.

LIPKIN, John P. & Robert F. Lawson "Perspective on Multiculturalism in North America: Minority Education in Toronto and Montreal", Compare, 8:1 (1978), 31-44.

LIPKIN, John "Le sort des immigrants en France", CSSE Bulletin, 2:8 (Sept. 1974).

LIPPIMANN, Leopold & I. Ignacy Goldberg Right to Education: Anatomy of the Pennsylvania Case and its Implications for Exceptional Children. New York: Teachers' College Press, 1973.

LOMAX, A. & N. Berkowitz "Evolutionary Taxonomy of Culture", Science, 180 (June 1, 1973), 907-8.

LORENZO, Morris "The Politics of Education and Language in Quebec, A Comparative Perspective", Canadian and International Education, 5:2 (Dec. 1976), 1-38.

LOWENFIELD, B. The Visually Handicapped Child in School. New York: John Day, 1973.

LUPUL, Manoly R. "Bilingual Education and the Ukrainians in Western Canada: Possibilities and Problems" in Merrill Swain (ed.) *Bilingualism in Canadian Education: Issues and Research*. Yearbook of the CSSE, Vol. 3. Edmonton: University of Alberta, 1976.

LUPUL, Manoly R. "Multiculturalism and Educational Policies in Canada", *Compare*, 8:1 (1978), 45-50.

LUPUL, Manoly R. "The Portrayal of Canada's 'Other' Peoples in Senior High School History and Social Studies Textbooks in Alberta, 1905 to the Present", *Alberta Journal of Educational Research*, XXII:1 (March 1976), 1-33.

LUPUL, Manoly R. *Ukrainian Canadians, Multiculturalism and Separatism: An Assessment*. Edmonton: University of Alberta Press, 1978.

LYSONS, Heather "The Language Question and Quebec Education" in Terence Morrison & Anthony Burton (eds.) *Options: Reforms and Alternatives for Canadian Education*. Toronto: Holt, Rinehart & Winston, 1973, 317-339.

MACDONALD, Robert J. "Education, Language, Rights and Cultural Survival in Quebec, A Review Essay", *Journal of Educational Thought*, 9:1 (April 1975), 49-64.

MACKAY, Robert "Children's Intellectual Rights", *Interchange*, 8:1,2 (1977-78), 109-118.

McALLISTER, Jim "Ethnic Participation in Canadian Legislatures: The Case of Manitoba", *Canadian Ethnic Studies*, 3:1 (June 1973), 77-94.

MCDIARMID, Garnet & David Pratt *Teaching Prejudice*. Toronto: Ontario Institute for Studies in Education, 1971.

McDONALD, Lee C. (ed.) *Human Rights and Educational Responsibility*. North Hollywood: CLIO, Western Publications, 1979.

MCLEOD, Keith A. "Ethnic Relations and Schooling: The Case of Western Canada Since the 1870's", *Compare*, 8:1 (1978), 51-68.

MCLEOD, Keith A. "Canadian Society, Ethnic Pluralism and Education" in Terence Morrison & Anthony Burton (eds.) *Options, Reforms and Alternatives for Canadian Education*. Toronto: Holt, Rinehart & Winston, 1973, 308-316.

MCLEOD, N. Bruce "Human Rights and the Law" in Keith A. McLeod (ed.) *Multiculturalism, Bilingualism and Canadian Institutions*. Toronto: Guidance Center, Faculty of Education, University of Toronto, 1979, 16-22.

MCPHERSON, N.J. *Toward a Multi-Cultural, Multi-Lingual Education System in the North West Territories.* Saskatoon: Indian and Northern Education Program, College of Education, University of Saskatchewan, 1975.

MAGNUSON, Roger "Education and Society in Quebec in the 1970's", *Journal of Educational Thought,* 7:2 (Aug. 1973), 94-104.

MAGSINO, R.F. "Student Rights in Canada: Nonsense Upon Stilts", *Interchange,* 8:1,2 (1977-78), 52-70.

MALLEA, John R. & Edward C. Shea *Multiculturalism and Education: A Select Bibliography.* Toronto: Ontario Institute for Studies in Education, 1979.

MANLEY-CASIMIR, Michael E. "The Rights of the Child at School", *Education Canada,* 19:3 (1979), 9-13.

MANONCHEHR, Ganji *The Realization of Economic, Social and Cultural Rights: Problems, Policies and Progress.* New York: United Nations, 1975.

MARACLE, Shirley "Indian Children: Strangers in the Classroom", *ATA* (May 1972), 28-32.

MATTSON, L. "Should Teachers Cross Picket Lines?", *Saskatchewan Bulletin,* 41 (March 14, 1975), 3.

MAXWELL, Thomas R. *The Invisible French.* Cambridge: Wilfrid Laurier University Press, 1977.

MIGUS, Paul M. *Sounds Canadian: Languages and Cultures in Multi-Ethnic Society.* Toronto: Peter Martin Associates, 1975.

MOORE-EYMAN, Evelyn "A University's Search for a System of Delivering Basic Skills to Canadian Native Peoples - A Concurrent Approach" in Vincent D'Oyley (ed.) *The Impact of Multi-Ethnicity on Canadian Education.* Toronto: Urban Alliance on Race Relations, 1977, 129-146.

MORRIS, Lorenzo "The Politics of Education and Language in Quebec: A Comparative Perspective", *Canadian and International Education,* 5:2 (Dec. 1976), 1-38.

MORRISON, T.R. "Reform as Social Tracking: The Case of Industrial Education in Ontario", *Journal of Educational Thought,* 8:2 (Aug. 1974), 87-110.

MUNDY, J.H. "Language Teaching and the Young Immigrant", *Trends in Education,* 20 (Oct. 1970), 21-26.

MURRAY, John et al. *Toronto Educational Governance/Multiculturalism Case Study*. Toronto: Ontario Institute for Studies in Education, 1977.

NCTE issues criteria to combat racism and bias in texts. *Library Journal*, 96 (March 15, 1971), 1070.

NEWLAND, T. Ernest *The Gifted in Socio-educational Perspective*. Englewood Cliffs, N.J.: Prentice Hall, 1976.

NOSEWORTHY, J.W. "Education - A National Responsibility", *Canadian Forum*, 18 (Feb. 1939), 338-343.

OBRIEN, Kenneth *Retention of Other Tongue by Ethnic Minorities*. Toronto: Ontario Education Communications Authority, 1974.

OESTREICHER, Paul "Human Rights - The Experience Since the War", *Manchester Guardian Weekly*, 121:10 (Sept. 2, 1979), 8.

Ontario Human Rights Commission *Life Together: A Report on Human Rights in Ontario*, 1977.

Organization for Economic Cooperation and Development *Review of National Policies for Education, Canada*. Paris: OECD, 1976.

"Other Languages", *McGill Journal of Education* (Special Issue) XIII:2 (Spring 1978).

PACHAI, B. *Canadian Black Studies*. Halifax: International Center, St. Mary's University, 1979.

PALMER, Howard & Harold Troper "Canadian Ethnic Studies: Historical Perspectives and Contemporary Implications", *Interchange*, 4:4 (1973), 15-23.

PANIO, John (Jr.) "Tenure Does Not Mean Security", *Saskatchewan Bulletin*, 43 (Oct. 1976), 3,4.

PARENT, Alphonse Marie P.A. et al. *Royal Commission of Inquiry on Education*. Quebec: Government of the Province of Quebec, 1963 et seq. (4 Vol.).

PARKER, Margaret *The Joy of Excellence*. Kaslo, B.C.: Kootenay Center for the Gifted, 1975.

PASSOW, A. Harry *Education and the Law*. New York: Columbia University, 1976.

PAULSTON, Rolland G. "Ethnicity and Educational Change, A Priority for Comparative Education", *Comparative Education Review*, 20:3 (Oct. 1976), 269-277.

PELLETIER, W. "For Every North American That Begins To Disappear, I Also Begin To Disappear", This Magazine is About Schools, 5:2 (Spring 1971), 7-22.

"Plain People, The Mennonites near Elmira". National Film Board of Canada, 1976, 27 minutes.

POGREBIN, Letty Cottin "Born Free: A Feminist Fable", McGill Journal of Education, XII:1 (Spring 1977) 111-123.

PORTER, John "Dilemmas and Contradictions of a multi-ethnic society". Royal Society of Canada, 4th Ser. 10, Transactions (1972), 193-205.

PORTER, John "Ethnic Pluralism in Canadian Perspective" in Nathan Glazer & Daniel P. Moynihan (eds.) Ethnicity, Theory and Practice. Cambridge, Mass.: Harvard University Press, 1975, 267-304.

PORTER, John The Measure of Canadian Society: Education, Equality and Opportunity. Toronto: Gage, 1979.

PRENTICE, Alison L. & Susan E. Houston (eds.) Family, School and Society in Nineteenth Century Canada. Toronto: Oxford, 1975.

PRENTICE, Alison "Fertility: State Control or Human Rights?" CSSE News, IV:1 (Oct. 1977), 7-8.

PUGLISI, D.J. "Disadvantaged or Different? Two Approaches to Minority Group Education", Educational Leadership, 32:2 (Dec. 1974), 173-175.

RAPHAEL, D.D. Political Theory and the Rights of Man. Toronto: Macmillan, 1967.

RAY, Douglas "Alternative Scenarios for Managing Educational Contraction", Canadian Journal of Education, 6:1 (1981), 65-72.

RAY, Douglas "The Canadian Educational Take-Off", Canadian and International Education, 3:2 (Dec. 1974), 1-23.

RAY, Douglas "Can Technology Provide Cultural Security?" Paper for CIES, San Antonio, 1973.

RAY, Douglas "Ethnicity and Reorientation of the Curriculum in Canada", Comparative Education, 14:1 (March 1978), 19-32.

RAY, Douglas "The Management of Educational Collapse" in Robin Farquhar & Ian Housego (eds.) Canadian and Comparative Educational Administration. Vancouver: University of British Columbia, Department of Extension, 1980, 297-304.

RAY, Douglas "Teacher Education in Canada and the UNESCO Recommendation Concerning Education for International Understanding, Cooperation and Peace and Education Relating to Human Rights and Fundamental Freedoms", <u>Canadian and International Education</u>, 10:1 (1981) 61-76.

RAY, Douglas "Multiculturalism in Teacher Education" in Keith A. McLeod (ed.) <u>Intercultural Education and Community Development</u>. Toronto: Faculty of Education, University of Toronto (1981), 79-86.

RAY, Douglas (ed.) "Multi-cultural Societies and Education", <u>CSSE Bulletin</u> 2:1 (Sept. 1974).

RAY, Douglas "Personalized Education", <u>Teacher Education</u> (Oct. 1979), 74-80.

REMNANT, R. "Italian Students in Toronto Schools: Equality in Difference", <u>CSSE Bulletin</u>, 2:8 (Sept. 1974), 2-7.

<u>Report of the Royal Commission on The Status of Women in Canada</u>. Ottawa: Information Canada, 1970.

<u>Rights of Children (The)</u>. Reprints from <u>Harvard Educational Review</u>, 1974.

"Rights of Mentally Retarded Persons", <u>Journal of Special Education</u>, 7:1 (1973), 49-50.

ROBERTS, Joan I. & Sherrie K. Akinsanya <u>Schooling in the Cultural Context</u>. New York: David McKay, 1976.

ROBERTSON, A.H. <u>Human Rights in the World</u>. Manchester University Press, 1972.

ROBINSON, Paul <u>Where Our Future Lies: Students and Textbooks in Atlantic Canada</u>. Halifax: Atlantic Institute of Education, 1979.

ROCHER, Guy "Formal Education: The Issue of Opportunity" in Dennis Forcese & Stephen Richer, <u>Issues in Canadian Society: An Introduction to Sociology</u>. Scarborough: Prentice-Hall Inc., 1975, 137-161.

ROWLANDS, Peter <u>Gifted Children and Their Problems</u>. London: Dent, 1974.

Royal Commission on Bilingualism and Biculturalism <u>The Cultural Contribution of the Other Ethnic Groups</u> (Vol. 4). Ottawa: Queen's Printer, 1970.

Royal Commission on Bilingualism and Biculturalism <u>Education</u>. Ottawa: Queen's Printer, 1968.

Royal Commission on Bilingualism and Biculturalism, <u>The Official Languages</u>. Ottawa: Queen's Printer, 1967.

Royal Commission on Bilingualism and Biculturalism <u>The Work World</u> (2 Vol.) Ottawa: Queen's Printer, 1969.

RUSSELL, Marlene "Still Few Women in Educational Administration". *Challenge in Educational Administration*. XVIII:1 (1978), 7-9.

SAID, Abdul Aziz "Pursuing Human Dignity", *Society*, (Nov./Dec. 1977), 34-38.

SAMUDA, Ronald J. *Psychological Testing of American Minorities*. New York: Harper and Row, 1975.

SAVARD, Jean Guy *Multilingual Political Systems: Problems and Solutions*. Quebec: Laval University Press, 1975.

SCHIFF, Alvin "On Intermarriage and Jewish Education", *Jewish Education*, 47:2 (Summer 1979), 18-21.

SCHLICHTMANN, Hansgeorg "Ethnic Themes in Geographical Research on Western Canada", *Canadian Ethnic Studies*, 9:2 (1977), 9-41.

SCHMEISER, D.A. *Civil Liberties in Canada*. Toronto: Oxford University Press, 1964.

SCHOENFIELD, Stuart "The Jewish Religion in North America, Canadian and American Comparisons", *Canadian Journal of Sociology*, 3:2 (Spring 1978), 209-231.

SCOTT, Frank R. *Essays on the Canadian Constitution*. Toronto: University of Toronto Press, 1977.

SEALEY, D. Bruce "Children of Native Ancestry and the Curriculum" in Terence Morrison & Anthony Burton (eds.) *Options: Reforms and alternatives for Canadian Education*. Toronto: Holt, Rinehart & Winston, 1973, 199-206.

SEALEY, D. Bruce & Anoine S. Lussier *The Metis: Canada's Forgotten People*. Winnipeg: Manitoba Metis Federation, 1975.

SEVIGNY, Marc "La participation des parents dans l'école: Du principe à la réalité", *Education Québec*, 9:7 (May 1979), 10-17.

SHACK, Sybil *The Two-Thirds Minority*. Toronto: Guidance Center, Faculty of Education, University of Toronto, 1973.

SHACK, Sybil *Women in Canadian Education* (The Quance Lecture for 1975). Toronto: Gage, 1975.

SHANES, Bert "Child Abuse: A Killer Teachers Can Help Control", *Phi Delta Kappan* (March 1975), 479-482.

SHEFFE, Norman *Issues for the Seventies, Canada's Indians*. Toronto: McGraw Hill, 1970.

SHORE, Bruce M. "Teacher Training for the Gifted and Major Issues in Gifted Child Education", *Canadian Journal of Education*, 4:3 (1979), 75-88.

SMUCKER, Donavan E. *The Sociology of Canadian Mennonites, Hutterites and Amish* (A Bibliography with Annotations). Waterloo: Wilfrid Laurier Press, 1977.

SOMAN, Shirley Camper *Let's Stop Destroying Our Children*. New York: Hawthorn Books, 1974.

SORIANO, Marc "Children's Books and Human Rights", *Prospects*, VII:2 (1977), 204-225.

SPINKS, Sarah "Sugar and Spice", from Satu Repo (ed.) *This Book is About Schools*. New York: Vintage, 1970, 32-50.

STACEY, Judith, Susan Bereaud & Joan Daniels *And Jill Came Tumbling After: Sexism in American Education*. New York: Dell, 1974.

STASSINOPOULOS, Arianna *The Female Woman*. London: Davis Poynter, 1973.

STEER, Michael "Fostering Positive Attitudes Toward the Handicapped", *Education Canada*, 19:4 (Winter 1979), 36-41.

STENING, Bruce W. "Direct and Stereotype Cultural Differences", *Journal of Cross Cultural Psychology*, 10:2 (June 1979), 203-220.

STEPHENSON, Marylee *Women in Canada*. Toronto: New Press, 1973.

STOPSKY, Fred "The School as a Workplace: Extending Democracy to Schools", *International Review of Education*, XXI:4 (1975), 493-506.

SULLIVAN, J.A. "Native American - Right to be Different", *Christian Century*, 93 (Nov. 3, 1976), 960.

SWAIN, Merrill "Bibliography: Research on Immersion Education for the Majority Child", *Canadian Modern Language Review*, 32:5 (May 1976), 592-596.

SWYRIPA, Frances *Ukrainian Canadians: A Survey of their Portrayal in English Language Works*. Edmonton: University of Alberta Press, 1978.

TARASOFF, Koozma J. *Pictorial History of the Doukhobors*. Saskatoon: Prairie Books Department, Western Producer, 1969.

TARNOPOLSKY, Walter *et al*. "The Bill of Rights: Help or Hindrances". CBC Phonotape, 1971.

TAWNEY, R.H. "Equality" in Harold Silver (ed.) Equal Opportunity in Education. London, Methuen, 1973.

TAYLOR, Alton L. Protecting Individual Rights to Privacy in Higher Education. San Francisco: Jossey Bass Inc., 1977. (Special Issue of New Directions in Educational Research, 14 (Summer 1977).

TIEDT, Pamela & Iris Tiedt Multicultural Teaching, A Handbook of Activities, Information and Resources. Boston: Allyn & Bacon, 1979.

TROPER, Harold & Lee Palmer Issues in Cultural Diversity. Toronto: Ontario Institute for Studies in Education, 1976.

TRUDEAU, Pierre Elliott A Canadian Charter of Human Rights. Ottawa: Information Canada, 1968.

UNESCO Human Rights: Comments and Interpretations. London and New York: Allan Wingate, 1949.

UNESCO Some Suggestions on Teaching About Human Rights. Geneva: UNESCO, 1968.

UNESCO Education on the Move. Paris: UNESCO, 1974.

United Nations and Human Rights. New York: United Nations, 1968.

United Nations, Human Rights Division Human Rights: A Compilation of International Instruments of the United Nations. New York: United Nations, 1973.

United Nations Yearbook(s) on Human Rights. New York: United Nations.

VALDEKO, Virunurm & Roger N. Gaunt "Safeguards for the Protection of Individual Records in Computerized Data Banks", New Directions in Institutional Research 14 (Summer 1977), 55-70.

VALENTINE, C. "Deficit, difference and bi-cultural models of Afro-American behavior", Harvard Educational Review, 41 (1971), 137-159.

VALLEE, Frank G. "Multi-ethnic Societies: The Issues of Identity and Inequality" in Dennis Forcese & Stephen Richer (eds.) Issues in Canadian Society: An Introduction to Sociology. Scarborough: Prentice Hall, 1975, 162-202.

VAN STOLK, Mary The Battered Child in Canada. Toronto: McClelland & Stewart, 1972.

VESA, Unto "The UNESCO Recommendation and Peace Education", International Peace Research Newsletter, XIV:5 (1976), 10-13.

WALKER, James W. The Black Loyalists: The Search for a Promised Land in Nova Scotia and Sierra Leone, 1783-1870. Halifax: Dalhousie University Press, 1976.

WASSERMANN, Selma "Teacher as Decision Maker, or Who Shapes Educational Practice?" Teacher Education 9 (Spring 1976), 79-82.

WATTS, Ronald Lampman Multi-cultural Societies and Federalism. Ottawa: Information Canada, 1970.

WEAVER, Sally M. "Indian Women, Marriage and Legal Status" in K. Ishwaran (ed.) Marriage and Divorce in Canada. Toronto: McGraw Hill Ryerson, 1978.

WELISCH, S.A. "Ethnic Educational Promises and Perils", Educational Forum, 40 (May 1976), 543-550.

WINKS, Robin Blacks in Canada; A History. New Haven, Conn.: Yale University Press, 1971.

WOLFGANG, Aaron Education of Immigrant Students. Toronto: Ontario Institute for Studies in Education, 1975.

Women and Education (Special Issue of McGill Journal of Education) X:1 (Spring 1975).

Women Around the World (Special Feature) The Center Magazine (May/June 1974), 44-80.

WOOD, Dean D. Multicultural Canada: A Teacher's Guide to Ethnic Studies. Toronto: Ontario Institute for Studies in Education, 1978.

WOODCOCK, George & Ivan Avakumovic The Doukhobors. Toronto: Oxford University Press, 1968.

WOODCOCK, George "I'm a WASP, Which Minority do you belong to?" MacLean's Magazine, 84:14, 71.

WOODSWORTH, J.S. Strangers Within Our Gates. Toronto: University of Toronto Press, 1972 (originally published by The Methodist Church in 1909).

WORTH, Walter H. A Choice of Futures. Edmonton: Queen's Printer, 1972.

YALDEN, Max "French Language Instruction as a National Issue". Interchange, 9:4 (1979), 4-11.

YOUNG, John R. "Multiculturalism and its Implications for Youth" in Keith A. McLeod (ed.) Multiculturalism, Bilingualism and Canadian Institutions. Toronto: Guidance Center, Faculty of Education, University of Toronto, 1979, 102-111.

YOUNG, Jonathan C. "Education in a Multicultural Society: What Sort of Education? What Sort of Society?", *Canadian Journal of Education*, 4:3 (1979), 5-22.

NOTES ON CONTRIBUTORS

James Brown is Associate Professor of Curriculum and Instruction in Social Sciences at The University of Western Ontario. He has published extensively on topics defining and proposing educational rights and how they may be secured.

Anthony Burton is Assistant Headmaster at the Toronto French School. He has taught in several Canadian universities. His publications include personal and edited collections plus many individual papers. Most concern the foundations of educational thought rather than classroom procedure.

Janet Collins is now studying law after teaching Biology at Dalhousie. Her avocation led to close association with human rights promotion, analysis of social injustice and practical steps for community action.

Vincent D'Oyley is Professor of Education at the University of British Columbia. His many publications, public addresses and organizational talents are devoted to social analysis and public responsibility, especially in a multicultural society.

John Kehoe is Professor of Curriculum (Social Studies) at the University of British Columbia. His research and publications address the reasons for particular classroom procedures and propose new targets and approaches.

J. Roby Kidd was Professor of Adult Education at the Ontario Institute for Studies in Education. A prolific author, global traveller and respected confidant of leaders in many nations, Roby's 1982 death was mourned around the world.

Michel Laferrière is Associate Professor of Education at McGill. His work in education of minorities has won acclaim from the Multiculturalism Directorate, Canadian Ethnic Studies Association and Sociologists in Canada, the United States and Europe.

Jacques Lamontagne is Associate Professor of Education at the University of Montreal. Formerly the editor of Canadian and International Education, he has usually written about education and sociology. An accomplished linguist, Jacques has just completed two years of academic work in China, editing, consulting and lecturing in Chinese.

MarySue McCarthy is Associate Professor of Education at York University. Her work usually links psychology to social analysis. She is best known for her frequent television appearances.

Grant McMurray is Professor of Psychology and Education at The University of Western Ontario. His current research includes special education and teacher 'burn-out', both clearly related to human rights.

Douglas Ray is Professor of Educational Policy Studies at The University of Western Ontario. His research and writing link international topics with Canada, usually focussing on how society affects schools.

Danny Zawadski is a teacher of History in Brantford.